THE OUTCOMES BOOK

THE OUTCOMES BOOK

Debate and Consensus after
the WPA Outcomes Statement

edited by

SUSANMARIE HARRINGTON
KEITH RHODES
RUTH OVERMAN FISCHER
RITA MALENCZYK

UTAH STATE UNIVERSITY PRESS
Logan, Utah

Utah State University Press
Logan, Utah 84322-7800

Manufactured in the United States of America
Cover design by Barbara Yale-Read

Library of Congress Cataloging-in-Publication Data

The outcomes book : debate and consensus after the WPA outcomes statement / edited by Susanmarie
Harrington ... [et al.].
    p. cm.
 This volume of essays reflects on the process that led to the development of the "WPA outcomes state-
ment," and includes debate on the many theoretical, pedagogical, political, and assessment issues that
the outcomes statement raises.
 Includes bibliographical reference (p.) and index.
 ISBN 0-87421-604-4 (alk. paper)
 1. English language–Rhetoric–Study and teaching–United States. 2. Report writing–Study and teach-
ing (Higher)–
United States. I. Harrington, Susanmarie.
 PE1405.U6O94 2005
 808'.042'071073–dc22
                    2004029702

WPA Outcomes Statement
for First-Year Composition

Introduction

This statement describes the common knowledge, skills, and attitudes sought by first-year composition programs in American postsecondary education. To some extent, we seek to regularize what can be expected to be taught in first-year composition; to this end the document is not merely a compilation or summary of what currently takes place. Rather, the following statement articulates what composition teachers nationwide have learned from practice, research, and theory. This document intentionally defines only "outcomes," or types of results, and not "standards," or precise levels of achievement. The setting of standards should be left to specific institutions or specific groups of institutions.

Learning to write is a complex process, both individual and social, that takes place over time with continued practice and informed guidance. Therefore, it is important that teachers, administrators, and a concerned public do not imagine that these outcomes can be taught in reduced or simple ways. Helping students demonstrate these outcomes requires expert understanding of how students actually learn to write. For this reason we expect the primary audience for this document to be well-prepared college writing teachers and college writing program administrators. In some places, we have chosen to write in their professional language. Among such readers, terms such as "rhetorical" and "genre" convey a rich meaning that is not easily simplified. While we have also aimed at writing a document that the general public can understand, in limited cases we have aimed first at communicating effectively with expert writing teachers and writing program administrators.

These statements describe only what we expect to find at the end of first-year composition, at most schools a required general education course or sequence of courses. As writers move beyond first-year composition, their writing abilities do not merely improve. Rather, students' abilities not only diversify along disciplinary and professional lines but also move into whole new levels where expected outcomes expand, multiply, and diverge. For this reason, each statement of outcomes for first-year composition is followed by suggestions for further work that builds on these outcomes.

Rhetorical Knowledge

By the end of first year composition, students should

- Focus on a purpose
- Respond to the needs of different audiences
- Respond appropriately to different kinds of rhetorical situations
- Use conventions of format and structure appropriate to the rhetorical situation
- Adopt appropriate voice, tone, and level of formality
- Understand how genres shape reading and writing
- Write in several genres

Faculty in all programs and departments can build on this preparation by helping students learn

- The main features of writing in their fields
- The main uses of writing in their fields
- The expectations of readers in their fields

Critical Thinking, Reading, and Writing

By the end of first year composition, students should

- Use writing and reading for inquiry, learning, thinking, and communicating

- Understand a writing assignment as a series of tasks, including finding, evaluating, analyzing, and synthesizing appropriate primary and secondary sources
- Integrate their own ideas with those of others
- Understand the relationships among language, knowledge, and power

Faculty in all programs and departments can build on this preparation by helping students learn

- The uses of writing as a critical thinking method
- The interactions among critical thinking, critical reading, and writing
- The relationships among language, knowledge, and power in their fields

Processes

By the end of first year composition, students should

- Be aware that it usually takes multiple drafts to create and complete a successful text
- Develop flexible strategies for generating, revising, editing, and proof-reading
- Understand writing as an open process that permits writers to use later invention and re-thinking to revise their work
- Understand the collaborative and social aspects of writing processes
- Learn to critique their own and others' works
- Learn to balance the advantages of relying on others with the responsibility of doing their part
- Use a variety of technologies to address a range of audiences

Faculty in all programs and departments can build on this preparation by helping students learn

- To build final results in stages
- To review work-in-progress in collaborative peer groups for purposes other than editing
- To save extensive editing for later parts of the writing process
- To apply the technologies commonly used to research and communicate within their fields

Knowledge of Conventions

By the end of first year composition, students should

- Learn common formats for different kinds of texts
- Develop knowledge of genre conventions ranging from structure and paragraphing to tone and mechanics
- Practice appropriate means of documenting their work
- Control such surface features as syntax, grammar, punctuation, and spelling.

Faculty in all programs and departments can build on this preparation by helping students learn

- The conventions of usage, specialized vocabulary, format, and documentation in their fields
- Strategies through which better control of conventions can be achieved

Adopted by the Council of Writing Program Administrators (WPA), April 2000. Reprinted by permission.

*For all the teachers who played a part
in developing the Outcomes Statement*

*May the dialogue you began
continue in classrooms and hallways
to the benefit of your students.*

CONTENTS

ACKNOWLEDGMENTS

Almost as soon as the idea of an Outcomes Statement was under consideration, the idea for a book like this was, too. From the earliest days, those involved with the Statement recognized that in many ways a short statement of common outcomes would be the most useful statement, but that a short statement would also be the most risky statement in many ways. A short statement would necessarily be simple, and potentially over-simplified. No one wanted a statement that would seem to give aid to those who might wish the teaching of writing could be reduced to teaching grammar. We hoped that the publication of a book debating outcomes in conjunction with the Outcomes Statement would draw attention to the many complications any such statement raises. There are many, many people who deserve thanks for helping this book find its audience.

First, we thank the many teachers who attended Outcomes events between 1996 and 2001. Subscribers to WPA-L first gave the project energy with their initial discussion, and an informal meeting at the 1996 CCCC led to the first of a series of workshop and forum proposals. Participants in those forums at CCCC, Computers and Writing, the Council of Writing Program Administrators Summer Conference, and other smaller conferences helped shape the Statement, but more importantly, helped raise many issues and questions which have been taken up by the authors of this volume. The years of running debate about teaching practice and theory as well as about the language of the Statement helped shape the scope of this volume.

Chet Pryor deserves special thanks for his role in Outcomes process. Of those who have not contributed chapters to this book, he has been the most persistent booster of the project. His many contributions, from ideas to encouragement to special color-themed pens, helped to feed and sustain the process at many critical moments.

We are also indebted to the contributors to this volume, whose willingness to revise has helped the manuscript re-invent itself several times over. Michael Spooner's enthusiasm for this project helped with the last‾and most profitable‾overhaul of the manuscript, and we appreciate the way his vision for the project helped us highlight the collection's strengths.

INTRODUCTION
Celebrating and Complicating the Outcomes Statement

Susanmarie Harrington

The WPA Outcomes Statement (OS) had innocuous beginnings: one plaintive question in an electronic discussion group for writing program administrators wondering whether or "a pithy and effective list of objectives for writing (and maybe speaking!) programs" existed. This simple question immediately generated enthusiasm and skepticism. A few participants immediately shared local documents describing courses or programs. Some participants in the discussion, sensitive to the role of local context in matters of curriculum and assessment, thought that outcomes were best discussed locally. Others, looking at a discipline centered on first-year composition, thought that our theoretical commonalties could lead to practical commonalties as well. And still others saw a challenge: what would happen if we could construct a description of program outcomes that could be used in very different settings?

Several years and thousands of hours of discussion and drafting later, the Outcomes Statement is an official document of the Council of Writing Program Administrators—and more importantly, it has been used in numerous ways by individual teachers and programs to guide the development of teaching and learning.

This collection celebrates the Outcomes Statement; it also complicates it. The Outcomes Collective, as the group that developed the statement playfully yet seriously called itself, worried a great deal about potential uses of the statement. Would a simple list of outcomes be co-opted by bean-counting administrators swooping in to do quantitative evaluations? Would the list of goals and outcomes become so large as to be unwieldy? Would a focus on what can be easily measured or counted force outcomes to value what can be simply assessed rather than what is valued in the field? Any short statement of outcomes could easily be turned against a writing program, and the developers were always concerned about how the statement would be read by audiences with different levels of involvement in composition programs. Passionate debates and inquiries into all these questions characterized the work of the Outcomes Collective, and also illustrated why the group gravitated toward the term *collective*. *Committee* didn't fit, as there was neither the structure nor sponsoring organization that the term implies; *task force* similarly seemed too formal. *Collective* characterized the playful chaos that swirled around core questions, a chaos that eventually formed into the Outcomes Statement.

The collective's awareness of the many audiences for composition programs energized its work. Knowing that students, parents, deans, legislators, and teachers at other levels all had a stake in what happens in first-year composition programs led the developers to craft a statement that is plain enough to speak to those outside the discipline, yet rooted in disciplinary language enough to have status in the field. For many of the statement's developers, the experience of collaborating over time with colleagues from many different institutions, looking at the Outcomes Statement from many different perspectives, and soliciting many different views was a formative professional experience. The statement's several drafts were revised at various points to make the language more complex yet more simple, to build bridges with high school teachers or with colleagues in other departments or programs, to build connections between different types of institutions. Articulating what are the primary features of a composition sequence, and then whittling away and refining that articulation in order to make the statement shorter, was a formidable challenge—and an exciting one. Participants in the process explored their dearest assumptions about teaching and learning. Working with the Outcomes Statement, cyclically reflecting on their own practice and on the evolving document, the collective tussled with minor issues of usage and major issues of substance. The aim: a one-page statement that captured the essence of composition programs, that pointed to the further work students could do as writers, and that helped faculty in all programs consider how to teach students to become increasingly effective writers. Simple yet complex.

This book attempts to do justice to the complexity of those issues by publicly engaging them, in the hope that faculty will be encouraged to work with the Outcomes Statement. For departments, programs, and individuals, the Outcomes Statement encourages engagement with fundamentals. What kinds of experiences should students share? What concepts should students learn? How does learning happen? How do our ideal concepts and performances fit in a curricular sequence?

The Outcomes Statement isn't perfect. Even as it went off for publication, most of those involved in drafting the statement could find a word or two to tweak, or a bullet or two to modify or to add. The Outcomes Statement is important because of the processes it should evoke, and we represent that here by inviting critiques of the statement from scholars who have not been a part of the drafting process. We invited theorists Peter Elbow, Richard Haswell, and Marilyn Sternglass to critique the statement with an eye toward curriculum and development theory. Their chapters illustrate some of the ways in which the Outcomes Statement is a floor, not a ceiling, for composition programs. The Outcomes Statement does not prescribe curriculum; rather, it encourages conversation about curriculum. It's arguably not comprehensive: it doesn't attend to personal writing or to nonacademic writing; it may privilege awareness of rhetoric over performance of rhetoric; some readers may find that the tone of the statement is too formal, or not formal enough. This collection celebrates responses to the statement and invites others.

Following this introduction appear four sections that focus attention on crucial areas related to outcomes articulation and assessment. The opening section, *Contextualizing the Outcomes Statement*, provides background on the emergence of the statement. Edward M. White puts the search for outcomes in the context of the field's history, and a collaboratively authored chapter by original members of the collective (Keith Rhodes, Irvin Peckham, Linda S. Bergmann, and William Condon) sets out the working history of the statement. Chapters by Kathleen Blake Yancey and Mark Wiley distinguish outcomes from standards, with Yancey offering useful definitions and Wiley exploring ways those who work with outcomes can avoid the political problems that have plagued standards-based reform efforts. Cynthia L. Selfe and Patricia Freitag Ericsson close the section with a challenge to readers to consider technology as fundamental to writing-course outcomes. This section, then, makes the case for considering outcomes and lays open some unsettled controversies about the language of the statement.

The second section, *The Outcomes Statement and First-Year Writing*, focuses on ways the Outcomes Statement has been used to articulate and implement first-year composition programs. Chapters in this section highlight each of the four domains of the statement, offering a close look at the complexities inherent in each part of the document. Stephen Wilhoit's chapter offers the Outcomes Statement as a bridge between university, high school, and writing across the curriculum efforts. J. L. McClure situates the Outcomes Statement as the cornerstone of a community college's assessment efforts. The next four chapters examine each domain of the Outcomes Statement carefully. Linda Adler-Kassner and Heidi Estrem complicate issues surrounding critical thinking, reading, and writing, and Barbara Little Liu tackles the implications of genre theory for teaching and learning rhetorical knowledge. Duane Roen and Gregory R. Glau offer a detailed look at the ways the Outcomes Statement's attention to processes helps structure dialogue between students and teachers at the end of the semester. Looking at issues surrounding grammar, mechanics, and usage, Donald Wolff takes his classroom experience to investigate the possibilities and limitations of the Outcomes Statement's language on conventions. Patricia Freitag Ericsson closes this section with an overview of the myriad ways the statement has been used in different institutions, arguing that continued attention to the statement is necessary for it to reach its full potential.

The Outcomes Statement always intended to raise issues beyond first-year writing; each section of the statement closes with a reminder that faculty in other departments have a responsibility to build on the experiences of that first course (or course sequence). *The Outcomes Statement beyond First-Year Writing*, this volume's third section, examines what happens when the statement is used beyond first-year composition. Martha A. Townsend explores connections between outcomes and writing across the curriculum, while Susanmarie Harrington looks at connections between first-year writing and the English major. Barry M. Maid's description of the way the statement was the core document in the establishment of a new technical writing program offers an interesting example of the statement's use in building a program, while Robert O'Brien Hokanson's chapter illustrates the way the statement can add to an already well-defined campus assessment effort. Finally, Rita Malenczyk sets the statement in the context of the Boyer Commission's work, enabling those working with general education reform to become savvier campus politicians.

The collection's final section, *Theorizing Outcomes*, critiques and examines the Outcomes Statement from varying perspectives, providing a challenge to all of us. Ruth Overman Fischer's chapter explores the role of theory in the drafting of the statement, while chapters by Peter Elbow, Richard H. Haswell, and Marilyn S. Sternglass examine the statement from the point of view of expressivist and developmental theory. Each of these critiques points out ways in which the statement could, perhaps, have been more broadly conceived, and each points out ways in which users of the statement have much to consider as they get to work on pressing local issues. Kathleen Blake Yancey, past president of the Council of Writing Program Administrators, wraps up the collection with a look at the ways the Outcomes Statement process represents successful efforts at curricular reform and with a reminder that successful reform is an ongoing process. The dialogue must continue.

All in all, the contributors demonstrate the multiplicity of ways the statement can promote dialogue, debate, and action—all in the service of promoting interesting writing instruction. Our hope is that this collection will encourage you to do three things: first, read the Outcomes Statement; second, consider your syllabus, your curriculum, and your program in light of the Outcomes Statement; third, do something. Call your colleagues. Share the statement with them—or with your students. Use the Outcomes Statement to examine your own work—and use your work to examine the Outcomes Statement. Challenge yourself, challenge the statement.

PART ONE

Contextualizing the Outcomes Statement

1

THE ORIGINS OF THE OUTCOMES STATEMENT

Edward M. White

The question I posted to the Council of Writing Program Administrators (WPA) listserv in 1996 was based on a series of frustrating experiences as a consultant to college and university writing programs. Typically, I would be asked to advise the program faculty on an assessment device that would place students in the appropriate course for them, the one in which they were most likely to be challenged and succeed.

"Sure," I would reply, sitting down at a conference table with the teaching faculty. "Tell me what is being taught in your courses." This would be met with an embarrassed silence. Most of the time nobody really knew what was taught in the various sections of the various writing courses listed in the college catalogue—that is, in any course besides the one a particular teacher was teaching, with the door to the classroom shut. So I would turn to the faculty member on my left and ask what that person expected students to be able to do at the end of the class.

"Do?" I would hear echoed back with perplexity. "I teach sentence structure [or grammar or paragraph structure or the reading of poetry or journal writing or James Joyce's *Ulysses* or a dozen other curricular ideas]. I suppose students should know . . ." and the sentence would tail off into a series of indefinite abstractions. Like most other college faculty, the person on my left had focused on what the teacher did and hardly at all on what the student results were supposed to be. I would then canvass the others. "Are those your goals as well?" Not at all, would come the reply. What the first teacher sought to accomplish in English 45, Basic Writing, the second teacher taught in English 101, College Composition, and the third teacher taught in English 306, Advanced Composition. By the time we had gone halfway around the table, it was clear to everyone that we could not begin to talk about assessment until the program had some kind of structure. As long as every teacher did whatever seemed personally appropriate, and as long as more advanced work went on in some of the "basic" courses than in some of the "advanced" ones, there was no point in trying to place students in the curriculum. The problem was not so much with the different approaches taken by different teachers—that could in fact be considered a strength—but with the differing goals and expectations they expressed.

But how was the writing program to gain the needed structure? Again typically, each teacher was more or less on his or her own, at best guided by a few generalizations about the kind of reading material and writing assignments to use in each course. It seemed somehow wrong to limit a teacher, however new to the profession, however untutored in rhetoric or composition studies, by stating just what a particular writing course was supposed to accomplish. That is, an understandable resistance to making every teacher do the same thing had become a less defensible objection to developing common goals for a particular course. As long as the focus was on what the teacher did, rather than on what the student learned, there seemed to be no good answer to my uncomfortable questions.

Such a situation is absurd, unfair, and unprofessional, I have come to believe. Can we imagine a mathematics department in which Math 101 has widely different goals depending on which teacher happens to be teaching it, with some working on beginning arithmetic while others are starting calculus? So, during term break on March 13, 1996, I posed the following question to the WPA listserv, WPA-L: "Is it an impossible dream to imagine this group coming out with at least a draft set of objectives that might really work and be usable, for instance, distinguishing comp 1 from comp 2 or from "advanced" comp? We may not have professional consensus on this, though, or even consensus that we *should* have consensus. How would we go about trying?" (White 1996)

From that acorn has grown this oak. As it turned out, the question struck a major nerve on the list, epitomizing problems vexing many WPAs around the country, and rousing intense controversy and creativity. While composition studies has flourished as a graduate enterprise, with sixty-five Ph.D. rhetoric/composition programs now producing scholars and teachers, the first-year composition course has remained chaotic and confused, too often in its practice denying the professional work of the graduate programs flourishing on the same campus. It was time for the profession to start professionalizing the first-year composition course. The first step had been taken some years prior in a statement by the Conference on College Composition and Communication on the "principles and practices" for staffing that course (Conference 1989). Now we were ready to turn to the curriculum. What should its goals be? What should students be able to do when they leave the course at different levels with a passing course grade? The book you hold is the result of a long and arduous effort to grapple with these questions and provide guidelines for answering them.

But meanwhile a whole host of objections to an outcomes statement appeared, many of them based on long experience with American composition programs. I will focus here on three of the most prominent:

- There are many and conflicting visions of just what the first-year course should accomplish. Whose outcomes should prevail?
- Most of those teaching composition courses in American colleges and universities have little training in composition studies and little support from their institutions. Isn't it unfair to measure outcomes from young and inexperienced teachers? Is this a way to further harass the lowest-status teachers on campus?
- The struggle to define writing programs has become—perhaps always has been—highly political. We must resist giving ammunition to the enemy, who seeks to define our work as narrowly grammatical, conventional, and socially stratified.

Let's consider each of these reasonable objections in turn, with a particular eye to the way in which the Outcomes Statement attempts to meet them.

Whose "outcomes" should prevail? The loose collection of writing program administrators who volunteered to form the "outcomes group" represented all levels of postsecondary education and many different kinds of institutions. As the Outcomes Statement began to take shape, this group held workshops and gave presentations at professional conferences, testing drafts against realities of writing programs around the country. To everyone's surprise a general consensus did begin to take shape. Key to the process was a set of crucial distinctions: outcomes are different from standards, and agreement on outcomes does not require agreement on a single best way to achieve those outcomes.

Outcomes are often confused with standards, but they are quite different concepts. An open-enrollment community college and a highly selective private college can share the same desired outcomes, while their students may achieve them at different levels. The outcomes statements of the two institutions may be quite similar, while the standard of performance may be different, for all kinds of reasons. Thus, the outcomes group early on determined that it would deal with outcomes but not standards, which must be set by each institution for its own students. Again, since no one wanted to remove teacher initiative or creativity from the classroom, the outcomes group firmly rejected any proposal to suggest "best" curricula, textbooks, or teaching procedures. Some institutions, particularly those whose teachers have little or no professional training in rhetoric and composition, may prefer to proceed with such requirements for their teachers, while other institutions will be content to allow every teacher to try to reach the outcomes in his or her own way. Kathleen Blake Yancey's chapter in this collection ("Standards, Outcomes, and All That Jazz") addressees this issue in considerable detail.

Once the concept of outcomes was divorced from standards and from teaching methods and materials, we found it possible to reach a consensus that appeared to meet the needs of the wide range of institutions we represented and consulted. While that consensus is always subject to revision, and the outcomes group expects the present statement to be revised periodically as the needs of students change, we present a statement of desired outcomes from the first-year composition course that is generally applicable across American higher education in the first decade of the twenty-first century.

Isn't it unfair to measure outcomes from young and inexperienced teachers? The key to assessing student outcomes is to recognize that, however much teachers may labor, students must ultimately take responsibility for their own learning. We much regret the labor practices of many colleges and universities, which are often exploitative for those teaching the first-year writing course. At the same time, we know that those teaching composition in American colleges and universities on the whole do an excellent job under most difficult conditions. As writing program administrators, we have a primary responsibility for evaluating and improving our writing programs. The Outcomes Statement looks at campus writing programs, not individual writing teachers.

We must resist giving ammunition to the enemy, who seeks to define our work as narrowly grammatical, conventional, and socially stratified. One professional problem the Outcomes Statement is designed to address is the common reductive definition of what writing programs seek to accomplish. We have allowed others to define us, and some of those definitions have little to do with our actual work. Few college programs spend much time on vocabulary drill, spelling rules, or handwriting practice, for instance. The Outcomes Statement gives us a sophisticated and mature view of what college writing programs seek to do, demonstrating why these writing courses belong in the college curriculum, usually at the center of general education, and what other faculty should expect their students to have learned in those courses. We hope that a widespread understanding of these outcomes will benefit students, as other teachers expect them to transfer what they have learned in composition to other courses, and help these teachers to reinforce what we do as they ask for writing in their own fields.

I am pleased that the questions I posed seven years ago (at this writing) have opened into so many different avenues, each in turn raising new questions about the purposes and the objectives of the course required by almost all American colleges and universities. The Outcomes Statement that has emerged suggests some of the answers that thoughtful and reflective practitioners have in turn produced. But all answers produce new questions, and this book explores many of the questions that have emerged over the last few years as a result of the use of the Outcomes Statement, a document whose time at last has come.

2

THE OUTCOMES PROJECT
The Insiders' History

Keith Rhodes
Irvin Peckham
Linda S. Bergmann
William Condon

If ever there has been a project that won't really fit into a nutshell, the Outcomes project is it. This project began in frustration over the apparent inability to share or even specify widely what goes on in first-year composition. We—the Outcomes Collective, as we called ourselves—proceeded with a grassroots effort to do that, if only for ourselves. We ended with a document that, though it is addressed to an audience of writing program administrators and writing teachers, nevertheless supplies information that the various stakeholders in first-year composition—students, administrators, parents, legislators, the public at large (in addition to teachers and WPAs)—have some right to know. And more importantly, we ended with a document that can be used to promote smart and essential conversations about writing.

Before going on, we need to provide an aside about this chapter. This history of the Outcomes Statement book project has a history of its own. When the Outcomes Statement was new, we turned our gaze inward and backward. The statement was freshly created and had not yet been adopted by anyone. The Outcomes Collective conceived of this book as one that would explain the origins and motivations of that statement. The four authors to which this history is attributed wrote separate essays exploring different aspects of those origins and motivations. We sought to generate the sort of understanding that would lead to uses. As it turns out, the uses came on their own; and as they did, the purpose of the book evolved, so that it needed to focus outward and forward. We had woven a rich and self-satisfying historical tapestry; but eventually it became simply too much of a good inside game. The original need for such essays had mostly been met without them, so they have now been reduced and combined into this one.

Thus, the process of writing this chapter started with our needs and circumstances as writers, but then shifted to a concern for audience. As might be expected, that is the same process that this chronicle will describe in the history of the statement itself. Yet the "writer-based" motivations may still influence the interpretation of the final product; and so we hope to illuminate some of the key features of that process and of the Outcomes Statement's rhetorical situation by presenting some part, at least, of the inside story in the inside voices. We will not be so dramatic as to make this an obvious dialogue; but along the way there will be some obvious changes in voice, some disjunctures of flow. Rather than smooth them all out, we have left just a bit of a textual reminder of the multitude of voices that came together in the statement itself.

THE COMMUNITY OF COBBLERS

There was a good bit of joy and a lot of community in the building of this document, and that is why those of us who worked on it have maintained a commitment to it. What has been most gratifying about working with the Outcomes group is that not only did the group collaborate in the mode described by John Trimbur as "engaging in a process of intellectual negotiation and collective decision-making" (1989, 602), we also formulated a document that we all can live with pretty well—no one negotiated away the farm. We worked as a team, parceling out the work when necessary, for every one of us has been repeatedly or continually swamped with work of our own and with the demands of personal and professional responsibilities. In formulating proposals for panels and workshops, drafts of the Outcomes Statement, and this book itself, the process worked something like this: Someone would notice an impending deadline and send out a call for ideas. Ideas would tumble in. Controversies would arise—should the Outcomes Statement include a technology plank, for example—and sides would be taken. Inevitably someone would start a round of bad jokes or puns. Ed White would calm us down like a good uncle, and David Schwalm would structure our options like the dean that he is. And then someone—perhaps Susanmarie Harrington, Karen Vaught-Alexander, Bill Condon, or most often Rita Malenczyk—would outline a format. Everyone would red-pencil it into submission. A face-to-face planning meeting would be scheduled, we'd review our plans, and another panel would set off to present the idea and the draft to another assemblage of writing teachers.

The archived discussions read like a textbook exercise in collaborative writing. Moreover, the colorful electronic discussions throughout the year meant that when we met face-to-face, once or twice yearly at conferences, we were not at all strangers—we were friends, with much work and conversation in common, and we could work together easily and efficiently to push the document on to the next stage. However—and this is crucial—we all worked to keep the collaboration open to new members and expanded constituencies. Each conference and meeting was an opportunity to bring in new voices; we wanted this to be a document adopted and adapted by as many people as possible, because it filled a felt and expressed need. Almost before the ink was dry on the first draft, it was being tried and tested: Karen Vaught-Alexander, Chet Pryor, Mark Wiley, and others brought to conference sessions accounts of using it to articulate courses within and between programs and to design writing programs and projects in numerous venues. The collaboration we envisioned was always extending outward; the idea was to let the Outcomes Statement fly and see what happened, not to try to contain it. Occasionally a query would come from someone who wanted to change a part of the statement here or there for local reasons or to fit an institutional need. Our sense was that the Outcomes Statement would give the strength of professional validation to local formulations of outcomes and standards, but should not impose unsuitable restrictions on them. The statement is a device to formulate and validate—not to constrain—the development of local programs. The collaboration was open to anyone who wanted to join it.

The material result of the first informal meeting at the 1996 Conference on College Composition and Communication in Milwaukee was the plan to propose sessions for the 1997 CCC Convention in Phoenix and for the 1997 Council of Writing Program Administrators summer conference in Houghton, Michigan. The initial wide-ranging discussion of the Outcomes project on the WPA-L discussion list became the prototype for each phase of the project, from early discussions about whether an outcomes statement was even possible to later convention sessions examining particular versions of the OS. These discussions shifted to a specialized electronic form, the Outcomes discussion list, which was begun in February 1997; but the cobbling process continued.

In 1998, the Outcomes group hosted a full-day preconference workshop at CCCC in Chicago, at which time discussion group leaders and workshop participants compared the early draft of the Outcomes Statement with assessment tools used in various states and at various universities. At this workshop, a new statement was drafted that would pretty nearly define the shape and scope of the "final" document. By the end of the workshop, after considerable haggling over wording and phrasing, the participants had achieved a thoroughly revised draft of the statement with which the workshop had begun. At this time, the introductory phrases were added: "By the end of first-year composition, students should be able to x" and "Faculty in other departments and programs can build on this preparation by helping students learn x"; these phrases were intended to build in a relationship between first-year composition and the writing done in other courses, without, we hoped, making impossible claims for first-year composition.

The work of writing and revising the Outcomes Statement was primarily the work of writing program administrators. We tried to embed in this document the knowledge derived from several decades of research and practice in composition, without taking sides in the arguments that separate, say, the expressivists from the social constructivists. Because the Outcomes group drew members from different parts of the country and different kinds of institutions, with different theoretical positions, curricular requirements, and student bodies, we had many, many disagreements, both practical and theoretical. However, we kept returning to the point that we were looking for what we have in common, what best ideas and best practices we could all agree on. Flurries of disagreement were most commonly resolved by moving to a level of generalization that could accommodate multiple positions. When there was a major argument in 1999 about whether the Outcomes Statement should mandate computer technologies, the issue was resolved with a line about technologies in general, to keep the issue open enough that it would not exclude particular institutions in the present or become obsolete a decade hence, when who-knows-what will be the desired technology.

The Outcomes list chatter and joking that accompanied preparing for panels and presentations helped build the sense of community among the Outcomes group and reaffirm our common humanity. Chet Pryor distributed "party favors" at WPA and CCCC sessions on the OS—one year a pen, another a pin—and these brought attention to the document—and new voices into the community. The everyday life at the edges of our discussions also brought us together and kept us aware of the human communities behind our postings. In the archived discussions, I see the flow of lives through the project, as we made our plans for meeting at conferences, said our good-byes to the list as we left for vacations, disclosed pregnancy and birth, illness and recovery, retirements and job changes. The human factors helped keep our debates civil—for the most part—and helped build the community of human respect that allowed for this collaboration of cobblers.

TURNING TOWARD READERS

As we grappled with revising the evolving Outcomes Statement, we confronted an unpleasant fact: the term *first-year composition* varied widely in meaning. Indeed, as many of the ensuing discussions revealed, the term was hotly contested among the very people in charge of administering it. So, we asked ourselves, if *we* couldn't agree what first-year composition should be, how could we ever account for what we do? How could we explain what we do, even within our own institutions, let alone beyond them? How could we expect students transferring from one institution to another to understand why one school was—or wasn't—willing to accept another institution's first-year composition course for transfer credit? If we could not define the course in anything other than essentialist terms—what *we* do, in *our* program—how could we hope to convince even our own administrations that our course exemplified good practice, that it was worthy of its funding, that it provided the institution something to be proud of? Without the ability to define the course beyond what was taught at a single institution, how would we ever fight the tendencies of legislatures to seek accountability by establishing reductive tests? These questions and others led us to a discussion about possibilities.

The great and intractable differences among local settings legislated against any agreement about standards—about how well a student exiting first-year composition should write. Outcomes, however—what students exiting first-year composition should know and be able to do—might prove workable. We could specify *what* students should do in first-year composition in terms that could work within any of the variations we knew about; and we could leave decisions about *how well* students should perform those outcomes where those decisions belonged—in the local context.

Most of us working in the group were ourselves WPAs, so to the extent that the Outcomes Statement addresses the interests of WPAs, we had an immediate test audience within the Outcomes group and a much wider test audience among the six hundred or so members of WPA-L. In addition, since on a given campus the WPA is the person who must account for her or his program to wider audiences, the group had a direct interest in devising a statement that would work not only within but also beyond specific programs. We wrote a statement that could help us WPAs as we work on tasks that WPAs have in common—training teachers, devising curricula, administering assessments, arguing for resources, conducting research, and so forth. Most important, we were writing a document that we ourselves could *use*. We were our own first audience.

Turning toward other audiences was unusually complicated in this case. As many as twenty-five people spearheaded the writing and over forty contributed phrases and ideas. Not only did we have a complicated reader who might lie anywhere on a continuum from rhetorician to concerned parent, we also had a complicated author. The number of authors expanded and their identities changed as some dropped out and new authors entered. The problem of revising for a complicated set of readers was additionally complicated by having to change a document with no recognized authors. But if we were to convince anyone that we can practice what we preach, we needed to demonstrate that we knew how to read the rhetorical situation effectively and write appropriately. We finally decided, for instance, that we wouldn't gain much, rhetorically, if we talked down to secondary and tertiary audiences by including sidebar discussions explaining our statements for the other readers. To make this document work, we had to say it cleanly for all readers.

The issue of appropriate language has been one of these conversations central not only to the final version of the Outcomes Statement but also to how we teach writing. This answer depends on the answer to another question: Who is the audience? And this question intersects with our purpose, i.e., what change did we hope to effect by making the statement? Or as Lloyd Bitzer (1968) would have put it: what was the exigence, and how did we hope to answer it? And who are we?

From this discussion emerged the following declaration in the penultimate draft:

> we expect the main audience for this document to be well-prepared college writing teachers and college writing program administrators. We have chosen to write in their professional language.[1]

The penultimate draft of the document consequently remained largely in our professional language—not impenetrable to noncompositionists but not friendly either. Here is an example of the prose that might appear unfriendly to, let's say, a public school board member who has a bachelor's in business administration and who has been running a small business in investment services for twenty years:

As writers move beyond the first-year course, their writing abilities do not merely "increase." Rather, students' abilities both diversify along disciplinary and professional lines and move into whole new levels where expected outcomes statements would expand, multiply, and diverge.[2]

Nothing in this language is particularly mystifying—none of the vocabulary is even discipline specific. But it might put off our imagined reader. Perhaps it is the context within which words like *disciplinary* and *professional lines* occur or the series of abstractions (abilities, diversify, disciplinary lines) and the abstract nature of having abilities diversify and statements expanding, multiplying, and diverging. As Joseph Williams has put it in *Style: Ten Lessons in Clarity and Grace* (1999), we don't have an agent and action that tell a nice simple story. We had to reconsider writing in our professional language and solely to readers for whom—to quote from the preface to the final version of the Outcomes Statement—"terms such as 'rhetorical' and 'genre' convey a rich meaning that is not easily simplified."

There are of course more issues than phrasing that determine the appropriate register of any discourse. There is, for example, the problem of syntax. Academic readers tend to be more tolerant than general readers of long introductory elements: e.g., in our first drafts, we wrote:

> By defining the common knowledge, skills, and attitudes sought by the wide variety of approaches to first-year composition currently used in American postsecondary education, we seek to describe a set of common outcomes for those first-year composition classes.

To paraphrase Joseph Williams again, we should worry if it takes more than a few words to get past the subject and verb. In the example above, it took us twenty-four words to get to the subject. The final version pared this down to

> This statement describes the common knowledge, skills, and attitudes sought by first-year composition programs in American postsecondary education.

Some of us were still not entirely happy with this sentence, but the editing, like the writing, was an exercise in negotiation and compromise. The final document goes a long way toward finding an acceptable medium between discipline-specific and the general discourse available to most readers.

The notion of tone gets to the center of our problem. Professional language, characterized by words like *rhetoric, genre,* and *conventions* (and

register), is useful to people who have grown used to a common set of asso-
ciations, including the historical uses of the terms. But to others, it smacks
of snotty language people use to show that they understand because they
are on the in—and of course people who don't understand are on the
out. Having earned our Ph.D.s, we sometimes display our badges through
our language; people who have not similarly emblazoned themselves may
interpret that display as self-privileging. Whether they are correct, we
need to admit the possibility of this interpretation. Language is always
ideological; words are replete with the histories of their use, full of varied
meanings that include some and exclude others.

EDITING FOR CONCISENESS

The Outcomes Statement authors also faced decisions about the overall
scope of the document. The statement needed to communicate potentially complicated matters. Further, those who make writing their business
have a fundamentally different understanding of writing than do most
potential readers. Most critically, nearly all "outsiders" believe the best
approach to better writing is more grammar. "Insiders" have good reason
to suspect, based on years of research (e.g., Hillocks 1986; Hartwell 1985;
Haswell 1991), that nothing could be worse than more grammar. Yet the
statement must reach, somehow, readers who mostly want us to wield a
keen red pen. The brevity of the document has the virtue of accommodating limited patience and attention spans, but it probably hides much of
what we really need to say to readers who badly need to understand the
"insider" viewpoint. In sum, the brief statement leaves out a great many
highly important points.

Even so, there is perhaps little real loss in that brevity. Those of us who
worked on the statement quickly found that our goals for our students
diverged far less than anything else about us, from theoretical viewpoints
to pedagogical methods. Ed White, of course, had predicted this consensus around aims from the start; but the reality was, if anything, more
uniform than anyone seemed to expect. Indeed, this uniformity of goals
would persist even if we wrote in much more detail. We don't mention,
for example, that we expect students who go through our programs to
be able to summarize challenging texts, yet agreement on this point was
unanimous at every meeting. We don't expressly say that we aim to have
students write in a style that makes a human connection, but again this
was a strong consensus at our every meeting. Yet the expanding range of
uses for the statement described later in this book amply demonstrates

that the statement can function in this brief form, most likely because it can be "unpacked" in light of this broad agreement.

The question remains whether the statement actually functions *best* in brief form, however. Despite the disclaimers in the Statement's preface, we were always intensely aware of how we might be read by audiences other than our peers. We wanted readers to know that we were not radical relativists, that we *had* standards even if we were not writing them down; and yet we wanted readers to know that we had moved well beyond a simplistic interest in correctness, that we had a complicated rhetorical project in mind. The result is a somewhat timid and restricted document, one that does not extend itself comfortably into areas like writing for citizenship, or into areas that are common features of cultural studies composition classes. We can certainly argue that our interest in rhetorical knowledge and particularly the power of language can be reconstituted into full support for a cultural studies curriculum. Alternatively, we could argue that our interest in genre and critical thinking can support exercises like Peter Elbow's "looping," where writers explore a number of imaginary situations that call out various voices and genres. Indeed, the drafters and revisers did argue these very points among themselves while condensing the document into its current form. Still, the result ventures into such controversial and specific areas only by inference. Meanwhile, the concise document is not exactly "reader friendly." Instead, its brevity and "professional" language conveniently allowed the drafters to gloss over many of these controversies.

The steering committee that finished the drafting worked diligently and thoughtfully at expressing what the entire effort had generated, solving many rhetorical problems along the way. Yet by that point, global revision was barely possible, and even more questionably wise. That committee was only a small group, working without steady reference to all the other voices that had contributed bits and pieces of the language. It could not entirely recall the reasons for some of the phrasings we considered changing, much less unpack all the thinking and discussion that had gone into them. While we had kept archival materials, no record could presume to speak for the entire collective. That committee decided that its proper role, then, was to bring out the message of the document with greater clarity, not to rethink it wholesale. For that reason, the finished version is essentially an edited and rhetorically refined version of the brief draft that came out of the one-day workshop—a draft that has never truly been revised thoroughly in a reflective way. No one along the way even experimented with a more detailed, specific, and thus necessarily more complex document. Whether this fact indicates a prudent restraint or simply convenience (and possibly exhaustion) remains an open question.

CONCLUSION

When the Council of Writing Program Administrators adopted the Outcomes Statement, the Outcomes Collective became, as the term "*adoption*" metaphorically suggests, its birth parent. The statement will always carry our genetic material, but its life will be shaped—already has been shaped—mostly by its new social position. This chapter offers some hereditary information that might be useful in a health crisis, but perhaps it is mostly an act of letting go, with a small plea to be remembered.

3

STANDARDS, OUTCOMES, AND ALL THAT JAZZ

Kathleen Blake Yancey

Before we talk about standards, outcomes, and all that jazz, we best talk about objectives, the forebears of standards and outcomes.

In the 1970s I taught eighth grade in Washington County, Maryland. In addition to teaching, of course, we were expected to perform other tasks—everything from playing basketball in the faculty shoot-out to identifying objectives and standards for learning. Now this last task might not be as easy as you think it is. For instance, should all thirteen-year-olds know how to use the semicolon? Should they use it only to separate independent clauses or to separate items in a long list, especially one marked by other internal punctuation? Suppose you decide to test this objective by creating a basic test of semicolon usage. Exactly what will the test look like? Will students be asked to *identify errors* in semicolon use? Or will they be asked to *identify correct instances* of semicolon use? How will you score these items? Will they all be at the same level of difficulty? And on a test of ten items, how many items do students need to complete correctly in order that we might say that they could use them correctly? What them? Oh, yes: semicolons.

Given a test of ten items asking students to use the semicolon correctly to signal the boundary between independent clauses, they will get 70 percent of the items correct.

Fortunately—or not?—no one asked us to determine if students were using the semicolon in *their* writing at all.

Fast-forward two decades, and the paradigm shifts: from objectives to standards. Of course, interest in standards isn't limited to education. At a certain level, we all want standards, and we all rely on those standards being met. We want the physicians caring for our loved ones to be board certified, and we want that certification maintained. And most of us want teachers who likewise meet certain standards, though we might disagree on what those standards should be and how they might best be implemented. In general, we think standards are a good thing because through them, we have some assurance that products and services are "trustworthy": they have met some minimal level of safety or quality.

Standards in education are meant to function similarly, in this case to assure that students meet certain levels of achievement. Recently, educational standards have been linked to school reform, especially in the K–12 context. As Richard Murnane, an advocate of reform-based standards, explains, the recent drive for standards includes a quest for quality in student performance. At the same time, however, the emphasis on standards in the context of school reform is equally informed by a desire to level the educational playing field for all students. According to Murnane, standards that are required *uniformly*—of all children in all schools—can lead to *equal educational opportunities.* So while Murnane concedes that the standards-based reform is imperfect, he argues that the pressure they bring and their connection to reform exert an equalizing effect (Murnane 2000).

Murnane understands that educational standards are a vehicle, not the goal. Consequently, he suggests two checks: (1) low-income and minority children must be assured high-quality instruction; and (2) committed and successful educators should not be hamstrung by the accountability systems associated with standards. He also argues that testing formats are often too narrow to permit access to children's critical thinking abilities, and he believes that too much time is spent on test-taking skills (Murnane 2000). Still, Murnane believes that standards work toward equal access to quality education.

An appetite for standards is likewise taking hold in postsecondary education. Ronald Henry, provost at Georgia State University, makes an argument for standards that parallels Murnane's and, in some ways, goes beyond it. At Georgia State, standards are being used to generate two initiatives, both connected to creating a more coherent curriculum: "The first aims to establish standards for exit and transfer, and the second establishes disciplinary standards within undergraduate majors. For both projects, the goal is to foster an integrated curriculum, helping students to make more coherent course selections and to gain a better understanding not only of the ways that those courses intersect but also of the material in the courses" (Henry 2000, 19).

But curriculum isn't the whole story at Georgia State. Standards there also signal a basic shift—from a credit-based method of accounting for competence or proficiency to a mastery-based system. As Henry explains,

To set standards is to demand a certain level of mastery, rather than asking students merely to complete a set of credit requirements. In order to be effective, those standards should be high, achievable, and creditable to all parties, including students, faculty, the lay public, and potential employers. . . . Equally important, we anticipate that the process of establishing academic standards will make our educational goals a matter of public record and debate, bringing transparency to the educational system, pre-school through baccalaureate (P-16). (Henry 2000, 20)

In these terms, standards act as a check on the students as well as on courses. The courses themselves, in other words, are insufficient proof: something more is required. As important, standards themselves provide a kind of language that makes sense of schooling from kindergarten through college graduation.

What many—parents, teachers, even students—fear is that standards and standardized texts will lead to a standardized curriculum—which is exactly what has occurred in the United Kingdom. There the curriculum is implemented in a highly hierarchical, centralized way. A central team trains Local Education Authority (LEA) trainers, who then train "literacy coordinators" from each school, who in turn train colleagues on professional days and in "twilight" sessions" (Lofty 2000, 99). Although this system has been operating for only about three years, anecdotal evidence suggests that teachers there do see a "gain" in the curriculum in terms of "coverage, balance, and rigor." At the same time, they see those gains offset by serious losses: "fewer curricular innovations" and "less imaginative teaching." That the teaching would be less divergent is not surprising, given the way that curriculum is delivered—and then tested.

Advocates of standards, then, see them as helpful for many purposes: communication, high achievement, equality, and reform. Which is not to say that everyone likes standards, of course, and a brief examination of standards and their effects in Texas helps explain why.

Some time ago, Texas implemented a system of standards—or levels of achievement—for K-12 students. Students demonstrate that they can meet the standards by performing well on a standardized test. In other words, the measure of quality for the standards is achievement on a set of standardized tests. When people refer to standards in Texas, then, they can mean (1) the levels of achievement stipulated by the state; (2) the tests themselves; or (3) both. A fourth meaning is only implied, but all too common. Because Texas has articulated what's expected and because it requires students to meet those expectations, there is an accompanying assumption that Texas standards are high, that Texas schools are good, and that Texas students are learning well if they score well on the tests. In other words, the standards themselves are translated to mean excellence.

As it turns out, both from the point of view of opponents of standards and from researchers at the Rand Corporation (Klein et al. 2000), standards don't promise excellence, and meeting them doesn't assure it either: and this confusion about what standards mean is problem two. Critics of standards have suggested that Texas students have performed so well on the tests because the benchmarks are so low. If this is an accurate description, then the standards aren't producing the desired effect, which is a rise in achievement. And even if these critics are wrong, the Rand Corporation researchers who reviewed the test results say that whatever the students' performance on the tests, they can't do what the tests are supposed to measure, that is, think critically and imaginatively. In other words, the effects of the standards in Texas, according to this research report, is to produce students who can take tests but do little else.

The motivation for standards, as we have seen, can be admirable, in keeping with the best intentions of a democracy. At the same time, however, what the word *standards* can mean varies widely, they can be implemented very differently one place to the next, and they can yield effects contrary to their intent.

Outcomes provides another way of talking about and understanding curricular work. Rather than focusing on the specifics of a semicolon or on the level at which students should perform, outcomes focus on what we might call the *what* of education. Through thinking about what is it that we want students *to know, to understand,* and *to do* at the conclusion of a course, a program, a major, we begin to articulate our expectations: or, *outcomes.* A significant difference between outcomes and objectives is that objectives tend to be very specific statements of achievement, and the standards for achievement for each objective—the correction of semicolons at 70 percent, for instance—are likewise stipulated. While outcomes articulate the curriculum, they do not specify *how well* students should know or understand or do what the curriculum intends. In other words, because outcomes are not benchmarked against levels of performance, individual programs or institutions can have the same curricular outcomes but have different ideas about when and how well they want students to perform. A second significant factor is that outcomes tend to act as curricular frameworks: this is important because it means that an institution could have more than one framework operating simultaneously. For example, as in the case of the Outcomes Statement, several composition programs have their local outcomes plotted against these national outcomes. More generally, then, we might say that outcomes provide a kind of curricular stability without being very invasive—which in part explains their appeal.

Another important feature of outcomes is that they tend to be used as much (or even more) for program assessment than for individual assessment. In other words, tests connected to objectives have always been targeted to the individual student; and while results of standardized tests are sometimes aggregated so that we can talk about a general kind of performance—say, that of a school or even a state—that aggregation is based on a *summing of the tests results from every student.* Program assessment operates quite differently precisely because it seeks to answer questions about the course, the program, the district, or the institution. Accordingly, it tends to look at both product and process; it prefers real problems and rhetorical situations to items with predigested answers; and it can make observations by examining the work of a selected sample of students. To illustrate, then, program assessment doesn't ask how much a specific student has learned, but how much learning is taking place among all the students, why that learning is taking place, and how we can help more and better learning take place. In other words, outcomes-based program assessment tends to address both teaching and learning and is vested in helping both, as outcomes-oriented questions like these suggest:

- What knowledge, understanding, and skills do students acquire as a function of participating in this program?
- At the conclusion of this program, what do students know? What can they do?
- How does this compare with the kinds of thinking, knowing, and doing we saw in the beginning of their student careers?
- What has contributed to students' development? What has hindered it?
- How can you take what you have learned in this process and enhance your program?

In addition to the kinds of questions associated with outcomes, what's also interesting about them is the freedom they allow for curricular specifics—for different teaching styles, diverse pedagogies, multiple kinds of assignments, direct and indirect response strategies, and so on. What's

important, from an outcomes perspective, is the students' final performance, and there is an implicit recognition within outcomes assessment
that there are many legitimate ways to get to Rome. Such an approach—
the mirror image of the UK standards—permits maximum and appropriate freedom—for both students and faculty.

It may appear that I've muddied the waters some: on the one hand,
I'm talking about outcomes assessment, and on the other I'm talking
about outcomes as curriculum. As in many things, however, it's not really
either/or. Let me explain.

The original impulse for outcomes came from a need to understand
and enhance programs: it was an assessment impulse, true enough. And
accrediting agencies, interested as they are in motivating enhancement,
encouraged outcomes assessment. Now what's germane here is the balance between the local and the global that we see in the actions of accrediting agencies. In one sense, they act as an agent for the global since they
ensure that institutions in fact enact their own missions: that's the global
mandate that they enforce. On the other hand, the institutions' missions
are unique one to the next: each is the embodiment of local. So there is
a balance in this assessment that includes both local and global.

At the same time, as I've worked more with outcomes generally, with
this statement particularly and with a number of different groups across
the country, it seems increasingly clear to me that outcomes assessment
is, ironically, an exercise in curriculum much more than in assessment.
It is through articulating our expectations that we create outcomes, that
we then have these to share with students, that we begin to think not of
what's barely doable, but of what's visionary for our students—and for
ourselves.

In calling ourselves and our students to what's visionary, we create very
new and different outcomes indeed.

4

OUTCOMES ARE NOT MANDATES FOR STANDARDIZATION

Mark Wiley

Although official acceptance of the Outcomes Statement can provide needed coherence, stability, and political power for writing programs and composition courses, these outcomes can also be misinterpreted and consequently put to uses detrimental to the spirit within which they were deliberated, drafted, and publicly advocated. Examining criticisms of recent standards-based reform efforts can be instructive in terms of possible consequences that those of us who worked on this Outcomes project hope to avoid.

NEED FOR STANDARDS IN THE CONTEXT OF DISCIPLINARY REFORM

The push for national standards in subject-matter disciplines began in earnest in the early 1990s on the heels of Goals 2000 legislation. Certainly, such reform efforts are not new and demonstrate how the discipline of English has responded to larger political and socioeconomic changes. The current standards movement, particularly in the language arts, is the culmination of several reform efforts over the last one hundred years. Miles Myers (1994) identifies five key areas where shifts have occurred as the result of such nationally organized disciplinary projects as the NEA's Committee of Ten, Project English, the Dartmouth Conference, and most recently the English Coalition Conference.

1. English is no longer a course for the few, but for the many.
2. The definition of the learner has shifted from passive receiver to active constructor of meaning.
3. The role of literary studies is no longer to deliver readings of moral touchstones, but to construct readings within diverse cultural settings.
4. Education has moved from strictly local agencies to an interaction of school sites with federal and state agencies.
5. The public policy role of national subject-matter organizations has shifted from a minimal to a major role. (274)

As Myers indicates, education is no longer solely under local control, and national subject-matter organizations play a much larger political role in terms of public policy issues. Playing a larger role in public policy is necessary because the discipline of language arts (along with history) is a key area in public education where cultural conflicts are most clearly visible. What gets taught in "English" class as well as what standards of language usage are identified and enforced will always be issues debated not only within the discipline but in the wider public realm as well. The reading wars and debates over whole language have made headlines throughout the 1990s, while recent examples more germane to composition studies are the well-publicized battle over course content at the University of Texas–Austin as well as current battles in several states over the place of remedial education on university campuses.

CRITICISMS OF STANDARDS

The setting of disciplinary standards is both a pragmatic and political response to what the media sometimes implies is a growing incoherence in and irrelevance of the field of English studies. Nonetheless, standards-based reform, though gaining momentum in school districts throughout the country, has also generated its share of criticism. One of the prevalent charges is that setting standards means standardization—that is, standardizing the curriculum in a given subject-matter area so that teachers have no choice in what they teach. Severe constraints on what is taught can also often limit how one teaches. Adding substance to this charge of standardization is the fact that state and national assessments are at the top of the agendas of many politicians. Standardization therefore means teacher compliance, with compliance managed and enforced through standardized testing.

Critics contend that setting standards and enforcing them through testing encroaches on teachers' freedom and undermines confidence in their ability to judge what is appropriate for their students. Moreover, Susan Ohanian (1999), a strident critic of standards, argues that those who set them overlook variability in student ability and individual development. She fears that standards will force students to march lockstep through a given curriculum, with each student expected to achieve at the same level at the same time. The differences in the ways students learn and develop would become a liability, and instead of the promise offered by proponents of standards-based reform that all students will be expected to demonstrate proficiency, only those who can be molded into the new one-size-fits-all curriculum will be successful. Ohanian labels those putting forth standards "standardistos" who she claims ignore the needs of real students. "I know that being a teacher means honoring and nurturing oddball kids, kids who don't meet the neighborhood's standards. Being a teacher means giving kids time and space to work out some kinks. In the name of 'preparing the workforce of the twenty-first century, ' Standardistos insist on a uniformitarian curriculum delivered on schedule; taking a nineteenth century, instrumentalist position, they treat education as a commodity to be regulated (but not paid for) by the government. They see education as something external to the child, as something that can be shrink-wrapped and delivered like meals to a jumbo jet" (14).

The idiosyncrasies of learning and the unique profiles of individual learners, as dramatized in such recent works as Mel Levine's *A Mind at a Time* (2002), lend indirect support for Ohanian's criticisms that standards in practice do not enable so much as confine each child in an educational straightjacket. Tom Fox (1999) criticizes the standards movement as a veiled attempt to limit access to educational opportunities for traditionally excluded groups. Historically, Fox argues, the use of standards does not level the educational playing field for all but instead creates additional institutional barriers for immigrant students and students of color. Fox is not arguing against standards in principle but against the seeming inevitable harmful social and political uses to which they are put.

In his even-handed critique of standards, Elliot Eisner (1998) notes that current reform efforts echo long-familiar goals in education: to be precise about what we teach and to deliver instruction as efficiently as possible. Eisner recognizes the value of clear standards in setting high expectations and infusing rigor, substance, direction, and coherence into the curriculum. However, he also reminds us that the quest for certainty in terms of what we can expect our students to achieve was the hallmark of the "'efficiency movement' in education," a reform effort popular in the early part of the twentieth century and based on Frederick Taylor's goal to make business and industry less wasteful and more efficient. The quest for certainty and efficiency also characterized attempts in the 1960s to establish behavioral objectives for student learning. Eisner observes that both of these movements failed. With behavioral objectives, it soon became apparent that hundreds of them needed to be specified, and the result was that teachers were overwhelmed. Too much specificity proved to be counterproductive; a few objectives were much better than the minutiae contained in the hundreds. In attempts to "taylorize" education, administrators soon discovered that even if one could provide teachers with scripts of what to do hour to hour in the classroom, students would not follow them (177–78).

Repeating a theme in Ohanian's criticism of standards, Eisner goes on to claim that setting standards is futile and counterproductive if such efforts fail to recognize the variability in human development: "If you examine the patterns of human development for children from age five to eighteen, you will find that, as children grow older, their rate of development is increasingly variable. Thus the range of variation among children of the same age increases with time" (184).

As an example of this variability, Eisner cites the average range of reading achievement as approximately two years. He claims that in second grade some students read at the first-grade level, some at the second, and some at the third. But at the fourth-grade level, the range in reading achievement is about four years, while in the seventh grade some students read at the fourth-grade level and others at the tenth-grade, with everyone else falling somewhere in between (184–85). "Variability, not uniformity, is the hallmark of the human condition," Eisner argues, so students cannot be expected to meet grade-level standards with any consistency.

I share Eisner's, Ohanian's, and other critics' concerns over standards as an attempt to severely limit and micromanage education while ignoring the facts of variability in how (and when) human beings learn. But these negative consequences need not be the inevitable results of setting standards when standards are used to provide direction and goals for teaching. The Outcomes project was not intended to "standardize" postsecondary composition curricula, but to provide guidance for course and program design and to inform the curricular and pedagogic decisions of individual teachers. I recognize, though, that just as standards can be misused, so can the Outcomes Statement.

UNINTENDED EFFECTS

It is possible that at some institutions these outcomes will be misinterpreted precisely in order to impose a uniform curriculum upon the composition program. Individual teachers might be forced to use a common syllabus, text, and a reductive form of assessment to evaluate student writing at the end of the term. I don't believe, though, that knowledgeable writing program administrators will so narrowly interpret and apply the Outcomes Statement. Rather, misinterpretation is more likely to occur in situations where writing programs are being pressured to show measurable results of their efforts. Pressure from upper-level administrators on the composition program to demonstrate its value through measurable results might force some WPAs to select and translate aspects of the document that can be reliably quantified through end-of-term exams. Since the Outcomes Statement does not specify how each of its elements is to be weighted, some local program directors could isolate and privilege a few of the individual outcomes while ignoring the remainder. They could, for instance, decide to force all students to meet the conventions of Standard Edited English since this is one outcome most suitable to assessment by narrowly conceived empirical measures and one the public typically identifies with what teaching "English" is all about. Current pressure felt by colleges and universities nationwide to assess student learning can, unfortunately, feed into this impulse to reduce writing to its lowest common denominator, i.e., "basic skills" of grammar, usage, spelling, and punctuation, and formal elements of essays associated with formulaic writing (see Wiley 1999a).

The pressure to standardize writing curricula based on the Outcomes Statement may be worse at institutions where program directors and faculty are unaware of research and scholarship in composition studies, and who see the Outcomes Statement as an opportunity to get all faculty to follow the same syllabus in order to ensure consistency from section to section in the first-year composition course. Since writing program directors often do not have as much power as other administrators, and since the writing faculty are typically either graduate students or part-timers, this pressure to standardize easily wins out. Adding to this pressure to conform, the job performances of writing faculty could be based on student achievement on end-of-semester exams that measure how many outcomes were reached.

As a result, unintended "outcomes" of the document could be that nothing changes: in one scenario, the Outcomes Statement is interpreted as a mandate to prescribe a writing curriculum no different from the previous one, except that now this "new" curriculum acquires status because it has been advocated by recognized national authorities. In the second scenario, the Outcomes Statement becomes a rationale for returning to a locally interpreted version of a reductive basic skills curriculum.

A HAPPIER ENDING (WHICH IS REALLY A BEGINNING)

Let me emphasize that the Outcomes Statement is not meant to dictate course content nor to specify performance criteria. The term *outcome* is defined as the knowledge, skills, and understanding students have actually achieved as the result of their educational experiences. In this sense these outcomes for composition are similar to the national content standards in the language arts developed jointly by the NCTE and IRA, which are intended to guide, not to dictate, local curricular decisions (see the National Council of Teachers of English/International Reading Association's 1996 *Standards for the English Language Arts*, 2).

Since the term *standard* is used in several quite different contexts, it can be confusing. Content standards are not "performance standards" and not to be confused with other standards for assessment of students or teachers, or with standards specifying opportunities to learn (see Cross 1994; Loveless 1994; Atkin 1994). Content and performance standards, though, are closely linked: the former is much more meaningful when levels of performance are gauged. In other words, determining what students should know and be able to do is instantiated in performance standards that describe levels of achievement and articulate various ways students can demonstrate proficiency.

The Outcomes Statement does not articulate performance standards! Rather, these outcomes offer general goals for writing programs that can serve as a heuristic for designing various curricula and pedagogies whose ends are similar, but at the same time vary in form and content, emphasis, and sequence. These outcomes can inform the design of a single composition course or a sequence of two or more courses. There is no underlying assumption that all students will achieve these outcomes to the same degree of proficiency within the same time frame. In fact, we would expect variation depending on the type of program, the institution, and the students involved. Since students will demonstrate their developing competencies in a variety of ways, performance levels should be described locally by faculty participating in the writing program, who know their students well and who understand the level of writing ability necessary for success within a given course in a particular sequence. Local policy should also dictate what consequences follow for students who complete the required sequence of courses but who are still not able to demonstrate competency. It may well turn out that one or more of these outcomes is not realistically attainable by all students taking writing courses at a given institution. Some outcomes may need to be more finely articulated and perhaps even replaced.

Since the point of these outcomes, like the NCTE/IRA standards, is to provide direction and coherence, they should function more as foci to begin local conversations about curriculum and assessment, and about writing development and the institutional practices affecting that development. Again, like the term "standard," *outcomes* possesses a dual meaning. In the sense that these outcomes establish a basis for equity, they are a measure of what composition teachers share in common, a standard measure of what all students should be able to do after going through the composition program. These are educational experiences to which each student has access. But the other meaning of "standard," and one these outcomes also embody, is that of an emblem of quality, an emblem heralding high expectations for our students (see Wolf). As an emblem, these outcomes represent what the profession of composition values in terms of classroom practice. In this way these outcomes become objects of continued inquiry for practitioners and for WPAs. They allow us to focus on what we do in the classroom and to consider the value of our activities. Because these outcomes are not set in stone, we must continually ask: Are these emblems of our professional practice what we truly value?

In the spirit of inquiry, then, the Outcomes Statement must be subjected to continual scrutiny, to debate, to criticism, and to revision. We know as writing teachers that the criteria we bring to bear on judging a piece of student writing can be quite subjective. Often we are not even aware of some of these criteria until something a student writes grabs us unexpectedly, surprises us in such a satisfying way that our reaction causes us to reflect on the qualities we find in the writing that have pleased us. In trying to articulate these qualities, we achieve some measure of growth in our own knowledge of how we read and what we value. Such reflection can then enrich our practice as we try to translate into our teaching what we have come to know about what we value. These outcomes can thus create a productive tension between our interpretations of them and our students' performances. By engaging in this dynamic, reflective process, both students and their teachers continue to learn from one another.

Rather than this Outcomes document leading to standardization, to a one-size-fits-all curriculum, the hoped-for result is for WPAs and composition teachers to pursue a strategy the opposite of standardization. Instead of trying to be the same, we actively encourage and model diversity; we show how diversity of content and approach across sections and courses in writing programs reflect the spirit of the Outcomes Statement. We use these outcomes to encourage what Eisner calls "productive idiosyncrasy"(1998, 182); that is, as we invite students to exercise their judgment as they make rhetorical and linguistic choices, their written products will particularize these general outcomes at a concrete individual level. Perhaps the most significant long-term benefit that follows adoption of and acting and reflecting on these outcomes will be that the political power of WPAs within our respective institutions can be strengthened, as we become more skilled in devising assessment measures that concretely represent the protean ways these outcomes might be demonstrated through the variety of artifacts our students produce.

5

EXPANDING OUR UNDERSTANDING OF COMPOSING OUTCOMES

Cynthia L. Selfe and Patricia L. Ericsson

In a recent conversation among colleagues about the concerns and responsibilities of WPAs, it was suggested that our professional efforts might be better spent if we focused on more traditional outcomes of writing instruction—if we avoided diluting our efforts by paying attention to the texts generated within computer-based composing environments and the newly emerging forms of electronic composition that students and others are developing in these environments. This argument seems to underlie the Outcomes Statement as a whole, which focuses largely on traditional writing outcomes, with only the briefest nod to emerging technologies and their impact on literacies.

We find the logic of this argument difficult to accept—and, indeed, dangerous.

To our way of thinking, WPAs (or more accurately, as we argue below, CPAs)[1]—especially during a time of rapid and dramatic social and cultural transformation such as that characterizing the rise of the information age[2]—need to be more open in our intellectual understanding of the outcomes of composing and composition instruction, not more constrained. We need to recognize, study, and address not simply a limited set of such outcomes, but rather a full range of them—not simply those generated within the context of currently accepted literacies but also those generated within the contexts of newly emerging literacies and fading literacies.[3] And we need to understand more about how the standards of such literacies operate to shape texts, and the outcomes of composing, within specific historical periods and cultural ecologies.[4] We need to do this work so that we can help students negotiate and reconcile the contested values and practices of composing that they will encounter and produce during their lifetimes. And we need to do this work in order to negotiate these radical changes of composing practices and values for ourselves. In our view, the Outcomes Statement barely begins to address these complicated issues.

Our difficulty in accepting goes further. We would argue that some of our print-based expectations for writing instruction and our revered curricular practices will hold a declining relevance for many students as well as for the general public. We find evidence of this fact in the changing standards engendered by e-mail and online exchanges that resist traditional spelling and grammatical standards, in the Web-based texts that resist conventional organizational and authorial standards, and in the multimedia compositions that resist an alphabetic dependence altogether.

If we don't expand our traditional notions of composing outcomes beyond those of print-based texts to include visually based texts, multimedia and multimodal compositions, texts composed not only of printed words, but also of animations and images and sound, we run the risk of missing out on articulating new ways of making sense of a changing world (we encourage colleagues to read Bill Cope and Mary Kalantzis's (2000) outstanding edited collection which grows out of the work of the New London Group: *Multiliteracies: Literacy Learning and the Design of Social Futures*). If we don't think about expanding our *writing* programs into *composition* programs—we might well see these programs experience a rapid decline of relevance to young people and to the larger public.

How do we begin such a task? We can expand our own understanding of composing outcomes by observing students' online literacy practices as closely as we do their more traditional writing practices and by listening closely, and with open minds, to what they are saying about the role of new-media compositions in the world they inhabit. Although nothing in the Outcomes Statement would prevent such observation, little in it encourages it, either. We need to look through and beyond the OS in order to cultivate such a vision.

We can also expand our understanding of composing outcomes by studying the practices, values, and approaches of other composition specialists: multimedia designers and artists, digital photographers, poets who work in multiple media, and interactive fiction authors, among many others. We must extend our own understanding of "composing" practices to include a range of other behaviors: reading and composing images and animations; creating multimedia assemblages; combining visual elements, sounds, and language symbols into alternatively organized and presented forms of communication on the Web, in chat rooms, over networks.

To WPAs who work in institutions that lack material and electronic resources—often, but not always, the same institutions that serve large populations of students of color or poor students—it may seem almost frivolous to focus the kinds of new-media texts we have mentioned. In fact, these are the very best—and most important—sites for an expanded understanding of composing outcomes, and WPAs in such locations should continue to fight vigorously for students' access to electronic composing environments and for their own access to these environments. Unless we can help students of color and poor students compose rhetorically effective texts in these environments—and be critically aware of their own and others' rhetorical success in doing so—they run the risk of being "have-nots" in a culture that increasingly associates power with technological reach, of being passive consumers of electronic texts but not being able to produce these texts. Electronic composing environments are essential for such students *because* they are sites of political activism and power. As Manuel Castells explains in *The Power of Identity* (1997), such environments are places within which individuals can connect with others who share their interests, values, political commitments, and experiences. It is through these electronic connections, Castells continues, that individuals can participate in forging the new set of "codes" under which societies will be "re-thought, and re-established" (360) during the rest of this century. Hence, our failure to address technology may have serious implications for the future of writing programs, but it may have even more important implications—and dangerous ones—for students.

And here is one last argument. In 1992, Lester Faigley wrote about his concerns when he observed the fragmentation, alienation, contradiction, disaffection, loss of authority, and rejection of responsibility that characterized students' online conversations in one of his classes. Seven years later, in 1999, Marilyn Cooper tried to provide some comfort to those of us who shared Faigley's concern by focusing on the nature of responsibility in a postmodern world. She suggested that these students' exchanges—the outcome of their collective composing efforts—might be interpreted to illustrate not the rejection of responsible communication, but rather the practice of a new kind of responsible composition shaped by the conditions of postmodernity. Responsibility within postmodern contexts, Cooper pointed out—building on the work of Foucault (1983) and Bauman (1993)—rests *not* on an allegiance to traditional authorities like teachers and conventional texts, *not* on modernist authority figures or value systems rooted in the Enlightenment, but rather on a personal "willingness" to relate to other humans, on a personal "impulse to be responsive to and responsible for" others, on a "willingness" to approach authentic problems arising from the postmodern condition (Cooper 1999, 153) and to learn about their complexity with the help of concerned teachers.

It is this willingness to respond to others, Cooper argues, that students seem to have in abundance, although—we would add—we do not always recognize the importance of this fact or deal effectively with it as a prime exigence for composing. Sometimes, it seems as if we willfully ignore the newer forms of relating to one another and to the world that students have identified as the most valuable outcomes of composing.

Maybe we can start learning about these new compositions, these new outcomes, by opening our minds as widely as we ask students to open theirs.

PART TWO

The Outcomes Statement and First-Year Writing

6

THE WPA OUTCOMES STATEMENT GOES TO HIGH SCHOOL

Stephen Wilhoit

During the 2001–2 academic year, the English teachers at Oakwood High School in Oakwood, Ohio, began a systematic review of the school's writing curriculum. The teachers were particularly interested in determining whether the writing program offered students the reading, writing, and thinking skills they would need in college. As part of that review, I was asked to offer interested teachers a workshop on "college writing expectations." That workshop led to a much larger project—working with a small group of teachers to develop a writing-in-the-disciplines (WID) program for students in grades 9–12. This program is a year old now, and one result has been the creation of a new writing center staffed by peer tutors. The WPA Outcomes Statement played an important role in all three projects, helping us clarify college writing expectations, develop a high school WID program, and train tutors for the school's writing center.

PROJECT 1: A WORKSHOP ON COLLEGE WRITING EXPECTATIONS

In March 2002, the director of curriculum, instruction, and assessment for the Oakwood school system asked me to develop a workshop that would help high school teachers better understand college writing expectations. I pointed out that writing requirements vary widely at colleges and universities across the country, but agreed to offer what help I could. Thirty-five high school teachers from across the curriculum attended the workshop along with the high school and junior high school principals and several school system administrators, including the superintendent.

I began by asking the workshop participants to make a list of the writing assignments and projects they most often employ in class. After they shared their lists with each other, we compiled a comprehensive master list on an overhead transparency. The list was dominated by narrative, descriptive, and creative writing assignments plus essay tests. Other teachers mentioned literary analysis essays, summaries, reports, and research papers.

Setting this list aside for the moment, I then asked everyone to reflect for a few moments on two questions:

- What is your definition of "college writing"?
- On what is that definition based?

After a few minutes, I asked the teachers to share their answers with the group and composed another master list on an overhead transparency.

As might be expected, responses to the first question varied widely. Some defined college writing expectations in terms of specific assignments, such as research papers or essay tests. Some focused on critical thinking skills, such as the ability to analyze and synthesize texts. Others focused on certain academic conventions, such as correct documentation, or on certain rhetorical aspects of writing, such as the selection and arrangement of evidence or the ability to write for an academic audience. In responding to the second question, most of the teachers said they based their conceptions of college writing expectations on their own experience as college students or on what they have heard from former students who went on to college.

Next, I shared the results of eleven surveys of college writing assignments published over the past three decades (see appendix to this chapter, p. 50). Together, we engaged in a meta-analysis of these survey results to determine what they could tell us about the types of assignments students are typically asked to write in college and the skills students need to complete these tasks successfully. As we moved through these study results, one trend emerged—the ubiquitous nature of source-based writing assignments. According to these studies, students across the curriculum were most frequently being asked to summarize, analyze, critique, and synthesize source texts of some kind—textbook chapters, course readings, research results.

We then briefly discussed the limitations of the studies we just reviewed. Most were dated and many were based on the study of just one institution. Some of the findings were based on faculty surveys and others on student surveys. A few examined the assignments faculty actually distributed in class, but most did not, relying instead of self-reported data.

I next gave the participants a copy of the WPA Outcomes Statement, briefly explaining its genesis and purpose. I suggested that the Outcomes Statement could offer us a more recent view of how active members of the profession view college writing expectations. We then discussed the statement section by section with two goals: to be sure we understood what the document was saying about college writing expectations and to determine how well Oakwood's writing program was preparing students to meet those expectations.

The teachers were most familiar with the outcomes related to writing processes. The English department at Oakwood High School long ago moved to a process-oriented pedagogy that had spread to teachers across the curriculum. Our discussion of this outcome focused instead on the notion of helping students develop "flexible" composing strategies for classes across the disciplines and the role technology can play in the composing process.

For example, the teachers concluded that they should try to identify which composing strategies transferred most effectively across disciplines. Since no genre-based curriculum could prepare students to compose the wide range of writing assignments they would likely encounter in college, the teachers decided that a process-based curriculum that emphasized transferable reading and writing skills might best help students achieve the outcomes outlined in the statement.

The statement also sparked some discussion about technology, writing, and writing instruction. While no decisions concerning technology emerged from this particular workshop, the Outcomes Statement raised awareness of the issue, generated ideas that later informed the design of Oakwood's WID program, and led to a brainstorming session on ways instructors could make better use of the high school's existing computer lab when teaching writing and research skills.

The discussion then turned to questions concerning another outcome: the students' ability to employ "appropriate voice, tone, and level of formality" in college writing across the curriculum. The teachers wondered whether it was possible to identify standards of voice, tone, and register applicable to college writing across the disciplines or whether these standards were entirely discipline specific. Questions about genre also emerged: Do high school teachers and college faculty share common definitions of academic discourse? Do high school teachers and college faculty conceptualize "research papers," "response essays," "literary analysis essays," or "summaries" in similar ways? Do they share similar standards when evaluating these types of essays? They wondered how high school teachers can come to understand how these genres are defined in college courses and modify their curriculum to better prepare students for the demands of college writing.

Similar issues were raised in our discussion of the outcomes related to writing conventions. The workshop participants posed questions familiar to anyone involved in a WID program: What role should composition classes play in helping students learn discipline-specific conventions of writing? What role should teachers in those disciplines play? How can instructors best teach those conventions? Which conventions, if any, hold for writing across the curriculum?

Perhaps most helpful, though, was our discussion of the outcomes related to critical thinking, reading, and writing. We began by drawing connections between the assignment surveys we reviewed earlier and the statement's outcomes concerning writing, inquiry, learning, thinking, and communicating. Both the surveys and document emphasized the importance of "finding, evaluating, analyzing, and synthesizing appropriate primary and secondary sources" in college writing. The teachers agreed that this was a particular strength of Oakwood's writing program, but one they could also work to improve. A few participants also questioned whether their current curriculum, with its heavy emphasis on narrative and descriptive writing, could adequately address this outcome and suggested that the high school find ways of assigning more source-based writing projects.

To close the workshop, I again placed on the overhead projector the list of writing tasks the teachers currently asked their college-bound students to complete. Given all that we have been discussing, I asked them, how would they assess the adequacy of their writing curriculum? I did not have to offer any assessment myself. The teachers and administrators quickly identified ways their curriculum might help students achieve the outcomes included in the statement and acknowledged where their instruction could be improved.

We had little time left in the session to discuss ways to improve the curriculum. Instead, the high school principal announced that the teachers would take up that question at the next faculty meeting. A few weeks later, the school district's director of curriculum, instruction, and assessment sent me an e-mail. What intrigued many of the workshop participants, she wrote, was the Outcomes Statement's suggestion that faculty across the curriculum could play a key role in helping students develop their reading, writing, and thinking skills. Many of the teachers were interested in developing a WID program at Oakwood High School that could eventually be extended into the junior high. The director asked me if I could develop a series of WID workshops for interested faculty and administrators to attend during the last few weeks of the 2002 spring term (for a fuller narrative of the program's beginnings, see Scalzo, Koenig, and Wilhoit 2003).

PROJECT 2: OAKWOOD WRITING TO LEARN

After our discussion of the Outcomes Statement, Oakwood's teachers and administrators became especially interested in developing a WID program that would encourage students to employ writing-to-learn activities across the curriculum and master discipline-specific research skills and writing conventions. This initiative, called Oakwood Writing to Learn (OWL), initially involved fifteen high school teachers from across the curriculum, the high school principal, and several school system administrators. To get OWL started, I designed four workshops, summarized below.

Workshop 1. Writing to Learn: History and Theory

At this first workshop, we discussed the history and theory of writing-to-learn programs. The goal of the workshop was to help the participants form a clearer understanding of how writing can be used to improve learning across the curriculum, identify key elements of most writing-to-learn programs, develop a common vocabulary for discussing writing and learning, and develop a set of questions that would guide our future discussions about the connection between writing and learning across the disciplines.

Workshop 2. Writing to Learn: Critique of Current Practices

The following week we discussed a variety of writing-to-learn techniques commonly employed in classes across the curriculum. The goal of this workshop was to help the participants identify a wide range of writing activities and assignments that promote learning, understand how both formal and informal writing assignments can promote learning, and develop a set of criteria for evaluating writing-to-learn activities and assignments to determine which would be most applicable to Oakwood's new program and curriculum.

Workshop 3. Writing to Learn: Applications for Oakwood's Curriculum

Here we discussed specific writing-to-learn assignments and activities the participants currently employed in their classes or would like to employ in future classes. All of the participants brought for group critique copies of assignments or projects they believed promote student learning. The goal of the session was to help the teachers form a clearer understanding of which writing-to-learn assignments and activities their colleagues are currently using in class, consider how such assignments might be improved, and identify writing-to-learn activities and assignments they could jointly develop within and across disciplines.

Workshop 4. Writing to Learn: Where Do We Go From Here?

This fourth workshop involved a brainstorming session on how to move forward. The goal of the session was to help the participants develop a plan for engaging more faculty in OWL, form a strategy for assessing and documenting the effectiveness of the writing-to-learn assignments and activities they employ, decide on topics for future workshops, and identify steps faculty and administrators could take to support writing-to-learn initiatives and make OWL a success.

So many good ideas came out of this last workshop, we decided to meet one more time to identify specific steps teachers and administrators could take during the 2002–3 academic year to establish OWL and build on the momentum we had generated. We agreed to take the following steps:

- Establish a management team of high school teachers and administrators to oversee the program
- Develop an OWL Web site on the school system's server
- Develop and distribute an electronic newsletter to all faculty advertising OWL-related activities and initiatives
- Determine an agenda for a fall OWL workshop
- Develop an OWL-related teacher resource center in the high school
- Begin a "best practices" collection of writing-to-learn assignments and activities currently being employed by Oakwood teachers and place it in the teacher resource center
- Target one program or department in the high school for writing-to-learn workshops the following academic year
- Prepare presentations on the program for fall conferences or in-service workshops
- Collaboratively produce reports on the project for publication
- Establish a writing center in the high school to support student writing
- Decide how we would assess the program

The OWL leadership team met many of these goals during the first year of the program. They conducted follow-up workshops, collected material for the Teacher Resource Center, assembled a best practices collection, established a newsletter, published work describing the program, and established a writing center in the high school library.

The Outcomes Statement played an important role in planning these workshops and making OWL a success. First, Oakwood's WID program grew naturally from the teachers' desire to prepare their students for the demands of college writing. The Outcomes Statement helped them clarify those demands because it succinctly summarizes the "common knowledge, skills, and attitudes sought by first-year composition programs in American postsecondary education." The workshops were designed to help the teachers better understand outcomes; define them in terms applicable to their students, curriculum, and school; reflect on the effectiveness of the writing assignments and activities they already employ to promote learning; and envision how a cross-disciplinary, multiyear high school writing program might help students become more effective and confident college writers.

Second, the teachers believed that the Outcomes Statement could help convince their colleagues that OWL is a viable, important initiative. Since so many of the document's outcomes emphasize the epistemic aspects of writing, teachers across the disciplines may come to believe that using writing to promote inquiry, learning, and thinking is not just another passing educational fad. The statement further makes clear that leading experts in composition studies view writing to learn as a fundamental outcome of college composition programs. The statement also reinforces the message that student literacy is not the sole responsibility of a single department or program, that every teacher has an obligation to help students become critical readers, writers, and thinkers. The teachers believed their colleagues would welcome the document's specific recommendations concerning ways teachers across the curriculum can help students develop these skills.

Third, the multidisciplinary, collaborative view of writing instruction promulgated by the Outcomes Statement helped us design many elements of the program's support services. A central question the teachers and administrators participating in the workshops faced was this: If OWL hopes to achieve the outcomes outlined in the statement and encourage teachers from across the disciplines to promote learning and thinking through writing, what support services will the school system need to provide? This discussion quickly divided into two tracks: support services for teachers and support services for students.

Those interested in faculty support believed their colleagues would need little help addressing outcomes related to the conventions of writing. However, those related to rhetorical knowledge could prove more difficult for faculty to teach. For many instructors across the curriculum, the skills included in this section of the statement have become routine (for example, responding to the needs of an audience, using a structure and conventions appropriate to the rhetorical situation, adopting an appropriate voice). As experts in their fields of study, they employ these skills unconsciously themselves when they write. Such tacit knowledge is often difficult to articulate and teach. The OWL leadership team decided that collaborative inquiry was the best way to help their colleagues develop pedagogies that address rhetorical knowledge. They envisioned instructors working together in small, cross-disciplinary groups to develop ways to identify and teach discipline-specific critical thinking, reading, and writing skills; help students use writing as a mode of learning; and help both teachers and students understand the relationships among language, knowledge, and power in the academy. Finally, the teachers decided that all of the school's instructors could benefit from workshops that focused on multiple-draft writing, peer review, and technology.

Teachers interested in student support recognized that when OWL becomes fully established in the high school, they can expect Oakwood's students to be writing more often in many of their classes. Reviewing the Outcomes Statement for some guidance on developing support services, they concluded that establishing a writing center in the high school might be the best way to ensure students receive needed assistance. Peer tutors, they decided, could be especially effective in helping students master several outcomes related to rhetorical knowledge, writing processes, and writing to learn.

During the summer and fall of 2002, Oakwood teachers finalized plans for a writing center in the high school library. They worked successfully with the school system's administrators to obtain private funding to equip the center with new computers, printers, furniture, and software. When the school superintendent asked me to help train the peer tutors, I again turned to the Outcomes Statement for help.

PROJECT 3: TRAINING WRITING CENTER TUTORS

Tucked away in a back corner of Oakwood High School's library, the writing center began operations toward the end of the 2002–3 academic year with faculty tutors. Beginning with the 2003–4 academic year, it was staffed by juniors and seniors enrolled in the school's Honors or Advanced Placement English classes who volunteered for the position.

As I designed a three-hour training workshop for the first group of peer tutors during the summer of 2003, I again turned to the Outcomes Statement for help. I began the workshop by explaining what tutoring involves, how tutors tend to do their work, how tutoring sessions are typically run, and how tutors should work in concert with classroom teachers. I then distributed several sample papers I had composed for the workshop and asked the students to take turns role playing a scenario in which one of them was the author of the paper and the other a tutor. The student playing the role of the tutor had to answer the writer's questions and offer advice on how to improve the essay. After each session, we discussed the strengths and weaknesses of the interaction. Then the students switched roles and worked on another essay, followed by another round of discussion.

After a break, I turned to an examination of the writing process and the Outcomes Statement. First, I offered the students a model of the writing process, summarizing the activities writers typically complete during the pre-writing, drafting, revising, and proofreading stages of the process. Next, I turned the students' attention to an overhead transparency listing the statement's seven process outcomes and led a discussion of their implication for writing center tutors.

Process Outcome 1

Be aware that it usually takes multiple drafts to create and complete a successful text.

Tutors, I pointed out, need to reinforce the notion that good writing is usually the result of composing multiple drafts. I warned the workshop participants not to succumb to the common desire students have for tutors to "rewrite" or "fix" their papers. Instead, good tutors guide student revisions, helping writers understand various ways they can improve the next draft of their work.

Process Outcome 2

Develop flexible strategies for generating, revising, editing, and proofreading.

I reminded the tutors that they have succeeded as writers in part because they already possess flexible strategies for generating, revising, editing, and proofreading texts. Many of the students coming to the writing center for help will not have developed these skills. We discussed how tutors often serve as writing "coaches" who can share alternative composing and revising strategies with their peers or help their peers adapt the skills they already possess to complete new or difficult writing tasks.

Process Outcome 3

Understand writing as an open process that permits writers to use later invention and rethinking to revise their work.

We discussed how tutors can help their peers engage in reflective revisions of their work. Tutors can offer honest response to students' work and ask questions that need to be answered in the next draft of the essay. They can help students learn how to evaluate their own papers and develop a plan for improving the content of future drafts. In short, tutors are in an excellent position to help their peers understand the vital role revision plays in the writing process.

Process Outcome 4

Understand the collaborative and social aspects of writing processes.

This outcome gets to the heart of the tutoring process. Writing center tutors have to understand the collaborative, social nature of writing and their role in the composing process. They will work *with* the student to answer questions, solve problems, and make plans, avoiding the temptation to appropriate the client's text. Tutors can also help their peers understand that when they write academic papers, they are entering an ongoing conversation about the topic and need to decide what they would like to contribute to the discussion themselves.

Process Outcome 5

Learn to critique their own and others' work.

Tutors critique the work of other writers everyday. They model critical reading and revising skills their clients need to master. However, most tutors agree that working in a writing center also changes the way they look at their own writing. Tutors often learn as much or even more than they teach.

Process Outcome 6

Learn to balance the advantages of relying on others with the responsibility of doing their part.

A primary goal of tutoring is to help students become more self-sufficient writers. Tutors can work with students to identify the strengths and weaknesses of particular papers and offer strategies for improving the work, but they also need to encourage students to take on the responsibility of composing and revising themselves. Working with a tutor should help students learn how to take responsibility for their own work.

Process Outcome 7

Use a variety of technologies to address a range of audiences.

I noted that as writing center tutors, they may need to offer advice on how to use a range of technologies to locate audience-appropriate sources of information, obtain model texts, consult reference works, download graphics, or format and publish texts. Tutors have to be comfortable working with technology and understand the way technology impacts written communication.

After completing this workshop, I talked with several school administrators about offering future tutors a semester-long credit-bearing course on rhetoric, tutoring, and collaborative writing, using the Outcomes Statement as a curriculum guide. They enthusiastically endorsed the idea, and we are currently drawing up plans for the course.

CONCLUSION

The WPA Outcomes Statement has proven to be a highly flexible document, serving as a guide or source of information for several WID-related programs at Oakwood High School. As we collaborated on these projects, the high school teachers and I have repeatedly turned to the Outcomes Statement to gain a better understanding of college writing expectations, guide faculty development initiatives, and develop student support services. The statement has helped us bridge the gap that often exists between high school and college writing teachers, providing us with a common set of pedagogical and curricular goals and a shared set of terms for discussing what matters most to us—improving our students' reading, writing, and thinking skills.

Appendix

SAMPLE SURVEYS OF COLLEGE WRITING REQUIREMENTS

Behrens, Laurence. 1978. Writing, Reading, and the Rest of the Faculty: A Survey. *English Journal* 67.6: 54–60.

Bernhardt, Stephen A. 1985. Writing across the Curriculum at One University: A Survey of Faculty Members and Students. *ADE Bulletin* 82: 55–59.

Bridgeman, Brent, and Sybil B. Carlson. 1984. Survey of Academic Writing Tasks. *Written Communication* 1: 247–80.

Eblen, Charlene. 1983. Writing-across-the-Curriculum: A Survey of a University Faculty's Views and Classroom Practices. *Research in the Teaching of English* 17: 343–48.

Hale, Gordon, et al. 1996. A Study of Writing Tasks Assigned in Academic Degree Programs." TOEFL Research Report no. 54. Princeton: Educational Testing Service.

Horowitz, Daniel M. 1986. What Professors Actually Require: Academic Tasks for the ESL Classroom. *TESOL Quarterly* 20: 445–62.

Kroll, Barbara. 1979. A Survey of the Writing Needs of Foreign and American College Freshmen. *English Language Teaching Journal* 33: 219–27.

Ostler, Shirley. 1980. A Survey of Academic Needs for Advanced ESL. *TESOL Quarterly* 14: 489–502.

Rose, Mike. 1983. Remedial Writing Courses: A Critique and a Proposal. *College English* 45: 109–28.

Scharton, Maurice. 1983. Composition at Illinois State University: A Preliminary Assessment. *Illinois English Bulletin* 71: 1–22.

Zelman, Steven A. 1977. How College Teachers Encourage Students' Writing. *Research in the Teaching of English* 11: 227–34.

7

THE OUTCOMES STATEMENT AT A COMMUNITY COLLEGE
Verification, Accreditation, and Articulation

J. L. McClure

The first full draft of the Outcomes Statement, which came out of the Defining Outcomes from College Writing workshop at the 1998 Conference on College Composition and Communication (CCCC) in Chicago, was timely for the English department at Kirkwood Community College. Kirkwood, located in Cedar Rapids, Iowa, with sites in six surrounding counties, is a relatively large community college, with an annual enrollment of about thirteen thousand students. Each year about four thousand students enroll in our three-course composition sequence—Elements of Writing (our basic writing course, which about one-third of our students take), Composition I, and Composition II. In the spring of 1998, Kirkwood was in the middle of preparing for our ten-year accreditation review by North Central Association (NCA). A major focus of the NCA accreditation review is the assessment of student learning at the institution, including general education, which includes our composition courses. The first meeting of the Composition Assessment Committee, which had been charged with designing and implementing an assessment plan for our composition courses, was scheduled for the Thursday following the CCCC, and the Outcomes Statement became a central resource from the very beginning of our assessment process. Over the past several years, the Outcomes Statement has served to guide the committee in three areas: verification, accreditation, and articulation.

VERIFICATION

At that initial meeting, the Composition Assessment Committee agreed that the first step in assessing our composition courses was to identify what it was that we did in those courses. During the 1991–92 academic year, the English department had devised general objectives for its composition courses:

Critical Reading. We intend that students will develop the following abilities:
- To understand the writer's purpose and audience
- To analyze the writer's reasoning and support
- To become acquainted with the writer's context(s)
- To integrate new material with prior knowledge
- To relate individual experience to a broader world

Critical Writing. We intend that students will develop the following abilities:
- To employ a recursive writing process
- To adapt writing to purpose and audience
- To write with reasoning and necessary support
- To integrate new material with prior knowledge
- To relate individual values and experience to a broader world
- To use "Standard English"

Of course, there are varying degrees of emphasis of these general objectives in each of the courses in our sequence. For each of the courses, the department developed more specific objectives that represented the emphases for the particular course. For example, the objectives for Composition II, the final course in the sequence, focus more on argument and research than either Elements of Writing or Composition I:

Instructors [of Composition II] intend that students will do the following:
- Comprehend and analyze the *arguments* of others
- *Write logical arguments* that state claims clearly and provide appropriate and sufficient reasons and evidence to support those claims
- Locate, select, and evaluate appropriate *sources* and integrate information from sources in papers
- *Cite and document sources* using the MLA or other parenthetical documentation format
- Continue to improve critical reading, writing, and thinking skills
- Continue to gain understanding of the *process* of writing, including invention, thesis, rough drafts, final drafts, global revision, editing, and the importance of the writing community at various stages during the evolution of a composition
- Continue to heighten awareness of *audience* and *purpose* through various types of writing assignments, which may include summaries or analyses of readings, research papers, literary analyses, business letters, etc.
- Continue to improve command of *Standard English,* including punctuation and grammar
- Through these experiences, continue to build *confidence* in writing ability

Most of the first meeting of the assessment committee was to review these general and more specific course objectives against the Outcomes Statement draft that had come out of the CCCC's workshop. The consensus of the committee was that while the phrasing was not always the same and the emphasis was somewhat different (for example, because of the abilities of our students, we tend to emphasize reading skills more in our sequence than other colleges and universities might), the Outcomes Statement verified the objectives defined by our department as comparable to the national set of outcomes defined by representatives of college and university composition programs from around the country. This was an important first step in our process of program assessment and review.

ACCREDITATION

As part of the NCA accreditation review, an institution is required to provide evidence of the assessment of student learning in all of its programs and courses. After using the Outcomes Statement to verify our department's objectives as being appropriate, the assessment committee proceeded to develop two measures of student learning in our composition courses.

The first assessment method is an indirect measure, a survey that is given to students in all composition courses sometime during the last two weeks of the semester. The committee determined that some outcomes of composition courses—for example, attitudes toward writing, or behaviors involving the process of writing—were best assessed by asking students what they thought their abilities were and how their experiences in composition affected those abilities. The committee compiled the items for the initial survey by working simultaneously with the Outcomes Statement and the department's objectives. The survey went through two pilot administrations and revisions before the final version was approved (see appendix A, p. 57).

While the specific phrasing of the survey items and the emphasis on students' abilities may appear to have little direct correspondence to the Outcomes Statement, it certainly was an influence in the content of the items. Clearly, we needed to phrase the items in terms that are used by instructors in our program and that students will understand. We also wanted to balance the emphasis on the particular abilities represented in the survey with those of the curriculum in our overall sequence. Through the initial development and subsequent revisions of the survey, the Outcomes Statement was regularly referred to as a resource to assure coverage of what we want our students to have done and have learned in our composition sequence.

The second assessment method is a direct measure, an evaluation of student writing:

- Argumentative research papers (the culmination of the composition sequence) are collected from a representative sample of sections of Composition II from all county sites and all methods of delivery.
- All full-time faculty and several adjunct faculty meet to read and evaluate the set of papers (125–50), in groups of four or five (15–20 papers per group).
- The assumption at the beginning of the reading is that all papers are "2" papers on a scale of 3 to 1 (3 being "superior," 2 being "average," 1 being "inferior"). The groups read their set of papers, first each member individually, evaluating each paper, noting particularly papers that verge into the 3 or 1 categories. Then each group discusses its set of papers, negotiating which papers fall into the 3 or 1 categories. The goal is to determine what papers are 3 and what papers are 1 scores; each group must come to a consensus on these papers. (The 2 papers are assumed to be the majority.)
- Once the groups have agreed which papers are 3 papers and which are 1 papers, they then use the "Argument Research Paper Attribute Check Sheet" (appendix B) to, first, fill in the number of papers that fall into each of the categories. Then, most important, the group agrees to check four or five of the "Attributes of Superior (3) Papers" that describe the qualities of the papers they've culled out as 3 papers and four or five of the "Attributes of Inferior (1) Papers" that describe the qualities of the papers they've culled out as 1 papers.
- When all of the groups have completed the above process, the groups get together to compare notes and discuss the papers read and the assessment of the papers. By the end of the whole-group discussion, there should be some agreement about attributes that showed up on the superior papers among all the groups and about some of the attributes that showed up on the inferiorpapers.
- Having agreed on one or several areas of deficiencies in the inferior papers among all of the groups, as a department we solicit assignments and strategies from all faculty for teaching those attributes that tend to appear across several groups' analyses, and when appropriate hold workshops to help faculty focus on teaching and assessing those attributes.

Because this assessment focuses on a particular rhetorical mode, the criteria established in the "Argument Research Paper Attribute Check

Sheet" (appendix B, p. 59) were not directly derived from the Outcomes Statement; however, by the time of the development of this assessment, the Outcomes Statement had become inherent within the whole process of the assessment committee.

ARTICULATION

As a community college, Kirkwood is concerned with articulation in two directions: (1) as a feeder institution for state four-year colleges and universities; and (2) as an open-enrollment college, accepting students from area high schools without any requirements for acceptance.

Kirkwood has long-standing articulation agreements with all of the three state universities (University of Iowa, Iowa State University, and the University of Northern Iowa), as well as similar agreements with area private colleges (Coe College, Mt. Mercy College, Grinnell College, Luther College). There is no indication that any of these articulation agreements are in jeopardy; however, if the articulation question should arise in the future, the demonstrated comparability between Kirkwood's objectives and the Outcomes Statement (see "Verification" above) should help to make the argument for maintaining articulation of our composition sequence.

More important currently are questions of articulation between area high schools and Kirkwood. In the 1999–2000 academic year, Kirkwood began an initiative to work with area high schools to better align the curriculum of high school composition programs with the composition curriculum at Kirkwood. Of concern are issues of (1) students who take four years of high school composition and still are placed in Kirkwood's basic writing course on the basis of their test scores; and (2) the curriculum of dual-enrollment courses offered by some area high schools, where students receive both high school and Kirkwood credit for composition courses taught at their high schools.

The dean of English, the coordinator of English assessment (me), and two faculty members met with English faculty and counselors from three area high schools to discuss the issues of curriculum and articulation. In four meetings over the year, we had productive discussions of what students are taught as they progress through high school and first-year college composition, what is expected of them during that progression, and how we assess their progress. In the very first meeting, one of the high school English faculty, somewhat frustrated, simply said that he wanted to know what his students would be doing and expected to do when they got to college composition. I immediately ran off to my office, grabbed a copy of the Outcomes Statement, made photocopies, and ran back to distribute the statement. As the high school representatives looked over the document, one teacher of both AP English and a dual-enrollment course stated, "This is *exactly* what we need to know." She could see in the Outcomes Statement what hadn't been as clear in the various sample course syllabi we had distributed prior to the meeting. She could see and understand in an abstracted way what the overall experience and expectations are in our college composition sequence (I hesitate to refer to it as "first-year composition" in the context of people who teach composition to students for up to four years before the students get to us).

In all three areas—verification, accreditation, and articulation—the Outcomes Statement has become a kind of touchstone for a variety of activities we're involved in at Kirkwood. As we continue our assessment process, as we continue to review our program, as we continue to work with area high schools regarding articulation, the Outcomes Statement will remain a document at the core of our efforts.

Appendix A

COMPOSITION SURVEY

To the left of each statement below, rate your own competence in each of the skills. To the right, estimate how much influence your composition course has had on improving each of these skills. Circle the appropriate number for both competence and influence according to the codes.

Competence				*Skill*	Influence			
4 = Very competent					4= Strong influence			
3 = Somewhat competent					3= Some influence			
2 = Not very competent					2= Little influence			
1 = Not at all competent					1= No influence			
1	2	3	4	*Writing ability*	1	2	3	4
1	2	3	4	Ability to state a main idea	1	2	3	4
1	2	3	4	Ability to develop and support my main ideas	1	2	3	4
1	2	3	4	Ability to organize the ideas in my papers	1	2	3	4
1	2	3	4	Ability to plan papers before I write	1	2	3	4
1	2	3	4	Ability to research for information that supports my writing	1	2	3	4
1	2	3	4	Ability to adjust my writing according to the purpose of my writing	1	2	3	4
1	2	3	4	Ability to adjust my writing according to the needs of my readers	1	2	3	4
1	2	3	4	Ability to revise my papers	1	2	3	4
1	2	3	4	Ability to use other people's comments to improve my writing	1	2	3	4
1	2	3	4	Ability to integrate source information into my papers	1	2	3	4
1	2	3	4	Ability to document source information	1	2	3	4
1	2	3	4	Ability to judge my own writing	1	2	3	4
1	2	3	4	Ability to correct my own mistakes in punctuation and grammar	1	2	3	4
1	2	3	4	Ability to write logical arguments	1	2	3	4
1	2	3	4	Confidence as a writer	1	2	3	4
1	2	3	4	*Reading ability*	1	2	3	4
1	2	3	4	Ability to identify the thesis, main point, or issue in reading	1	2	3	4
1	2	3	4	Ability to distinguish the main ideas from details and support in reading	1	2	3	4
1	2	3	4	Ability to analyze the arguments of others in reading	1	2	3	4
1	2	3	4	Ability to read other people's writing critically	1	2	3	4
1	2	3	4	Ability to read and offer constructive criticism to other students about their writing	1	2	3	4
1	2	3	4	Confidence as a reader	1	2	3	4

Each week I spent about _____ hours on homework for this class.
I met with my instructor outside of class _____ times.
I visited the writing center _____ times.
I was absent from class approximately _____ times.
I was late for class approximately _____ times.
The grade I think I will get in this course is _____.

Appendix B

ARGUMENT RESEARCH PAPER ATTRIBUTE CHECK SHEET

1. In the table below, indicate the number of papers on which the group came to consensus for each of the three scoring points (3 = superior, 2 = average, 1 = inferior).

3	2	1	Total

2. In the table below, check in the left column those four to five (not more than five) positive attributes that best describe the papers scored by the group as 3 (superior) papers. And check in the right column those four to five (not more than five) negative attributes that best describe the papers scored by the group as 1 (inferior) papers.

Attributes of superior (3) papers	*Attributes of inferior (1) papers*
Topic is focused and engaging	Topic is unclear or trite
Purpose is clear	Purpose is vague
Adapted effectively to audience	No apparent awareness of audience
Thesis is clearly stated or implied	Thesis is unclear
Argument is credible, convincing	Argument is weak
Ideas are original, sophisticated	Ideas are platitudes, trite
Ideas are fully developed	Ideas are undeveloped
Support is relevant and substantial	Support is not relevant or is meager
Sufficient, relevant evidence is provided	Lack of relevant evidence
Research is sufficient, relevant	Research is minimal or inappropriate
Overall organization is purposeful	Overall organization is unclear
Introduction identifies topic and engages	Introduction is vague or misleading
Paragraphs are unified and coherent	Paragraphs are not unified or coherent
Transitions are provided where appropriate	Lack of necessary transitions
Conclusion provides effective closure	Weak or no closure
Tone is appropriate to topic, purpose	Tone is inappropriate or inconsistent
Sentences are complete, clear, varied	Problems evident in sentence structure, variety
Word choice is appropriate, accurate	Problems evident in word choice
Grammar, punctuation, spelling are accurate	Problems evident with grammar, punctuation, spelling
Documentation format is accurate	Problems evident with documentation format
Other:	Other:

8

CRITICAL THINKING, READING, AND WRITING
A View from the Field

Linda Adler-Kassner and Heidi Estrem

A Google search using the terms "critical thinking reading writing + college composition" came up with 225,000 hits. While findings based on search results may not be entirely conclusive, we feel safe in asserting that these numbers say something about the ubiquity of this phrase in relation to first-year writing. Chances are that when any of us discuss what we want our students to take from our courses, "critical thinking, reading, and writing" are among the first we mention. The question, though, is what we *mean* by "critical thinking, reading, and writing" when we work to implement these outcomes. As Donald Wolff points out in chapter 11, "Knowledge of Conventions and the Logic of Error," unless the WPA outcomes are problematized, their complexity is elided. Additionally, the power of the *terms* of the Outcomes Statement—the broad categories (Rhetorical Knowledge, Critical Thinking, Reading, and Writing, and so on), as well as the points delineated within those categories—lies in the commonalities that exist among the specific ways that these categories are enacted in different institutions and contexts.

We were mindful of the need to strike a balance between broad goals and our specific context when we revised the writing outcomes at Eastern Michigan University, where we teach. Particularly, we were (and are) leery about using the adjective "critical" with "writing," "reading," and especially "thinking" precisely because it is so widely used, but sometimes not specifically defined. Thus, working from the Outcomes Statement as a template, we thought carefully about what we wanted students to do, to know, at the end of their composition experience, how our outcomes would reflect that, and what pedagogical implications those outcomes would have. We sought to identify and make explicit key practices surrounding reading and writing that would *engage* students in a wide variety of experiences that would stretch their literacies. "Critical," then, for us encompassed many nuances (including reflection, negotiation, connection, and analysis, for starters)—as we'll explain below.

WRITING—AND READING

Like most composition teachers and WPAs, when we started thinking about how to adapt the OS for our own program, our first thoughts were naturally about *writing*. The questions that we asked when we considered what we meant by "good writing," however, led us to realize that attending to reading would be just as important. Where and how was critical reading positioned in the writing (and writing process) that we imagined? The word that has become emblematic of these conversations is "grappling." We wanted students' writing to reflect their own evolving thinking about the subjects of their writing. We wanted their written projects to engage them in helping their readers understand how they worked to achieve the kind of "critical reading" that they do as active participants in cultures inside and outside of the classroom and the university. What outcomes for critical thinking, reading, and writing, then, would enable this work? The WPA Outcomes Statement says that students should:

- Use writing and reading for inquiry, learning, thinking, and communicating
- Understand a writing assignment as a series of tasks, including finding, evaluating, analyzing, and synthesizing appropriate primary and secondary sources
- Integrate . . . ideas with those of others
- Understand the relationships among language, knowledge, and power

These gave us a starting point, but this language didn't focus specifically enough on the different kinds of texts or reading that students would need to engage in the kind of writing that we hoped for. Missing was language about the complex interactions between reading and writing that would privilege the kind of grappling with ideas (in written and other kinds of texts) that we hoped to see in writing in our program. Thus, EMU's critical thinking, reading, and writing outcomes for our two-course sequence read as follows:

In ENGL 120, students will practice with the following strategies. By the end of ENGL 121, students will fluently:
- Use writing and discussion to work through and interpret complex ideas from readings and other texts (e.g., visual, musical, verbal)

- Critically analyze their own and others' choices regarding language and form (e.g., in student texts or formally published texts)
- Engage in multiple modes of inquiry using text (e.g., field research, library-based inquiry, Web searching)
- Incorporate significant research (as above) into writing that engages a question and/or topic and uses it as a central theme for a substantive, research-based essay
- Use writing to support interpretations of text, and understand that there are multiple interpretations of text
- Consider and express the relationship of their own ideas to the ideas of others

Included in these goals, we think, is explicit attention to reading practices. The first and second bulleted points, which require students to work through and interpret ideas and analyze choices, focus on reading processes. Thus, when we teach our first-year courses, we know that we must incorporate activities that refer to processes. The first, second, and third call attention to varieties of texts (visual, musical, and verbal texts; student texts and formally published texts; and field research, library texts, and Web sources); we know, then, that these courses must incorporate and draw explicit attention to the features and conventions of different kinds of readings and texts. In their attention to engaging in multiple modes of inquiry, incorporating significant research, interpreting text, and considering and expressing relationships between their ideas and others', the final three points focus on uses of reading. Thus, we also know we must consider and give students the opportunity to perform and reflect on different kinds of reading in our courses.

READING PEDAGOGIES IN WRITING CLASSROOMS

Before explaining further the ways in which critical thinking, reading, and writing are enacted in our program, we want to reflect on some of the reading we were doing concurrently with using these kinds of reading strategies in our classrooms. Three books intended for students' use in the college classroom helped us to consider reading practices and processes: Wendy Bishop's *The Subject Is Reading* (2000), Bruce Ballenger and Michelle Payne's *The Curious Reader* (2003), and especially Rob Pope's *Textual Interventions* (1995). Pope's book, while not expressly about reading pedagogy, engages students in writing and closely reading a variety of genres for a variety of purposes; Ballenger and Payne's work complements Pope's approach by asking students to read self-consciously and reflectively with a variety of texts.

Other scholarly work helped us to consider the ways in which we framed the approach to reading in these outcomes and in classroom practice. Mariolina Salvatori's work (2003), for example, helped us to think about the theories underscoring different approaches to reading, as we describe above. The same holds true for Donna Qualley's "Using Reading in the Writing Classroom" (1993). Similarly, the recent *Intertexts: Reading Pedagogy in the Composition Classroom* (2003) features chapters by Salvatori and others who have devoted careful attention to reading theory and practice in the college classroom. Kathleen McCormick's *The Culture of Reading and the Teaching of English* (1994), a broad study of reading practices in composition/English classes that also focuses on reading pedagogies, helped us think about the relationships between students' cultures and reading.

Certainly, this handful of resources is valuable—yet, compared with the volumes of literature on writing pedagogies, it is but a grain of sand in a vast desert. Instead, within college composition, the scholarship on reading focuses more on instructor reading of student essays (e.g., Straub 1996; Straub and Lunsford 1995; Haswell and Haswell 1996) or students' reading of instructors' comments (Lunsford and Connors 1998; Sommers 1982). While these articles are useful for instructors to consider their own reading practices, they are not as immediately applicable to the challenge of developing a reading pedagogy.

Instead, most of the research on reading is rooted in and focuses on the reading practices of K-12 students, particularly middle and high school students. Much of this work seeks to extend the earlier theories of scholars like Frank Smith (1978), Ken and Yetta Goodman (1989), Yetta Goodman et al. (1980), Yetta Goodman and Sandra Wilde (1986), Alan Purves et al. (1990), and Louise Rosenblatt (1978) that highlighted the importance of engagement with a whole text in purposeful ways (rather than with isolated features of text, whether phonetical or literary). For instance, Jeffrey Wilhelm and Michael Smith have worked with the reading practices of adolescents; through close study of and with these students, they have extensively discussed reading pedagogies (see Wilhelm's *You Gotta Be the Book* [1997] and Smith and Wilhelm's *Reading Don't Fix No Chevys* [2002]). Similarly, Kylene Beers's *When Kids Can't Read* (2003, 28) focuses on helping teachers identify what we (and students) mean when we say they "can't read" (from "decoding single-syllable words" to "reads all types of text the same way") and then addressing those areas with students in meaningful, contextualized ways.

The work cited above reflects an emphasis in this research on actual student practices; the observations and pedagogical suggestions based on them can be invaluable for college teachers who want to focus more explicit attention on reading practices. This body of work also led us to consider issues of student engagement and helping students become lifelong learners, in addition to the emphasis on strategies for academic success reflected in a preponderance of the work in composition. When we thought about developing explicit reading strategies to enact our outcomes, then, we started with the literature on composition, but also with that from English education; this led us to also articulate affective dimensions that we hoped would result from students' work in our course. Like Beers, we believe that "simply improving the cognitive aspects of reading (comprehension, vocabulary, decoding, and word recognition) does not ensure that the affective aspects of reading (motivation, enjoyment, engagement) will automatically improve" (2003, 13). Thus, the affective dimensions of reading/writing instruction that we see emerging are:

- Helping students find meaning (personal, intellectual, otherwise) in their research
- Facilitating students' abilities to pique their own curiosity and at least wonder about, if not become in invested in, a question that could be pursued (at least partly) through "academic" research
- Building the confidence necessary for students to (1) engage in research writing as a public act; and (2) engage in research writing as a conversation with others interested in the same or related topics
- Helping students find value in reflection on writing and research processes

As these affective dimensions suggest, we think that if students enjoy their encounters with reading, they will become engaged in it (and their writing), and this will ultimately facilitate their investment in and acumen with strategies that will benefit their academic work.

CRITICAL THINKING AND PURPOSES FOR READING

Reflecting on and working with these outcomes in our curriculum has helped us to articulate more clearly what we mean by them and how they shape the work we do with students. This work also has helped us to develop teaching strategies to give students opportunities to practice what we say they will achieve by the end of our second-semester course. We can say now, for example, that we want students to engage generally in different kinds of reading for different purposes in these courses and to meet the underlying pedagogical imperatives outlined above. To achieve these readings, students must simultaneously enact the four roles of readers outlined by Peter Freebody: code breakers (or decoders of text), text participants (or "inferrer[s] of connection" between texts and contexts that shape the texts), text users (or users who can employ the texts in specific circumstances for specific purposes), and text analysts (or readers with "conscious awareness of the language and idea systems that are brought into play when a text is constructed and . . . that make the text operate and thus that make the reader . . . into its operator") (Freebody 1992, 1–10). We ask students, acting within these four roles, to perform reading within three broad categories: *content-based reading* (based in what the reading says), *process-based reading* (based in how the reading came into being), and *genre-based reading* (based in how the reading says what it says). In each, they must be decoders and text users, as their decoding is always framed by specifics: class, assignment, the student/writer's purpose for using the text.

Strategies within the broad category of *content-based reading* most frequently ask students to consider their interpretation of a reading and consider connections between that interpretation and a "dominant" interpretation. The first two strategies within this category, particularly, call on students to enact their roles as text analysts, identifying the text's preferred reading and considering why and how that reading is preferred. These include:

- *Reading to connect/refute.* This kind of reading practice is often what students expect to employ in school. It typically happens after the writer has explored a subject for some time, has come to an analysis, and recognizes that a source can provide evidence for that analysis. The writer's ideas might concur or digress from the ideas in the reading.
- *Reading to summarize/paraphrase.* Here, writers read to capture the dominant interpretation of a reading and repeat that interpretation in their own writing.

The second two strategies in this category leave more room for students to develop their own interpretations of the reading and enact with the reading as what Freebody and Luke (2003, 3) have called text participants. They are:

- *Reading to explore.* Writers explore ideas, experiences, or questions that they have developed. The purpose of this kind of reading is to discover more about those original ideas, questions, or purposes so that writers can read to extend, as described below.
- *Reading to extend.* This kind of reading might begin with expanded ideas, as above. Here, the writer reads to reflect on and extend ideas and/or frame of reference. For example, writers might discover that elements of experiences that they had considered relevant only to themselves extend to others, as well.

Using reading to explore and/or extend is an open-ended task because there are so *many* directions a writer can take their reading. Over time, we've articulated various ways students might use text in their writing; however, to use these strategies, students must first articulate (for themselves and for their readers) how they are using reading. Students can use reading:

- To support their ideas. Finding something that resonates with experience, something that seems to add depth or perspective to what they are writing about.
- To oppose their ideas. Finding something that does not resonate with experience, something that helps them to clarify what they do mean (or want to say) because it is not what they mean (or want to say).
- To frame their ideas. Finding a way of looking at or thinking about an issue or question that is different from what students are writing about, but which can be applied to their issue.

For readers familiar with Ellin Keene and Susan Zimmerman's *Mosaic of Thought* (1997), a popular text among secondary teachers, these connections will sound familiar—Keene and Zimmerman ask students to make and identify "text-to-self connections, text-to-text connections, and text-to-world connections" in their reading (55). Instructors in our first-year writing courses might bring a handout that includes these "ways of reading" (as well as others) to class; they might use this in conjunction with an activity where they ask students to look closely at a piece of reading and identify where the writer has used reading in these (and/or other) ways in *that* piece. (They then might move into looking at how the writer has done this, leading to genre-awareness activities described in genre-based reading, below.)

The second broad category is *process-based reading.* Here, the emphasis is on extrapolating from reading to identify processes used by authors so that writers can decide if and/or how they want to draw on those processes for their own work. To enact this kind of reading, students must occupy roles as text participants, recognizing the processes by which the text is constructed, and text analysts, analyzing the ideological positions enacted through that construction. In this category, the strategies encompass two main areas:

- *Reading to infer writerly behaviors.* This kind of speculative reading asks students to work from the finished product they see and articulate what "might have been"—that is, what might have been this writer's process of working from research to writing to publication. The purpose of this kind of reading is to help students see the energy lurking behind the text—the energy that compelled the writer to respond to the world in some way with his or her text.

- *Reading to infer research strategies.* Similar to the above strategy, this one helps students focus on how much research a writer might have done, what her or his motivations might have been, how the particular sources used might have been chosen, and why the writer might have been interested in the research in the first place. Reading this way can help bring "research" closer to students; its purpose is to help them see the real ways in which writers use research in their work.

In class, writers might be asked to look carefully at evidence compiled from research (observations, interviews, library work, artifact analysis, and so on) and extrapolate what the author did (looked for, asked, had as research questions, did in the analysis) to develop the evidence in the reading.

The third broad category in which we ask students to read, finally, is *genre-based reading.* For this kind of reading, as for process-based reading, readers must act as text participants and text analysts. Here, the emphasis is on reading to develop genre awareness so that they can make conscious decisions about how, when, or whether to use those conventions in their own writing. Writers might look carefully at the textual moves made in a piece of writing. They might look at the language, style, or form; they might look at specific conventional elements (such as how and where the reading employs evidence from reading). These strategies include:

- *Reading to analyze form.* Here, writers read in utilitarian ways, asking themselves, "What makes a _____ a _____?" (What makes a poem a poem? A newspaper editorial a newspaper editorial?) They may essentially ignore content, momentarily focusing only on what the particular features are of the genre they're reading and why those features make it recognizable as such.

- *Reading to understand the rhetorical situation.* With this way of reading, writers focus on deducing as much as they can about the rhetorical scene. Questions often considered include those that focus on purpose, audience, genre, context, and how all of these features might be operating within a particular text.

Implicit in genre-based reading is also a move that readers are asked to make as writers: as students consider when or whether to employ these conventions, they also must consciously reflect on what idea systems *they* are bringing into play, how these idea systems shape *their* writing, what roles they are asking readers of *their* texts to perform and why they are asking them to perform those roles.

To practice with this kind of reading, instructors might ask students to focus their energies on a close analysis of what *comprises* a reading or a photograph. Reading the first page of a reading together, they will ask about everything. ("What's this first paragraph doing?" "Why is there a page number there?") Such an activity accomplishes several goals simultaneously. First, it demystifies the reading because it helps students identify textual conventions that might be unfamiliar (for example, when authors of academic pieces refer to work that has informed their own or review relevant literature). It also can help students make decisions about what to attend to (or not) in a reading. This, in turn, can lead students to develop (and/or articulate) strategies for their own reading processes that, again, can lead to more conscious decisions about reading.

Other activities linked with increasing genre awareness can help students make conscious decisions about how, when, and where to incorporate those conventions in their own writing. For instance, in another activity we will distribute a page or so from an academic article to students and ask them to work together in groups to locate particular elements of the article:

- Where the author uses sources (How do you know?)
- Why the author uses the sources he or she does (How do you know?)
- How the author leads into the sources (How do you know?)
- The foci of the studies cited by the author (How do you know?)
- Where the author discusses the foci of those studies (How do you know?)
- Where the author uses direct quotes from the studies
- Why the author uses direct quotes (How do they help the article?)

After this analysis, we will ask students to return to their own drafts and apply these questions to their papers.

USES OF READING: STUDENTS' PAST AND PRESENT EXPERIENCES WITH TEXT

As we have used and adapted the strategies we delineated above as content-based, process-based, and genre-based reading strategies, we recognize that neither the categories nor the specific points underneath them are mutually exclusive—it is certainly possible, and often advisable, to mix them. However, it is useful to us, both as teachers working with new teachers of writing and as teachers of first-year writing ourselves, to separate them, at least initially. This is because, in our experience, students (both graduate student instructors and first-year students) have relatively little experience reading reflexively and thus have not devoted much thought to *how* or *why* they are reading. Instead, we have found that our students have primarily "read to connect/refute" or "read to summarize," reading experiences that reflect two dominant theories of reading that Salvatori (2003) has identified as ubiquitous in education. In the first, authors of texts (not students) are "visionary shapers of meaning," their texts "venerable repositories of those meanings." In the second, texts are "various thesis statements—cultural, political religious, and so on" (443–44). In both cases, readers' roles are to "extract" meaning from the text—literally, to pull out what the writer intended and/or what is necessary for the readers' work —and move on from there. As writers using sources, students see their role as that of a utilitarian treasure hunter who must find "sources" that "back" his or her ideas up. At the same time as they see their own writing as a flimsy construction in desperate need of support from the "real experts," they simultaneously plumb readings for *the* line that echoes their own ideas, rather than imagining how ideas might work in concert, or in conversation, with each other. In neither case, Salvatori points out, are readers expected to engage in a dialogue with the text; instead, they reflect the perspective advanced by an adolescent reader interviewed by Jeffrey Wilhelm (1997, 10) who told him, "'You're not really interested in how I read . . . no teacher would ever be interested in that.' What teachers are interested in, she told [Wilhelm], was 'my getting it right—or what you all think is right.'"

The challenge for critical thinking, reading, and writing outcomes (and strategies that reflect them), then, is to ensure that they make room for strategies that reflect alternative theoretical paradigms, ones that shift the relationship between reader and text. Asking students to read reflectively and reflexively—How are you reading? Why are you reading that way? How are you thinking about using reading in your writing?—is another classroom strategy that can help to affect this shift. Sheridan Blau (2003, 13) refers to this kind of reading as "metacognitive processing—thinking about and reporting on their own thinking in their encounter with a problem—[which] positions students and teacher in a pedagogical relationship that entails a shared or distributed expertise." Such reading can help students consciously articulate their movements through audience expectations, contexts where those are formed, and genre conventions; ultimately, this also will contribute to conscious choices about interacting (or not) with text, rather than reading as an activity performed on autopilot.

SUSTAINING READING PRACTICES IN FIRST-YEAR WRITING

To sustain what we are here referring to as critical reading, we had to develop models for writing that would support this activity. To this end, we have designed a broad framework for our two first-year courses that grounds the development of literacy strategies in specific contexts (academic and otherwise) and asks students to consciously and consistently analyze their own purpose(s) for writing and balance these with their audience's expectation(s) for writing. As they do so, students work on developing writing strategies to meet those expectations, but always consciously reflect on when, whether, and/or how to employ those strategies within a piece of writing. At every stage of this recursive cycle of analysis, development, and decision making, students employ critical reading strategies—reading texts, reading people, reading situations. Ultimately, students represent their work for the Celebration of Student Writing, a semester's-end fair in which students exhibit their research work for the larger campus community. For it, students create projects based on their research, discussing this work with the 650 to 1,000 participants and visitors who attend the event (the number fluctuates depending on the semester).

The Celebration, as it's now called, has become a pivotal point of reflection for us, particularly in relation to critical thinking, reading, and writing. Based on our work with students to prepare for this event and our observation of students participating in it, we have formulated new questions that lead us to continually rethink how to make these outcomes as tangible as possible. For example, one of the points under the outcomes is to "consider and express the relationship of their own ideas to the ideas of others." At the Celebration, they have the opportunity to engage (verbally and in writing) with a large number of others. Last year, we noticed that while students' projects showed that they had learned a lot about how to display their work for a larger audience, we hadn't done as good a job helping them develop strategies to engage with one another (verbally) about that work. This has led us to questions: how can we help students to articulate (in writing and speaking) additional questions about *content* ("What's your project about?"), *genre* ("How did you know how to make this genre?"), and *process* ("Why did you make the genre choices you did? How did you do the work that got you to this project?"). How can we help students develop strategies to engage in the kind of discussion that we outline about their projects—and about work in the academy more generally? In continuing discussions of reading with students into this unconventional, creative showcase of student (written) work that is the Celebration and about our entire first-year curriculum, we hope to blur the boundaries between coursework and personal interest, between first-year writing courses and writing across campus. Concurrently, continuing to work closely with reading pushes us to examine how we encounter and negotiate with a variety of texts—including the rich, changing text that is the pedagogy of teaching critical reading and writing.

9

MORE THAN THE LATEST PC BUZZWORD FOR MODES
What Genre Theory Means to Composition

Barbara Little Liu

In her *College English* introduction to the "WPA Outcomes Statement for First-Year Composition," Kathleen Blake Yancey notes what "such a document allows us to argue for—the role of genre in first year composition, for instance" (Outcomes Statement Steering Committee 2001, 323). The Outcomes Statement itself states that, with regard to "rhetorical knowledge," students completing a first-year writing course or sequence should be able (among other goals) to "Understand how genres shape reading and writing" and "Write in several genres." With regard to "knowledge of conventions," one of the stated goals is that students should "Develop knowledge of genre conventions ranging from structure and paragraphing to tone and mechanics." In a document, then, that takes up basically two pages in *College English*, the term *genre* is used three times: twice in the first, and I would say foundational, section, Rhetorical Knowledge, and once in the section on Knowledge of Conventions. Thus, genre is not a token or limited concept here. The concept of genre is enshrined in a "curricular document that speaks to the common expectations, for students, of first-year compositions programs in the United States at the beginning of the 21st century" (Outcomes Statement Steering Committee 2001, 323).

But what is the understanding of genre related in this document? And is it the same understanding had by the WPAs, tenure-track and adjunct faculty, and graduate teaching assistants (whether trained in rhetoric and composition or in literature, creative writing, or linguistics) who are doing the actual work of writing instruction in the various composition programs around the country? A May 1999 discussion on the WPA-L listserv between Irvin Peckham and Trish Roberts-Miller suggests that not everyone who might choose (or be called upon) to interpret and implement the Outcomes Statement will necessarily read the term *genre* in a way that is informed by recent genre theory. The discussion of genre came up in Trish Roberts-Miller's argument that outcomes should be determined locally rather than by any national consortium. In supporting this position she notes that genre isn't a term with much currency for a lot of people in English studies. Roberts-Miller uses the absence of serious considerations of genre in literary criticism as indication that it hasn't been recently or adequately theorized in a way that would make a term like genre central to a nationally devised set of curricular outcomes (qtd. in Peckham 1999). Elsewhere in this thread, Peckham names key works in genre theory, including some recently published pieces and the foundational work of Bakhtin. In reference to Bakhtin, Roberts-Miller responds, "I honestly don't remember Bakhtin saying a word about genres." For many of us familiar with genre theory, it hardly seems as if Bakhtin said a word about anything else. His work, especially "The Problem of Speech Genres" (1952), and that of Carolyn Miller, especially her essay "Genre as Social Action" (1984), are foundational in contemporary conceptions of genres as much more than just forms. Clearly, Roberts-Miller's background, her reading of Bakhtin, and probable lack of familiarity with Carolyn Miller's article or other important explications of genre theory have provided her with a point of view very different from that of Peckham and those he worked with in drafting the Outcomes Statement. And by saying this, I do not mean to dismiss her or insult her preparation or education as a composition instructor; indeed, I doubt that she is in the minority.[1] As Peckham is finally forced to admit, "one of the problems with genres is that people who haven't read very much about them think they refer to the modes."

One of the potential problems with implementation of the Outcomes Statement, then, is the fact that not everyone has read very much about genre. At least, not everyone has read the kind of genre theory Peckham references and that seems to be intended by the use of genre as a key term in the Outcomes Statement. Note how the statement uses the word genre: "Write in several genres"; "Develop knowledge of genre conventions ranging from structure and paragraphing to tone and mechanics"; and finally, what is perhaps the most complex use of the term, "Understand how genres shape reading and writing." In each of these cases the word "modes" or the phrase "different types of academic essays" could be substituted and make just as much sense.[2]

Therefore, it seems that the acontextual, undertheorized way in which the term appears in the Outcomes Statement may unintentionally reinforce some unfortunate misconceptions and relegate an interest in genre to a purely formulaic concern.[3] The more complex and theoretically informed view of genre that was at the core of the Outcomes Statement committee's intentions is one in which genre is not merely a finite product that writers produce, but an ongoing process in which writers take part. This is a key distinction because if genre is not fully conceptualized as a complex process, a genre-based approach reverts to a product-centered approach, and the writing process becomes a series of increasingly accurate attempts to replicate an ideal text rather than an engaged understanding of how writing and writers work within a complex world.

To more fully articulate an understanding of genre, it is probably wise to begin (as Peckham noted) with Mikhail Bakhtin, as Bakhtin was perhaps the first theorist to see genre as a dynamic, social entity. In "The Problem of Speech Genres," he writes: "We speak only in definite speech genres, that is, all our utterances have definite and relatively stable typical *forms of construction of the whole*. . . . Even in the most free, the most unconstrained conversation, we cast our speech in definite generic forms, sometimes rigid and trite ones, sometimes more flexible, plastic, and creative ones. . . . We are given these speech genres in almost the same way that we are given our native language . . . not from dictionaries and grammars but from concrete utterances that we hear and that we ourselves reproduce in live speech communication with people around us" (1952, 78).

For Bakhtin, our acquisition of generic forms (such as common greetings, pleas, arguments, etc.) is an essential part of our acquisition of language. Our speech and language are ordered by these recurring forms so that what we say can be interpreted by others: "If speech genres did not exist," Bakhtin argues, "speech communication would be almost impossible" (Bakhtin 1952, 79). The same can be said for written communication. The recurrence of certain forms of written discourse brings order to written communication. It lets a writer know what to say in a particular situation, and consequently makes clear to an audience the author's position and stand according to the genre chosen.

However, as Bakhtin notes, many genres are "subject to free creative reformulation," allowing speakers or writers to "reveal our own individuality" and "more flexibly and precisely . . . reflect the unrepeatable situation of communication" (Bakhtin 1952, 80). It is this interplay between the familiar and the novel, the static and the dynamic, that is key to various other reformulations of the term *genre* and the genre theory that results.

There have been numerous other attempts to provide a comprehensive and socially situated definition of genre (some before Bakhtin's work was widely available in translation outside of Russia). The impetus for much of the theoretical work in the United States and Canada was Carolyn Miller's important essay, "Genre as Social Action." Like Bakhtin, Miller sought to expand the definition of genre from its traditional emphasis on specific, reoccurring formal traits to the recurring, yet changing, social situations that engender them. Miller posited: "Genre refers to a conventional category of discourse based in large scale typification of rhetorical action; as action, it acquires meaning from situation and from the social context in which that situation arose. . . . A genre is a rhetorical means for mediating private intentions and social exigence; it motivates by connecting the private with the public, the singular with the recurrent" (1984, 37).

As others have worked to apply Bakhtin's and/or Miller's conception of genre to rhetorical criticism and/or composition theory, they have attempted to explicate the characteristics that constitute a genre. John Swales (1990) and Ann Johns (1997) attempt to list what it is that is shared by members of a community who recognize a particular genre or genres. Both Swales and Johns spend a great amount of time explicating the various elements of genre named in their definitions, attesting to the comprehensive understanding of social context, which is a goal of many genre theorists.

In *Genre Knowledge in Disciplinary Communication*, Berkenkotter and Huckin define genre by laying out five principles or a "framework" for genre theory:

- *Dynamism.* Genres are dynamic rhetorical forms that are developed from actors' responses to recurrent situations and that serve to stabilize in response to their users' sociocognitive needs.
- *Situatedness.* Our knowledge of genres is derived from and embedded in our participation in the communicative activities of daily and professional life. As such, genre knowledge is a form of "situated cognition" that continues to develop as we participate in the activities of the ambient culture.
- *Form and Content.* Genre knowledge embraces both form and content, including a sense of what content is appropriate to a particular purpose in a particular situation at a particular point in time.
- *Duality of Structure.* As we draw on genre rules to engage in professional activities, we *constitute* social structures (in professional, institutional, and organizational contexts) and simultaneously *reproduce* these structures.
- *Community Ownership.* Genre conventions signal a discourse community's norms, epistemology, ideology, and social ontology (Berkenkotter and Huckin 1995, 4).

Berkenkotter and Huckin's definition/framework seems comprehensive and relevant to me in that it includes many of the important elements of both Swales's and Johns's definitions (awareness of shared purposes, forms, contexts, cultural values, and intertextuality, for example).

Like Johns, Berkenkotter and Huckin call attention to the fact that a genre may both disseminate and participate in the ideology, epistemology, and culture of a community. They point out, for example, the ways in which the writing of graduate students begins to take on the formal characteristics common to work in their disciplines as they become more familiar and comfortable with the research methodologies of that discipline. One might say, as well, that an author's wish to publish his or her work is also an acknowledgment of the importance of the greater disciplinary community to the validation of that work.

Berkenkotter and Huckin's definition of genre, therefore, contains a key element found in Johns's definition—recognition of the ways in which genres instantiate and reinforce the culture and values of the communities that use them. Berkenkotter and Huckin also restate a key element of Swales's definition when they argue that "genericness is not an all-or-nothing proposition. . . . If texts arise out of discursive differences, as Bakhtin, Kress, and many others argued, such texts can be expected to embody different kinds of *recurring rhetorical responses* in different ways. Thus, rather than taking a holistic, normative approach to genre, as is done in traditional studies, we feel it makes more sense to take a more articulated approach in which individual texts are seen to contain heterogeneous mixtures of elements, some of which are recognizably more generic than others" (1995, 17).

When Berkenkotter and Huckin say that "genericness is not an all-or-nothing proposition," they echo Swales's assertion: "Exemplars or instances of genres vary in their prototypicality" (1990, 49). In other words, one instance of a genre may contain a great many of the elements usually associated with that genre, while another may contain far fewer—its author employing more creativity and individual initiative in its use; however, both would be readily recognized as members of the genre.

By naming *dynamism* as a key term in their theory, Berkenkotter and Huckin suggest that genres change and evolve over time as the situations they address change and as various members of a community bring their own practices and priorities to their enactment of genres. Berkenkotter and Huckin's *dynamism* hearkens back to a Bakhtinian term: *dialogism*. Dialogism supposes that utterances are always shaped in response to previous utterances, and that they, in turn, prompt future utterances. Thus, utterances, whether turns in a conversation or articles in academic journals, are formed as part of an ongoing dialogue between various conversants in a social sphere. Individuals may be able to use generic utterances "freely and creatively"; however, this "is not the same as to create a genre from the beginning; genres must be fully mastered in order to be manipulated freely" (Bakhtin 1981, 80). In working with a genre, authors are constrained by the generic expectations they inherit, but they are also free (to a degree) to contribute practices of their own that may then become part of the future constraints associated with that genre.

To sum up, this dynamic approach to genre that Berkenkotter and Huckin propose emphasizes both constraints and choices to a degree that is not consistently done in other explications of genre. An awareness of both the constraints that genres impose on writers *and* the choices writers can make as they manipulate genres has great significance for the application of genre theory to the teaching of writing. Discussion of constraints alone may cause writing instruction to revert to the teaching of standard forms alone, when a more critical understanding of social processes is needed.

If genre theory has had or will have any significant impact in composition theory, it will lie in the recognition that generic forms are not static—that they are constantly being socially constructed and reconstructed. Miller has argued that "the failure to understand genre as social action afflicts the typical first-year college writing program in the United States; it turns what should be a practical art of achieving social ends into a productive art of making texts that fit certain formal requirements" (1994, 67). As Miller's statement suggests, the tendency in many writing programs has been to focus on particular modes or forms for academic prose. While instructors have been, at the same time, concerned with the processes that help students write clearly in these modes, these processes are taught and employed so that students will produce generically defined products such as the "research paper," the "persuasive essay," the "problem/solution essay," and so on. While such genres may help students gain certain skills of production, they are primarily what Freedman and Medway would term "classroom genres," in that they do not bring students into any discourse community beyond the particular classroom. Freedman and Medway note that classroom writing "can effectively (at least to a certain level) support students' personal sense-making in the face of [complex topics in geography, such as] 'shifting cultivation.' . . .

It will not, however, make them geographers. Hence the strength of the argument for getting students into the standard discourses" (1994, 15).

Freedman and Medway use the journal assignments developed by Bruffee as an example of invented classroom genres. Such journal assignments, in which students are encouraged to write freely about their responses to readings, classroom activities, and various other prompts, are commonplace to many first-year writing classes. Writing across the curriculum programs have encouraged the use of journals in many other classes as well, touting the effectiveness of writing as a tool for better and more complete understanding of difficult concepts within various disciplines. Freedman and Medway note that while ostensibly these journals were meant to free students from attention to convention, allowing them to interact with the content of the classes in a reflective and intellectually stimulating way, "the rhetorical demands had not disappeared" (1994, 17). Successful students "learned to manipulate textual features to create an impression of artless expressivity" characterized by "a certain length, expressivity, unconventionality, and sparkiness"; they learned to "mix observations about the material with an indication of personal enjoyment, frustration, or amusement" if they were to please their reader (the teacher) and achieve their purpose (a good grade) (17–18). Thus, classroom genres, even when they are supposed to be ungraded opportunities for free expression, require students to discover and follow certain formal requirements.

Not all classroom genres are completely distinct from more authentic genres, however; the persuasive essay contains many features common to such varied projects as grant proposals, editorials, and policy statements. Nonetheless, in the face of a socially complex universe of discourse communities with equally complex, socially developed genres, it does little good to teach students standard written forms without giving them the capability to interpret and apply those forms in socially acceptable and novel ways. Thus, Charles Bazerman argues that the "largest lesson" of his research into scientific research genres "is not that there are simple genres that must be slavishly followed, that we must give students an appropriate set of cookie cutters for their anticipated careers, but rather that the student must understand and rethink the rhetorical choices embedded in each generic habit to master the genre" (1988, 8).

Bazerman is suggesting here that the teaching of writing should provide students not only with the ability to produce certain forms on command, but also with the ability to choose when and how they will adapt these forms when they are writing independently for a variety of situations. If, as many social views of rhetoric argue, "all learning is necessarily situated within communities of practice in which learners are enabled to perform by an intricately orchestrated process of coparticipation with old-time members," then "explication is not part of the learning process" (Freedman 1994, 197). While Freedman does concede that explicit instruction paired with immediate participation in the community may benefit student writers, active participation in actual communities is a crucial requirement. Drawing on Krashen's second language acquisition theory, she warns us that "the restrictions are severe . . . ; proximity in time to exposure to authentic models is crucial. Teaching business writing to high school or even college students, years before their likely exposure to the relative contexts, constitutes far too long a gap. In addition, the instructor must be sure that her or his descriptions of the genre are accurate. . . . Finally, for some students at least, there are dangers in explicit teaching; they may overgeneralize the rules . . . and distort their composing processes" (206).

The work of designing a writing curriculum that incorporates a full understanding of genre becomes even more difficult given the fact that most U.S. colleges and universities require only one three-credit course in writing. Perhaps the greatest first step that writing program administrators can take in an enlightened revision of their curricula is to revise their expectations. The major myths that inform many current first-year writing programs—that an introductory writing course (or two) can "cure" students of all their writing "ills" or can give students a specific set of writing tools that will serve them with equal ease in all their future writing—must be discarded. In place of these myths must come a new understanding that, as Ann Johns puts it, "students can begin, but not complete, their development of academic literacies in [first-year writing] classrooms" (1997, 19). Hence, a writing program should seek to prepare students for the lifelong work of learning to write by exposing them to a number of genres, developing their ability to look critically at communities and genres, helping them to see both the constraints and the choices within particular writing situations, and preparing them for both the rewards and the consequences of acculturation into new writing communities.

It is important to recognize that when a student becomes a member of an academic discourse community, he or she indeed becomes another kind of person. Becoming a part of a community means a change in the way a person thinks. It means thinking less like a member of the home community from which one came and more like a member of the community of which one is becoming a part. The adaptation seems at first an obvious advantage—the kind of upward mobility that is a primary goal of a college education in the first place—with writing as the tool to attain it. But for many, primarily those whose home communities are culturally furthest from the Anglo-dominated academy, this change of being is somewhat threatening and cannot be entered into lightly. Many theorists worry, like Sharon Crowley: "To the extent that [students] adopt the language of the academy, their entitlement to their native languages and cultures is compromised or diminished" (1991, 173).

However, linguist James Paul Gee suggests that "there happens to be an advantage to failing to master fully mainstream Discourses. . . . we become consciously aware of what we are trying to do or are being called upon to do, and often gain deep insight into the matter" (1996, 147). Thus, when a person cannot naturally acquire "full fluency" in a discourse, he or she can still develop a useful and empowering combination of "partial acquisition coupled with meta-knowledge and strategies to 'make do'" that Gee calls "mushfake." Mushfake, Gee explains, "is a term from prison culture meaning to make do with something less when the real thing is not available. So when prison inmates make hats from underwear to protect their hair from lice, the hats are mushfake." For Gee, the important skill is metalinguistic: the ability to think about and talk about language in ways that will enable a self-conscious approach to learning new discourses (Gee does not use the term *genre*), breaking them down into analytic bits, to talk about, describe and explain them, to see "how the Discourses you have already got . . . relate to those you are attempting to acquire, and how the ones you are trying to acquire relate to self and society" (141). That metalinguistic skill, then, allows for the production of mushfake, the discourse of approximation that allows the individual to make do.

Gee's metalinguistic skill is similar to what John Swales (1990) calls "rhetorical consciousness." Swales suggests that pedagogy informed by genre theory should involve two practices: first, helping students develop rhetorical consciousness by working with them to examine particular texts and explicate the ways in which those texts make use of or break from accepted practices; and second, helping students become ethnographers of discourse communities by getting them to look critically at the classroom communities and genres that they encounter in college. These critical capabilities will serve students as they continue to encounter new and different discourse communities and genres.

Recently, Mary Jo Reiff took Swales's claim one step further by claiming that when instructors lead students in conducting ethnographic research and writing genre analyses, they accomplish the criteria set by Aviva Freedman for authentic instruction in genres. Referencing Marilyn Chapman, Reiff notes that ethnographic research and genre analysis involve students in three important processes: learning a genre, learning about genres, and learning through genres. "students learn one research genre (ethnography) while they simultaneously use ethnographic techniques to learn about and through other genres" (2003, 555).

A synthesis of Gee, Swales, and Reiff (and Chapman via Reiff) reveals that a first-year writing curriculum steeped in genre theory would prepare students for what lies ahead, not by claiming to teach a set of so-called universal writing skills, but by making them aware of the fact that there are very few universals. Such a course should prepare students for the social processes that shape the genres of different communities by

- Exposing them to as many kinds of discourse and as many writing communities or situations as possible so that they will better appreciate the variety of writing that they might later encounter
- Helping them to develop the mindset of ethnography and inquiry that will assist them in understanding and acculturating to the writing communities that become important to them
- Investigating the political and ideological agendas of writing communities and the ways in which those agendas are enforced and enacted in writing, so that students can make more informed choices about which communities they will join and in what role
- Helping them to foresee the personal consequences both of wholly acculturating into a new community and of resisting the values of that community through writing in ways it may not accept

This is a *genre process* approach. Naming this approach genre *process* calls attention to a number of writing processes: the continual, lifelong processes of writing acquisition; the processes of entering and understanding a new writing community; and the processes involved in producing a particular piece of writing. The final of these three is the most related to compositionists' use of the term. However, *the* writing process needs to be reenvisioned so that student writers can imagine a variety of possible writing processes—as tied to specific writing communities and genres as all other writing practices are.

This means a first-year writing course (whether linked to another course through a WAC or WID program or housed exclusively within the English department) should give students opportunities to explore and practice genres valued in diverse contexts so that they can make comparisons between different disciplines' and communities' ways of writing and enact diverse problem-solving strategies to accomplish successful writing in a variety of situations. Ideally, a writing course should not settle down within any one discipline or genre, explicating its requirements for students, but rather it should engage students in a series of problem-solving situations, asking them to figure out what a particular situation requires, what texts and experts they can call on for modeling and experience, which of the writing practices already in their repertoire might suit this context and what kinds of practices they need to acquire. While each problem-solving situation in this series should be unique, instruction should bring cohesion to the course by requiring reflection and meta-awareness on the part of students. Students should, for example, compare situations and discuss differences and similarities; they should keep a list of problem-solving strategies and note when certain strategies worked and when they did not. Students should note which situations were most or least comfortable for them and speculate about why.

Instructors should also recognize that the ample guidance and individual feedback that is given to students in writing classes—through thoroughly articulated assignments and grading criteria, through copious written comments on multiple drafts, and through in-class and individual conversations with students—is not often replicated in the other contexts for which they will write. Perhaps, then, the writing instructor's tendency to initiate and dominate conversations about student writing is somewhat misguided. It might be more useful to help students practice initiating such conversations themselves, discussing, in the process, what kinds of questions might be appropriate to ask and of whom, and thus expanding student writers' vocabulary for such inquiry beyond the ubiquitous but vague, "What do you want?"[4]

Writing instructors could facilitate such practice by working with faculty in other disciplines to design assignments that (in both what they ask and how they ask it) simulate the kinds of writing students are asked to do in discipline-specific classes. The cooperating faculty member might then be invited to class as a visiting expert, fielding questions about the genre and his or her expectations as a reader. The class and instructor could work together to brainstorm appropriate questions as they examine models in the days before the expert's visit.

Students could also be encouraged to seek out other expert writers outside the context of a specific writing assignment. They could be encouraged to interview published writers and experts within their current or anticipated major field. These interviews could focus on the constraints that work on writers (generic expectations, refereeing of major journals, style sheets, taboo issues), the writers' strategies for assessing community expectations (who they ask to read drafts, the questions they ask of these readers, what they do with the responses and suggestions of editors,), and the choices writers make (what motivates them to write, where and how they write, in what ways do they break or bend the rules).

Ideally, practice in interviewing and questioning instructors and other expert writers would serve two purposes. First, it would give students greater insight into the expectations of various disciplines and communities outside the English classroom through interaction with working, writing members of such communities. Second, it would help students develop a mindset of ethnography—an attitude that allows and encourages curiosity and inquiry—making them less reluctant to seek out advice and ask questions in their future forays into new writing communities. They will come to realize that learning to write is an ongoing process, just as writing a particular text is a process. There is a process (or processes) involved in learning about how a particular genre functions and in then applying what has been learned to writing here and now—genre process.

These are only some of the ways a genre-process approach would manifest itself in the classroom and within a writing program, but they should begin to make clear that the application of genre theory to writing curricula is much more complex and demanding than might be imagined by many readers of the Outcomes Statement. If the steering committee of the Outcomes Collective and the Council of Writing Program Administrators as a whole embrace this task, they need to do more to help assure that their statement is read and applied as they would want it to be. Perhaps they could take as their model "NCTE's Statement on Students' Right to Their Own Language," which includes not just a listing of principles but an explanation of the research and theoretical foundations that ground them. That document also includes a bibliography that would allow those who wanted to act on the recommendations held within the statement to inform themselves and enlighten their constituents more fully about the nature of language differences. The Council could also publish collections of key articles or a readable and comprehensive guide to genre theory for the uninitiated.[5] This kind of work might also need to be done for other assumptions of the Outcomes Statement that may not be universally understood in the manner the committee meant them.

In the end, a document so brief cannot be expected to stand on its own, even if written by people from multiple kinds of campuses from across the country. Their choice to become involved in such a project, and their presence at the conversations (whether actual or virtual) that led to the final document place them in a much smaller, more coherent community of discourse and work than the one to which they are writing. I believe, working now in a department where there is no standard syllabus, where first-year writing courses are taught by a mix of tenured literature, linguistics, and rhetoric and composition faculty, along with a similar mix of adjuncts, that how theory gets put into practice is, in most of the country, a highly individualized matter. While my colleagues and I, for example, might—and to some degree have—tried to adopt the WPA Outcomes Statement for our writing program, how that gets read and put into practice in the classroom of individual instructors is always going to be somewhat up for grabs.

The Council of Writing Program Administrators is to be commended for trying to articulate a comprehensive set of goals that might allow diverse writing programs across the country to develop up-to-date and theoretically credible curricula that together comprise a coherent application of the best thought and practices in the field of rhetoric and composition. However, providing venues for more thorough explication and support of these goals will go a long way toward making the council's vision a reality.

10

PROCESSES AND OUTCOMES IN ARIZONA'S HIGHER EDUCATION SYSTEM

Duane Roen and Gregory R. Glau

In the fall of 1992, John Ramage, then acting director of English composition at Arizona State University, submitted to the dean of the College of Liberal Arts and Sciences a document titled "Proposal to Improve Writing Instruction at ASU." Among other things, the plan, subsequently approved by the provost, suggested changes to enhance the quality of instruction in the English composition program by establishing a set of goals:

- First, it called for the hiring of faculty with formal training in rhetoric and composition. To date, we have hired twelve lecturers (faculty with three-year, infinitely renewable contracts)—all with Ph.D. degrees and specializations in rhetoric and composition. We have also hired more than twenty instructors (faculty who reapply each year).
- Second, the plan recommended that TAs' teaching loads be reduced from four to three sections per year. Although we've been unsuccessful in achieving this goal, we have managed to lower enrollment caps in sections taught by first-year TAs.
- Third, the plan recommended salary raises for faculty associates (faculty who reapply each semester). To date, we've raised those salaries modestly.
- Fourth, the plan called for a Stretch 101 course—a course for basic writers that "stretches" the first-semester course out to two semesters and six credit hours. That program is thriving.
- Fifth, the plan called for the hiring of additional tenured and tenure-track faculty. We've been able to hire Patricia Webb, an assistant professor specializing in computers and composition, and Sharon Crowley, filling a position formerly occupied by Frank D'Angelo.
- Sixth, the plan called for a minor in composition. We do not have a minor, but ASU's faculty senate did approve our proposal for a writing certificate program in the fall of 1998.

Since 1992, we have frequently cited the Ramage plan as a very necessary commitment to quality instruction in undergraduate composition courses. In the spirit of improvement of undergraduate instruction, we have also sought and received support from the College of Liberal Arts and Sciences, as well as the Graduate College, to enhance the training of first-year TAs.

Although we think that we have served students well by implementing some of the measures described above, we realize that the Arizona legislature, the Arizona board of regents, and the general public want some demonstration that we are achieving the goals of actually improving the quality of instruction in first-year composition courses. They want to see what students have done in our courses. Since 1995, we have asked students to construct portfolios in our first-year courses so that they can begin to see the breadth and depth of their learning in the courses. More recently, with the connection of the Outcomes Statement to our students' portfolio assignments, we hope our composition program will be able to control, as Ed White puts it, our own destiny: "By calling for . . . portfolio assessment, teachers have hoped to gain power over assessment and hence over the definition of what is to be valued in education; they have attempted to impose the educational vision in which assessment is a vital support for the learner onto the institutional vision in which assessment is a sorting and certifying device" (1996, 9).

During the 1997–98 academic year, Duane participated in online discussions of the Outcomes Statement. In the spring of that year, at the annual CCCC meeting in Chicago, he participated in the day-long workshop in which participants revised a draft of the Outcomes Statement. As he thought about the Outcomes Statement and the portfolios that students construct in our courses, he realized that combining the two would allow the composition program to provide evidence that our students are accomplishing much in first-year composition.

In the summer of 1998, the two of us collaborated with several other colleagues (Deirdre Mahoney, Jackie Wheeler, and Bonnie Kyburz) to link the Outcomes Statement and students' portfolio work. That is, we constructed a portfolio assignment that asked students to use the items in the Outcomes Statement to reflect on their work in the first-year courses. Since then, we have revised the assignment each semester, and there are slightly different versions for each of the first-year courses.

For our purposes here, the version that Greg has revised for students in the Stretch Program will illustrate the functions and details of the assignment.

End-of Semester Portfolio Assignment

There are two parts to the end-of-semester portfolio:

- First, an end-of-semester semester letter that discusses your change (and, we hope, your growth) as a writer over the course of the semester. The "rhetorical considerations" section and others below provide more detail, but the idea here is to both explore and demonstrate in what specific ways you have further developed your reading, writing, and thinking skills as you "wrote your way" through the first part of this class.
- Second, a revision plan where you examine one of your writing projects and explain, in detail and with specific examples, how you'd go about revising that composition. Keep in mind that you do not do the actual revision; rather, you discuss what you would do if you had the chance to revise the project. Please include the final version of the text with my comments and then, attached to these, a detailed discussion of how you are seeing this paper differently and how you would go about revising it now. Be sure to comment on audience, purpose, goals, and so on for the essay and provide specific examples of what changes you'd like to make.

Rationale for the letter and revision plan

Following this project prompt, you will find a draft "Outcomes Statement" that composition faculty from all over the United States have constructed. The purpose of this document is to specify the kinds of knowledge and skills that students should acquire by the end of the first-year composition sequence. Because only some of that knowledge and some of those skills will be evident in any given project that you complete for the course, you need to provide a sampling of all your work in this course to demonstrate what you've accomplished as a reader, writer, thinker, learner. In general, this letter provides you with an opportunity to illustrate how you make informed choices as a writer.

Rhetorical Considerations

One purpose for this letter is to demonstrate that you have acquired rhetorical knowledge. Second, you should also demonstrate that you have further developed your reading, writing, and thinking skills. Third, you should demonstrate that you know how to use composing processes. Finally, as the Outcomes Statement suggests, you should demonstrate that you have gained further control over conventions of written language, especially by showing in your compositions what you are doing . . . and why you're doing it (that is, what's your rhetorical purpose?).

So: what can you give me copies of (learning logs, drafts, comments, commented-on papers, invention activities, etc.) and comment on to show what you've learned?

The Project

To complete this letter and the final portfolio for this course, you will need to save your written work throughout the semester—invention work, drafts of projects, "final" versions of projects, the post-composing reflections on each project, journal entries, written peer responses, and the like.

However, you do not need to submit all of your written work with your letter. Rather, you need only submit copies of whatever you consider necessary to demonstrate that you have accomplished the goals specified in the attached Outcomes Statement.

For this letter, I'm asking you to submit a letter addressed to me in which you explain what you've chosen to include in the portfolio and what each item in the portfolio demonstrates—so if you include some of your learning logs, discuss them in relation to the questions below. You'll want to include an early version and the final version of writing project #1, and you'll want to discuss it in detail in terms of the questions below, and so on.

For your letter, you need to be as detailed as possible, using examples from your writing projects #1 and #2 as well as the other work we've done to illustrate your growth as a writer, what you've learned from the invention, peer review, and other activities, and from the final "production" of the first writing project. Your letter should also include a paragraph or two in which you look to the future, commenting on how you plan to use your rhetorical knowledge and your composing skills in your academic, professional, personal, and/or civic lives.

For your revision plan, you want to be as detailed as possible about what you'd change, and where you'd change it, and what you'd add and where you'd add it, and what you'd delete and so on . . . the more detailed, the better your plan will be.

Activities and Approaches for Working Through the Reflective Letter and Revision Plan

You will be doing "early invention" work for the portfolio throughout most of the semester. That work will consist of all your written work in the course. As you do the work for the course, be thinking about the goals included in the attached Outcomes Statement. As you write the post-composing reflection at the end of each writing project for the course, you might use the Outcomes Statement to guide that writing.

For your letter, respond to each of the following questions in detail, using specific examples to show rather than just telling us:

- What goals have I reached at this point in the semester?
- What goals can I strive for as I complete the next project?
- How did I work differently for WP #2 than I did for WP #1?
- How have I used peers' responses to improve my work?
- What was the best peer response I got, and how did I use it?
- What excerpts from my projects illustrate what I've achieved?

Another and perhaps more detailed approach is to use the Outcomes Statement as a heuristic (a way to help you get started) in answering more specific questions about your portfolio.

In terms of rhetorical knowledge:

- Where and in what ways can I show how I focused on a specific purpose?
- Where and in what ways do I show that I'm able to anticipate the needs of different kinds of readers?
- What examples can I give to show that I can use the conventions of format, organization, and language appropriate to specific writing situations?

In terms of general reading, writing, and thinking skills:

- What examples can I provide to show that I'm able to use writing to record, explore, organize, and communicate?
- What illustrations can I include in my portfolio to indicate I'm able to find, evaluate, analyze, and synthesize appropriate sources (such as notes I've taken, comments I've received, etc.)?

In terms of processes:

- What materials do I need to include and discuss to demonstrate that I can use multiple drafts to improve my text strategies like brainstorming, outlining, and focused freewriting, during all stages of the writing process?
- In what ways can I show that I'm now able to use appropriate strategies to generate, organize, revise, and edit my compositions, and that those strategies are appropriate to the specific writing situation?

> (Note: the assignment continues here with drafting and peer review information and advice; current information and full samples are available at the Stretch Program Web site.)

When we first present and discuss this assignment in our classrooms, we are very aware that it asks students to do *a lot*, and often they feel overwhelmed by all of its components. Therefore, we let our students know that they're not expected to answer all of the assignment's questions (although we also tell them that the more detail they have, the more effective their final portfolio will be). Also, rather than simply handing it out "as your end-of-semester assignment," we work to integrate the various pieces into what we ask students to do at various times throughout the semester, so in essence they're working on the portfolio for fifteen weeks.

For example, we ask our students to construct a number of what we call learning logs (others might call them journal entries, or responses, or reflections). Here's an example of one of our learning log assignments that gets students started at answering some of what the OS statement refers to:

> Tell me how you are feeling about writing this writing project. What is the best thing about your writing project? What would you like to spend more time on? If you had to select the best idea in the writing project, what would it be? The purpose of this learning log is to ask you to step back a little from your writing and study it and think about it.

Here's another example: we ask our students to construct a midterm reflective letter, not only to give them experience at doing such work (which we'll ask for in much more detail at the end of the term) but also to give them a *starting point*, something they can build on for that end-of-semester assignment. As they then work with that first attempt with their peer reviewers and the list of prompts in the assignment (and the suggested peer-reviewer prompts), it's relatively easy for students to see what they've touched on and what they've missed, what they have some examples for and what they do not exemplify, and so on.

We also incorporate much of the OS into what we ask our students *to do* for each writing project. For instance, we ask students to turn in all notes, invention work, drafts, etc. when they turn in their final versions of each writing project—in line with this prompt from the portfolio assignment:

> What materials do I need to include and discuss to demonstrate that I can use multiple drafts to improve my text strategies like brainstorming, outlining, and focused freewriting, during all stages of the writing process?

Many of our students attach copies (often highlighted) of their work to *show* how they've used, say, brainstorming ideas, or to show how their drafts have changed. Consider how student Nikki Soper describes what she's including in her portfolio:

> [The] pieces that I feel I did well on, or that were better once they were workshopped I have attached to this letter. I have included pieces from LL #8, LL #10, LL #1, IA [invention activity] #2, WP #1 Version 1, and the final version of WP #1. The WP #1 Version 1 was my first draft that was workshopped by my peers. I feel in writing that another's view is important to your success. Therefore, when I had an extremely long introduction my reviewers pointed this out and this allowed me to change my introduction. It also helped me to rearrange my paragraphs into one, and place ideas from one paragraph to another. I really feel that the reviewers help the writer see things the writer himself may overlook.

Also note how Soper, in expanding how she describes what writing she's included in her portfolio, also explains specifically how she went about changing her introduction.

SOME EXAMPLES FROM STUDENT'S REFLECTIVE LETTERS

Perhaps the best way to illustrate what some of our students have done with the portfolio projects (both at midterm and end of the semester) is to examine some of their work in light of the OS and how we've adapted that statement to construct specific writing prompts that we ask students to address.

Here, notice how freshman Jami Coughlin uses many specific examples from her own texts to illustrate the points she's working to make:

> To show how I have grown as a writer, in this portfolio I have included copies of my learning logs, invention activities, peer responses to version #1 of writing project #1, peer responses to version #2 of writing project #2, the final version of writing project #1, and the final version of writing project #2. The goals of the learning logs are to get our minds heading in the right direction for a specific writing project. With that said learning log #3 did just that. In learning log #3 I had to make a list of at least twelve possible questions that I didn't know the answer to. That list of questions was helpful when trying to pick out a problem for writing project #1. In fact, from that list I was interested in the question, "Why isn't Arizona State a non-smoking campus?"

This student clearly is working hard to explain why her portfolio includes what it does and to provide some examples to show what she means. Jami is even more explicit later in her reflective letter as she works to answer these two assignment prompts:

- How have you used or not used previous peer responses in this revision? Why?
- If you did take advantage of the peer response you received, in what way(s) does that advice show up in your own composition? How could peer advice be more helpful in your next writing project?

Jami responds to these prompts with reflective comments about peer reviewing and also with specific examples from her text (in effect, "citing" herself):

After writing version #1, we workshopped our papers through peer responses. Peer responses have helped me tremendously with improving my work. . . . Sometimes the things that I think are well written may confuse the reader. Therefore, I can fix these portions of my papers so my final copy is almost flawless. For instance, one of my peers suggested to me, in version #1 of writing project #1, that I should give more examples of "Why college students begin smoking."

From that suggestion I created a paragraph in my final version, giving my opinions and other questions of why college students began smoking. Some of these include, "Was it because of peer pressure? Maybe their role models (mothers, fathers, older siblings, movie stars) as a child smoked, and they wanted to be just like them. How did these students as children have cigarettes in their possession when they weren't of age?"

Jami goes on to reflect on (and even to criticize) the peer reviewing we'd done in our classroom:

I think peer review is something that should be done in more classes. This semester is the first time I have ever used peer review and it has made a huge impact on the outcome of my papers. I try to take our peer review sessions very seriously because the more information and help I can get, the better. However, sometimes my peers are too nice and don't criticize my papers enough. I think being more critical is something our class needs to work on, because you can never get too many suggestions.

Other students responded in much the same way—with good examples and details that effectively demonstrated what points they were making. Becky Magos, for instance, cites both the comments she received and her responses to her classmates' suggestions when she notes:

An example of description in project two would be when I was negatively describing the red couches in the library. I described them as, "The dirty, stained, red couches, are so disgusting." I read all the suggestions that were given to me in the conference. In writing project two, I received a suggestion saying that I should explain what people were doing in the library. I incorporated this idea by describing what the people were doing in the couch area of the library, "Some lazy students fall asleep on the couches and begin to snore." I also added marks and suggestions of my own, in the margins, where I felt I needed to work on. I tried to use most of the suggestions that were given to me by my peer reviewers.

It's important to keep in mind that these students are responding to assignment prompts based on OS goals that students should be able to

- Understand the collaborative and social aspects of writing processes
- Learn to critique their own and others' writing
- Review work-in-progress in collaborative peer groups for purposes other than editing

By connecting the writing we ask our students to compose for their portfolio assignments to the Outcomes Statement, we move toward what Sandra Murphy and Barbara Grant (1993, 288) describe as a "constructivist perspective" on learning and assessment, for such a view "is contextualized, reflecting and supporting what students and teachers are actually doing in classrooms." As Murphy and Grant note, with such assignments: "Writing is conceptualized as a process, not a product, so that assessment . . . becomes an opportunity for [teachers] to learn what students know and are able to do. For students, assessment becomes an opportunity to practice authorship, that is, to assume ownership of and authority over their work rather than fulfill the expectation of others."

Consider how student writer Michael Henderson assumes such ownership of his texts as he responds to the assignment prompts asking how the writer reacted to and used peer comments. Michael writes:

When I first started this semester I believed that my writing skills were up to par and that this class was a waste of my time. But ever since that day I have been proven wrong, over and over again. I started to realize this right after the first peer review on writing project number one. In this paper I wrote about how college could be more enjoyable. When I got my paper back from the other students there were numerous remarks about how I did not use any examples of how college could be fun or just the opposite. I just had many reasons of why college is miserable "college is so different from high school. A disrespectful person thinks it is funny to pick on you. They are not attending college on their own free will." But I did not give examples of how these things ruin college. Also they pointed out how I only saw my topic from this point of view and could have brought up many more questions for the paper. Like I later inserted into my paper "Some students do enjoy college. Pick majors with easier classes. Or maybe they make it miserable for themselves."

It's important to note that Jami, Becky, and Michael all were addressing specific questions from the assignment prompt that led them not only to *reflect on* but also to *provide examples from* their own writing.

Another OS goal focuses on the use (and value) of multiple drafts. Student Lisa Brooke Konstanzer addresses (and reflects on) such concerns when she notes:

> Multiple drafts have done wonders for my papers. . . . When I rewrite, these points have been improved because I feel like the more times I revise, the more my paper improves. My problematic paper is a good example of this. I had two rough drafts for this assignment and I have learned the more rough drafts that I have, the better my paper is. My proof is from my peers. My peers were impressed by the improvement that I had made. . . .
>
> Multiple drafts are not only beneficial for gathering more complete thoughts, but they also help to recognize improvement for conventions such as spelling, grammar, and punctuation. Because I have had the opportunity to have multiple drafts, I have been able to control my grammar mistakes that I would normally overlook if I had not gone though numerous drafts. My spelling is naturally disgusting. And because it is so awful, I have had to resort to the dictionary many times for all three of my papers. This is nothing new to me, but I am more open-minded about it now because this class has motivated me to be a better writer in and out of class.

Our students have been constructing portfolios since 1995, and they have constructed Outcomes-based portfolios since the fall of 1998. We think that our portfolio assignments have encouraged students to do what Purves, Quattrini, and Sullivan see as the major purpose of constructing portfolios: "a deliberate effort to present oneself to the outside world as a writer or a student of writing" (1995, vi). We prefer to replace "or" with "and" in this sentence, though, because we hope that our students see themselves in both of these complementary roles.

It's been interesting to read teachers' individual variations in portfolio assignments. While teachers in our large program (approximately 145 teachers and 13,000 students each year) present the Outcomes Statement to students in language that reflects their individual teaching personae, pedagogical strengths, and writing practices, the general spirit of the Outcomes Statement seems to bring a real focus to teachers' expectations for students' portfolios. Because teachers adapt the Outcomes Statement to their own specific portfolio assignments, we don't encounter the problems (such as recycling the same paper through several classes) some associate with portfolios (Schuster 1994, 316–20; see also Larson 1993). At the same time, students also bring their own individual perspectives to the activity of portfolio construction. When these differing perspectives transact with one another and with the Outcomes Statement, they seem to interact as Bakhtinian "centripetal" and "centrifugal" forces. The Outcomes Statement focuses the discourse with its centripetal or unifying influence, but the individuals who use the Outcomes Statement to guide portfolio construction represent strong centrifugal influences. In these transactions, the Outcomes Statement does not remain a stable document; rather, it takes on a new life each time a student or group of students engage with it, interacting with student portfolios to enable "student learning that is active, engaged, and dynamic" (White 1994, 27).

Even though students have used the Outcomes Statement for a year to guide their portfolio construction, we have not yet begun using portfolios for large-scale program assessment. We realize that we soon need to begin such assessment, though, so that we, rather than external agencies, determine the nature of the assessment. We hope to begin planning for this kind of program—not teacher—assessment soon, because we think that the Outcomes Statement/portfolio connection will become an effective component in a useful assessment approach. We fully expect that the effort will demonstrate that students are accomplishing much in our courses.

In addition to assessing what is accomplished in our courses, we hope that the Outcomes Statement/portfolio connection encourages ongoing conversations about what we're doing in first-year composition. Teachers in our program already participate in formal and informal conversations about what constitutes effective curriculum and pedagogy. Putting the Outcomes Statement on the table, though, has helped us to focus some of those conversations, and it has helped refine some of the curricular goals that we have constructed. Further, as Pat Belanoff and Peter Elbow note, "We think the portfolio helps us deal with an essential conflict in program administration: Is it our program or the teachers'? . . . The portfolio permits genuine collaboration between us and our teachers" (1991, 26–27).

11

KNOWLEDGE OF CONVENTIONS AND THE LOGIC OF ERROR

Donald Wolff

The Knowledge of Conventions outcome sounds like "grammar first" all over again. While some will embrace going back to the basics, others will argue that emphasizing conventions marginalizes nonstandard dialects and seeks to supplant the voice, and hence the social identity, of those already linguistically, educationally, and culturally on the periphery (Smitherman 1999). This outcome hides so much of the real complexity of conventions, especially their relationship to dialects and socioeconomic background, that it is nearly bound to be misread and very likely misapplied.

Such objections demonstrate that an important part of understanding all the outcomes is the act of acknowledging their history within the discipline, of problematizing them, as Freire (1989) would say. In the case of the Knowledge of Conventions outcome, this means understanding error analysis and the logic of error, as they relate to the nature and function of American dialects and English as a foreign language.

I'll never forget one student. She was in the special section I taught for [Edited American] English as a Second Dialect designed for the weakest dialect writers—mostly African American and Chicano—admitted to the university. It was my job to hold them to university standards while addressing the particular writing and reading needs generated by their inexperience with the "Language of Wider Communication," as Weaver calls it (Weaver 1996). This particular student, who went on for an MBA, did very well, eventually producing A-level work—clear, cogent, well developed but still concise, and correct. I congratulated her and asked her how she liked being an A writer. She said she liked the grade just fine but hoped to avoid writing in the future because it was too much work.

On the one hand I felt that I had succeeded because she not only produced good work but had a clear understanding of what she had to do to produce it. On the other hand, I felt that I had failed, for my emphasis on academic prose had killed whatever joy she might have had in writing by making it grunt work. I take this as an emblem for a very real danger in stressing academic writing and its concomitant correctness.

Another African American student of mine asked me one day if I thought whites were smarter than blacks. He had just read some of the early arguments about the bell curve claiming that statistically blacks must be intellectually inferior to whites. I told him I didn't care what the statistics said—I had to teach everyone as if he or she could learn to write successful academic prose and I had had enough success to know that everyone could, if they were willing to put in the time and effort. The student just wanted to know where he stood and why he had to struggle so much. He was ready and willing to believe he was not intelligent enough.

It continues to surprise many both inside and outside the academy that grammar, including the study of conventions, is the most difficult aspect of writing for students to master. Grammar difficulty is surprising because those in charge and elite students find the "handbook" approach easy, effective, efficient, logical, mechanical. A few directives to avoid common errors like fragments, comma splices, and pronoun disagreement, and such students are ready to move on. However, most American students do not attend flagship universities, and even at such schools there is a significant number of students whose first language is not English or whose dialects differ in significant ways from the standard employed in most academic discourse. For these students, mastering the conventions presents repeated difficulties, especially if they have little experience with reading and writing, not to mention speaking the language (Matsuda 1999, 709). Teaching grammar is steady work for most teachers and the "handbook" approach doesn't work for most students. Why not?

It turns out we don't teach grammar rules at all, in the linguistic sense. Children have their grammar deeply embedded in their subconscious by the time they enter school, a view of grammar so counterintuitive that most people reject it out of hand, while many in composition embrace it all too readily in order to minimize the emphasis on grammar that has been too long identified as the essence of first-year composition (FYC). But we don't really teach grammar anyway. The grammar that enables us to produce novel sentences orally and communicate effectively day to day is learned deeply and well through everyday listening before we can talk and through conversation afterward. What we usually teach in FYC is a limited set of conventions governing academic prose, by means of the error hunt, hoping against all evidence (Weaver 1996, 16–23) that this approach will transfer to the students' actual writing.

For most students, the handbook approach creates a transference gap. The lessons easily applied by the top students hide the real complexity of the task. Editing is a "skill" only for those with enough literacy so that editing can be separated from attaining a new, more abstract level of discourse. Even successful drills, where students seem to master a convention enough to pass a quiz, many times will not result in a transference of the "skill" to the students' own writing. That's because it's not a skill; there's nothing basic about it, as we know from working with our weakest writers. There is a transference gap because the exercises are not grounded in the students' own writing; grammar is not taught in context, *even* if the exercises replicate the kinds of errors students make in their own compositions. If they're not connected more closely to the individual student's own writing, then making the transfer requires a greater level of abstraction, increased cognitive load, and we're back where we started—many students lose either fluency or correctness.

Teaching conventions is seldom as straightforward as we like to believe. Grammatical concepts, even "simple" ones like recognizing a subject, verb, or a complete sentence, are *very* difficult for native speakers, because by the time a child is six or seven those concepts are always already employed effectively in speech. The linguistic mind is very efficient and does not need to identify subjects and verbs, for example, in order to produce effective sentences orally. It is consequently difficult, in moving from oral to written proficiency, to get the mind to retain what for it is needless information, far removed from what's required to communicate effectively day to day. In addition, speech patterns may not match up well with the conventions of college-level prose. As a result, for inexperienced readers and writers a key component of mastering conventions is recognizing their own error patterns and seeing the logic behind their erroneous choices (Shaughnessy 1977, 10–11). The comma is a good case in point.

I have found the best way to teach comma use is through practice in sentence structure, where commas are linked to the higher frequency of complex structures in academic discourse, structures like subordinate and relative clauses. This leads to a conversation about bound and free (restrictive and nonrestrictive) modifiers, a concept that often governs whether or not a comma should be used. Linking sentence structure to articulation (of precise relations between elements in a sentence), to meaning, and to punctuation helps writers understand how readers process information at the sentence level. Such a lesson and perspective are more likely to stick than a review of conventions or avoiding the issue altogether, as some teachers are inclined to do, thinking the conventions are unimportant or that they will be picked up in the "natural" course of college-level reading and writing.

Students can't see where commas go and don't go because they can't *see* structure. However, they can *hear* structure, both phrases and clauses, and so that's a good place to begin. But often students mark syntactic units (clauses and phrases) with commas when something else is required, like a period or semicolon in the case of a comma splice. Or they mark a syntactic unit not usually marked, as in the case of putting a comma after the subject and verb of a clause embedded in some larger structure, or after a noun substitute (a phrase) acting as the sentence subject, so the comma intrudes between the subject and verb. Analyzing these patterns means recognizing their "logic."

The examples that follow are illustrative because they represent a range of problems at once idiosyncratic and familiar. In this case the comma errors stem from the writer's own perfectly consistent and even accurate linguistic intuition: in each case, a writer would be marking off a syntactic unit with a comma, even though these particular phrases are not usually marked with commas because they are bound:

> The students spent the first period, reading "The Story of an Hour."

The final six words are a verb phrase acting as an "indirect" object. That is, they function powerfully within the sentence as a single syntactic unit, added to what seems like a complete clause. At least, the part of the sentence before the comma has a subject, verb, and direct object, or a noun phrase ("the students") and a verb phrase ("spent the first period"). So the final phrase "feels" added on, even though it's necessary for the "completeness" of the sentence. The point is, the comma is not arbitrary but marks a phrasal unit. Actually, the sentence is a fairly complex construction, deceptively simple in appearance. Here's another example:

> He now asked more questions, than in the "Francis Macomber" discussion.

Here the comma marks the base clause off from the final modifying phrase. Again, the final phrase clearly acts as a single unit and "feels" tacked on to the base clause, which in fact it is, linguistically speaking. Here's another:

> She will read more carefully, with this in mind.

Now the writer sets off the prepositional phrase, again hearing the end of the base clause and marking it. As students expand their sentences, they often mark the end of the base clause because they have always been taught to mark the end of a sentence, which is what a base clause is. And they can't use a period here, so the default mark is a comma. Since no one has taught them about base clauses, modifying phrases, and bound and free modifiers (a knowledge often gained through sentence combining), they don't know how to ignore the clear message sent from their subconscious that a base clause like "I will read more carefully" *is* a complete sentence. Well, it is a complete sentence all right, but that doesn't mean one *must* mark the end of it. And I think one could even make an argument for keeping this particular comma, if the final phrase is referring to a big idea delineated in the previous sentence(s). It's a real option here for emphasis—sort of like "I'll be sure to keep that in mind." But it is also possible that the prepositional phrase might introduce the next sentence, in which case the writer may be avoiding starting a sentence with a prepositional phrase, which leads to so much trouble for so many: Introductory prepositional phrases often try to act like noun substitutes and perform as sentence subjects. Unfortunately, prepositional phrases can never be sentence subjects and often obscure the real subject of the sentence, in addition to creating a mixed construction.

Here's another common misuse of the comma, initially perplexing:

Although, the students haven't done a lot of reading this term, the teacher feels . . .

I see this a lot. And it looks like the exception to my argument since "although" isn't a phrase. However, it is a subordinator and therefore not only creates a dependent clause but it also precedes a base clause—what follows immediately is *by itself* an independent clause. So again, the writer has marked off a complete syntactic unit. The writer producing such sentences is remarkably consistent.

Grammar, of course, is also related to discourse, not only in terms of what counts as correct usage but also in terms of the writer's sense of agency, which brings us back again to questions of socioeconomic status and cultural identity. Most students don't see how to engage themselves in writing academically about issues that don't directly affect them, at least in their first year; some of them never discover how to operate in the specialized world of academic discourse. As a result, they try to effect an "objective" stance, which undermines their success. The distance between what they are attempting to write and where their interests really lie is the difference between academic writing and a prose that represents their personal interests, which often comes in "nonstandard" language or at least nonacademic prose. As inexperienced writers work their way through these conflicts, they will produce prose marked by errors created by moving back and forth between the two "voices," the personal and the academic. The problem, then, is figuring out a way to keep both in balance until the writers can move between them more or less effortlessly. Thus, errors in conventions can be intimately linked to the considerable rhetorical demands of advanced academic literacy, as we know from looking at early drafts of our own work, where errors often abound as we sort out the multiple demands of our subjects and audiences.

Needless to say, these are the kinds of sociolinguistic issues seldom considered in teaching conventions. The handbook approach is still operative today because it addresses the "basics" so many people think they embrace when they advocate a "back to basics" agenda. The difference between what grammar scholars advocate and what most people mean by teaching grammar creates a "hot spot," a politically sensitive issue where heated arguments occur in the public domain, played out in newspaper editorials and on the floor of legislative houses, as well as in our own professional journals and listservs. The teaching of grammar, like teaching many subjects, is politically charged, ideologically contentious. People tend to have *very* strong opinions about the subject. However, those who call for more grammar instruction usually are unaware of the transference gap and haven't thought about the logic of error. They haven't thought enough about grammar pedagogy and the sociolinguistic issues behind the Knowledge of Conventions outcome.

We need to understand error analysis as sociolinguistic practice. The dimensions of the problem were recently highlighted by the Oakland School Board "Ebonics" controversy. The board sought to declare Black English vernacular—an African American dialect—a separate language because the schools were not able to obtain enough funds in any other way to train teachers to appreciate the students' own dialect(s) while simultaneously moving them toward Edited American English. The issue is important enough to be the subject of the lead article in CCC's fiftieth anniversary issue (Smitherman 1999). Furthermore, the same volume closes with Debra Hawhee's "Composition History and the *Harbrace College*

Handbook" (1999), so that the special issue is framed by considerations of dialect and handbooks. When you think about grammar you're always current, always already embedded in the politics of grammar.

12

CELEBRATING THROUGH INTERROGATION
Considering the Outcomes Statement Through Theoretical Lenses

Patricia Freitag Ericsson

Since the Outcomes Statement has been adapted and adopted at myriad institutions, it is tempting to simply nod and celebrate it as a successful document. The many and diverse uses of the Outcomes Statement seem to make an uncomplicated argument for its success, and we can be tempted to say "Isn't that great!" and smile. But considerations of what has made the Outcomes Statement project so successful need to go beyond pats on the back. A serious, scholarly look at the statement is vital to our understanding of how projects like the Outcomes Statement work, how success is attained, and how we might replicate such successes. This chapter draws on technology theory, rhetorical theory, and public policy theory to provide us with a much clearer understanding of why the Outcomes Statement has been so widely adapted and adopted. This close examination of the way the Outcomes project was conducted and how the document has been used provide us with vital information about the project, the document, and its various implementations.

THE OUTCOMES STATEMENT AS A TECHNOLOGY AND SECONDARY INSTRUMENTALIZATION

Since the first part of this chapter relies partly on an understanding of the Outcomes Statement as a technology, clarifying that understanding is important before moving to considering implementations of the Outcomes Statement. It is easy enough to claim that goose quills, pencils, fountain pens, and computers are technologies because they are tools. They are, as Dennis Baron defines technologies, made of materials that are engineered "to accomplish an end" (1999, 16). A technology embodied as a tool is the most common way of thinking about technology. But when an object is made of disciplinary knowledge and its physical embodiment is a collection of words on paper or screen, the understanding of that *thing* as a technology is more difficult. However, a document like the Outcomes Statement is a technology. It is a product made from the materials of knowledge and words, engineered by highly skilled scholars and practitioners, and used to accomplish an end.

As a technology, the Outcomes Statement is more complicated than the document itself. Andrew Feenberg calls a technology "an elaborate complex of related activities that crystalizes around tool-making and –using in every society" (1999, 18). J. Macgregor Wise claims that a technology is an "aggregate of tools and their manipulations" (1997, 62). Operating with this expanded conception of a technology, Feenberg's two-part theory of technology can be utilized. In this theory, a technology that exists but has not been integrated into its supportive environment is at the functional point, or *primary instrumentalization*. The *secondary instrumentalization* occurs when the technology is "integrated with the natural, technical, and social environments that support its functioning" (205). During the secondary instrumentalization, the possibilities for agency open to groups other than those who created the technology. These groups influence whether a technology is actually used and how it is used.

As a published document, the Outcomes Statement is at a primary or functional point. It exists as a technical object, but has not yet become a part of any specific system of higher education in which it will ultimately function. In this state, the Outcomes Statement is underdetermined. What it will become as it is embedded in a specific college or university system is uncertain and will be influenced greatly by the system in which it becomes a part. As the table 1 and anecdotes in this chapter and this book demonstrate, the underdetermined, flexible Outcomes Statement technology has been broadly adapted and successfully implemented in a wide variety of venues.

Since the Outcomes Statement began in the WPA-L listserv, I began my study of the secondary instrumentalization of the Outcomes Statement by mining the list archives. Searching those archives provided evidence of several institutions adopting and adapting the Outcomes Statement for use in their programs. I also sent a query to the list for additional information about implementing the Outcomes Statement. The archives and inquiry responses provided a list of fifty-nine institutions that have implemented the Outcomes Statement. Not surprisingly, the most common use of the Outcomes Statement has been to define the first-year course: 88 percent of the fifty-nine schools have used the Outcomes Statement this way. The second most common use of the

Outcomes Statement has been in assessment. Although their assessment practices vary, seventeen of the schools (30 percent) have used the Outcomes Statement to help with assessment. Training TAs and adjuncts is the third most common way the Outcomes Statement has been used, with fifteen out of fifty-nine (25 percent) using the Outcomes Statement for this purpose. Finally, ten of the schools (13 percent) have used the Outcomes Statement in the first-year course itself. In each case, the institutions have adapted the Outcomes Statement to their own purposes. Some respondents called their adaptations "close," while others commented that their adaptations, while largely based on the Outcomes Statement, were considerably customized to fit local needs. The table below, "Uses of the Outcomes Statement," is a compilation of the research on Outcomes Statement use conducted in the WPA-L archives and through queries to the list. If the respondent included a Web site for his or her institution's adaptation of the Outcomes Statement, that URL is included.

Uses of the Outcomes Statement

Institution	Define course	Assessment	TA/adjunct training	In course itself
Alverno College	x			
Arizona State University http://www.asu.edu/english/writingprograms/teacherresources/wpgoals.htm	x			x
Atlanta Christian College	x	x	x	
California State University–Long Beach	x			
The College of New Jersey http://rhetoric.intrasun.tcnj.edu/WPArev1.doc	x			
College of the Mainland	x			
Community College of Denver		x		
Eastern Michigan University http://www.emich.edu/public/english/fycomp/outcomes/index.htm	x			

Eastern Washington University	x	x	x	
Georgia Southern University http://www2. gasou.edu/writling/ handbook/out- comes.html	x	x		x
Hannibal– LaGrange College	x		x	
Humboldt State University	x	x	x	x
Huston–Tillotson College	x	x	x	
Illinois State University	x	x	x	x
Johnson Community College				x
Kansas State University	x			
Kirkwood Community College		x		x
Louisiana State University	x			
Loyola University	x			
Mesa Community College	x			
Metropolitan Community College (Omaha)	x	x		
Metropolitan Community Colleges of Kansas City, Missouri				
Missouri Western State College http://www2. mwsc.edu/ eflj/eng100. html#Objectives	x			
Montgomery College	x			
Mount Union College	x			
Niagara University	x		x	
Northern Illinois University http://www.engl. niu.edu/FYCOMP/ outcomes_all.html	x	x	x	

Northwestern State University–Louisiana		x	x	
Oakland University	x	x		
Purdue University http://www.sla.purdue.edu/academic/engl/ICaP/106gmo.html	x			
San Juan College	x			
Southern Connecticut State University	x			
Southern Illinois University at Edwardsville http://www.siue.edu/ECPP/Statements/outcomes.html	x			
Stanford University	x		x	
University of Arizona	x			
University of California–Santa Barbara	x			
University of Colorado–Boulder	x			
University of Connecticut	x	x	x	
University of Delaware	x			
University of Illinois–Chicago	x			
University of Michigan–Dearborn	x			
University of New Mexico	x			
University of North Carolina–Chapel Hill	x			
University of Northern British Columbia	x			
University of San Francisco	x			
University of Tennessee–Chattanooga	x	x	x	x
University of Texas–Tyler		x		

University of Wisconsin–Eau Claire	x	x	x	x
University of Wisconsin–Green Bay	x			
University of Wyoming	x		x	
Utah Valley State University	x			x
Virginia Community College System	x			
Washington State University			x	
West Chester University	x			
West Virginia University	x	x	x	x
Winona State University	x			
Xavier College	x			
Xavier University of Louisiana	x			
Yeshiva University	x	x		x

To facilitate further investigation into the secondary instrumentalizations of the Outcomes Statement, more details were requested from several people who responded to the list inquiry. The extensive e-mail responses from these people illustrate the wide variety of uses to which the Outcomes Statement has been put and the diverse institutions that have chosen to adapt it.

At Mount Union College, a small liberal arts institution in Ohio, the Outcomes Statement was used as a foundation for the "Goals Statement for College Writers," which was adopted in 2000. Director of writing programs Kelly Lowe selected the Outcomes Statement as a starting point for collegewide writing goals because "the department wanted some kind of 'national endorsement' and having the WPA behind the goals made them easier to 'sell'" (Lowe 2003). He explained that instead of outcomes for a particular course, this Goals Statement is a declaration of what students should be able to do when they graduate from Mount Union. In reviewing the process of adopting these goals, Lowe recalled the politics that were involved and said that persuading the English department to adopt them was the most difficult. The small, traditional Mount Union English department (seven literature faculty and one composition faculty) resisted because of three factors: (1) "a long institutional history of Total Classroom Autonomy"; (2) "a fear that our one semester comp sequence 'couldn't do' all of the things in the outcomes statement"; and (3) "a (stated) fear that the 'comp guy' was trying to move the department away from liberal arts" (Lowe 2003). Lowe reported that getting the next constituency, the college faculty, to agree was easier. He attributed this to the fact that "they didn't really know what they were voting on." Recently, however, he has experienced resistance to the adopted goals as he has asked faculty in the WAC program to consider them. The third constituency that Lowe worked with was the dean, who asked Lowe to "simplify the statement" so that "someone with a degree other than Rhetoric/ Composition could understand it." The dean was supportive of the goals "early on," Lowe reported, which made getting it adopted easier.

Will Hochman of Southern Connecticut State University (SCSU, a state-supported institution with about six thousand undergraduates) recalled that work to adapt the Outcomes Statement for the local composition program was spurred by the National Council for Accreditation of Teacher Education's (NCATE) demand that they update an "ancient statement about teaching comp" (Hochman 2003). Hochman had previously believed that the SCSU faculty, which includes thirty-five full-time, tenure track and thirty-five part-time faculty, would "never come together and agree on a unified and strongly programatic set of goals." However, the NCATE demand, coupled with the Outcomes Statement document, provided the context for the development of these goals. The preface to the "Statement of Learning Goals for First-Year Composition at SCSU" notes that the statement is based on the WPA Outcomes Statement and recounts the series of Composition Subcommittee discussions and open workshops at which the Outcomes Statement were adapted for SCSU.

Another instance of adapting the Outcomes Statement to local use was recounted by a writing program administrator who has chosen to remain anonymous because of comments included about how the Outcomes Statement was received by the literature faculty in his department. Understandably, he does not want to have relations between the composition and literature faculty further eroded by public comment. To make writing and reading about this institution easier, the administrator is called "Doe" and the school "University of X" or "UX." In the beginning, Doe commented, "having the Outcomes Statement helped us tell ourselves that we were *not* off base in what we were doing" (Doe 2003). In addition to using the original Outcomes Statement, UX borrowed from customized statements that were developed (using the original Outcomes Statement as a base) at several other universities. The UX outcomes could be considered a third-level instrumentalization of the Outcomes Statement. By using the original Outcomes Statement as well as the secondary instrumentalizations from other universities, UX's outcomes are a complex hybrid instrumentalization of the original technology. In addition to using other versions of the Outcomes Statement, UX sought to make its outcomes even more understandable to different audiences. Faculty created student pages that interpret their outcomes in a more "student-friendly" way.

UX's outcomes have played well with administrators. The higher-ups at this university have been continually impressed that Doe and his colleagues "knew what they were talking about" concerning outcomes, and that Doe could get his "faculty committee to work up statements . . . because they were having trouble getting departments to understand what outcomes statements were" (Doe 2003). The set of statements that Doe's committee put together were used by the administration to show other departments on campus how setting up outcomes could be accomplished. Doe concluded that this process made Doe and the committee as well as the administration look very good and "They *love* it." Doe commented further that the Outcomes Statement work done on his campus has had a wider effect, as he accompanied an associate provost to a larger meeting of people working on outcomes statements at a larger campus. That group, too, was impressed with what UX had accomplished, which made both Doe and the administrator look good.

Other institutions have used the Outcomes Statement beyond first-year composition classes themselves by adapting it to inform writing across the curriculum programs, to set goals for developmental classes, and, as the next example illustrates, to advertise the composition program to other constituencies. David Stacey at Humboldt State University described using the Outcomes Statement to "advertise" that there is a national professional consensus about composition and to illustrate what his school is and is not doing compared to that national view (Stacey 2003). To introduce a new president to this disciplinary knowledge, Stacey presented a color-coded version of the Outcomes Statement comparing the national statement to what Humboldt State does in its one-semester first-year course: "black for what we do; blue highlighting for what we would like to do but really only touch upon; orange for what we'd like to do but don't really get anywhere near doing." Stacey used the same color-coded information at a collegewide general education outcomes meeting to "acquaint colleagues with what we do—and do not do."

At the University of Colorado at Boulder (UC–B), the Outcomes Statement was used to rebuild a writing program that Rolf Norgaard reported was "highly balkanized, the first-year course was woefully neglected, and political contentiousness abounded" (Norgaard 2002). In 2000, when the campus decided to reinvent the writing program, a new program for writing and rhetoric was conceived with a "newly conceived first-year course at its core." Norgaard's descriptions of what the Outcomes Statement meant to UC–B's efforts are remarkably positive. He called the Outcomes Statement a "welcome site for consensus building," noting that it provided a "neutral and flexible space for genuine dialog." According to Norgaard, the Outcomes Statement provided a "common space" and a "shared context" for discussions as well as a flexibility that allowed for "an opportunity for us to tweak the document in ways that address our more specific campus concerns and expectations about writing." Concluding these affirmative remarks about the Outcomes Statement, Norgaard says: "For us, the outcomes document was truly kairotic."

The University of Tennessee at Chattanooga (UTC) is one of the institutions that has used the Outcomes Statement in all of the ways listed in the table and is now using the Outcomes Statement beyond its institutional boundaries. In addition to using the Outcomes Statement to define the first-year course, to guide assessment, to train teachers, and to let students know about the goals of the course and their performance in it, UTC has begun using the Outcomes Statement to set up an "expectations" program based on the Outcomes Statement. Representatives of UTC, Chattanooga State Technical Community College, Hamilton County Department of Education, and the Public Education Foundation of Hamilton County collaborated to compose "Expectations for Entering College Writers," which is based on the Outcomes Statement. This document, which they refer to as the "Expectations Document," is being used to conduct workshops throughout the Hamilton County system to help middle and high school teachers understand what colleges and universities expect for entering college writers. The Expectations Document's five categories are similar to those of the Outcomes Statement: (1) rhetorical knowledge expectations; (2) critical thinking, reading, and writing expectations; (3) writing process expectations; (4) researched writing expectations; and (5) final draft concerns.

According to Lauren Coulter, the director of composition at UTC and leader of the first workshop on the Expectations Document, there were some objections to the Outcomes Statement because it did not include things like "specific modes of writing," but she indicated that these objections came largely from participants who were "out of the loop when it comes to current theory/research/practice of teaching writing" (Coulter 2003). These objections were met by including some language in the document that refers to "various organizing strategies" and then suggesting some methods of organization. The Expectations Document section on researched writing is not in the Outcomes Statement, but the committee members drafting the document knew that they would get "lots of specific questions about what our expectations are in that area" so they added it. As a help to teachers, they also added one annotated student paper (and will add more) so that teachers would have "papers that point back to specific expectations as a way to operationalize what some committee members thought were fairly abstract expectations."

At a spring 2003 workshop with master teachers from all subject areas, Coulter reported that the "group embraced the document wholeheartedly" (2003). Coulter was expecting some resistance, since teachers might have seen the Expectations Document as "yet another top down mandate about their teaching" and was prepared to meet the resistance with information about the composition of the committee that wrote the document (it included high school representatives). The group's surprising embrace was based, according to Coulter, on three main strengths of the Expectations Document: (1) it defines writing broadly, "as more than work done in English/Language Arts classes," and as more than writing about literary works; (2) it is a document that can "force their administrators to accept more theoretically-informed methods for teaching writing across the curriculum"; and (3) it "is a ticket to do some of what they have wanted to do with writing for a long time and haven't been able to do" because of administrators' clinging to outdated notions of what colleges want.

Although the workshops were not using the Outcomes Statement itself, they did use a document that is based on it. Coulter describes the process of arriving at that document: "we started with the Outcomes Statement and 'backed it up a year' to arrive at expectations for entering college writers" (2003). Using the Outcomes Statement, Coulter commented, made the "process of creating the Expectations document immensely easier, more efficient," and she recalls that when she was charged with creating the Expectations Document, she "immediately thought of the Outcomes Statement," realizing that in it she had "a position statement written by the best minds in the field; it had been deliberated over, discussed, scrapped and started over, and most importantly, ultimately ratified by the WPA."

The widespread use and broad adaptations of the Outcomes Statement in this chapter illustrate the variety of secondary instrumentalizations that the Outcomes Statement technology has undergone. In these instrumentalizations, the Outcomes Statement has been opened to input from new players—other teachers, other disciplines, administrators, and players at different educational levels. The social interests and organizational values of the particular institutions have played a vital role in how the Outcomes Statement is adapted and used—how, borrowing from Bruno Latour (2000), the technology is "enrolled" in the institutional networks in which it will function. The Outcomes Statement has proven to be highly adaptable—and ultimately, an exceptionally useful technology. The question that grows out of this claim of success is "Why?" Why is the Outcomes Statement a particularly successful document? That is the question that the second part of this chapter attempts to answer.

THEORETICAL ANALYSIS OF THE OUTCOMES STATEMENT AS SUCCESSFUL TECHNOLOGY

Simply claiming that the Outcomes Statement was the right technology at the right time and attributing it all to serendipity is tempting, but that simplistic approach teaches very little about the development and implementation of a good technology. In order to get beyond serendipity some theoretical tools are necessary. For this analysis, I enlist the rhetorical concept of *kairos* as well as ideas from Advocacy Coalition Framework, a public policy theory.

A revitalized definition of kairos that goes beyond the idea of timing helps in the investigation of the Outcomes Statement success. If kairos is defined as an analytical and generative concept used for both assessing the opportune time for a political move and guiding the force of that move, it can be particularly helpful in analyzing the Outcomes Statement. This richly defined kairos takes into consideration current political issues, the kinds of policies that are popular, and the problems that are receiving attention. Awareness of the current political climate was evident at the beginning of the Outcomes Statement project. Discussion of the Outcomes Statement began the same month (March 1996) that the

NCTE/IRA Standards for the English Language Arts (National Council 1996) were published. Although the NCTE/IRA standards and the outcomes were not directly related in the online discussions that spawned the Outcomes Statement, participants in the Outcomes Statement discussion were keenly aware of the standards movement and the troubled NCTE/IRA project. In an unpublished comment about the development of the Outcomes Statement, Kathleen Blake Yancey characterized the mood of "the larger culture" at the time the Outcomes Statement work began as "very standards rich" (Yancey 2003b). Those working on the Outcomes Statement were also aware of the *standards creep* that was taking place. The nationwide move toward standards-based education that began in the early 1980s with the *Nation at Risk* report had moved steadily up through the educational echelons and was making its way into higher education. Those involved in the Outcomes Statement movement realized that in short order, first-year composition would be a target of the standards movement. Preventing the first-year course from being defined by those outside the discipline was one of the prime motivators of the Outcomes Statement. Developing the Outcomes Statement was an offensive, proactive move based on a well-developed sense of kairos.

Development of the Outcomes Statement also took into consideration what kind of a document would be needed to allow different institutions to effectively use it. Some of the document's kairotic "force" was accomplished through the Outcomes Statement's extensive vetting in professional venues, its use of professional language, and its imprimatur by a national professional group. Those working to define the first-year course in differing institutions across the country voiced a need for a document that had a professional prominence and approval. The Outcomes Statement's development process gave the document just that—it carried the weight of a thorough vetting process and a "seal of approval" from the Council of Writing Program Administrators.

As the Outcomes Statement has been adopted, those promoting it have noted that the document and their awareness of it (because of extensive discussion of the Outcomes Statement in online venues and at multiple conferences) were also kairotic. It is a technology ready for use whenever it is needed and flexible enough to be adapted to all kinds of different situations and needs.

Consideration of Advocacy Coalition Framework, a public policy theory developed by Paul Sabatier and Hank Jenkins-Smith, can shed more light on the success of the Outcomes Statement. According to these scholars, effective advocacy coalitions must have "technical resources" so that they can participate in "prestigious" deliberations that are "dominated by professional norms" (1993, 50–54). The Outcomes Statement serves as the "technical resource" for those attempting to take part in discussions of the first-year course on multiple levels—from departmental to universitywide, to discussions beyond the university. In higher education, deliberations that are "dominated by professional norms" typically demand that participants have "professional training and technical competence" (Sabatier and Jenkins-Smith 1993, 53). This demand is often partially met by the Ph.D degree, but a technical resource like the Outcomes Statement is often needed to establish technical competence in policy deliberations. Such deliberations demand that the participants or advocates have a refined understanding of their own beliefs laid out in a comprehensible, rational form—a technical resource (Sabatier and Jenkins-Smith 1993, 42–43). The process of developing the Outcomes Statement provided for the clarification of the "beliefs" around which the first-year course is built and then turned those beliefs into a comprehensible resource.

The Outcomes Statement serves as a resource for what Sabatier and Jenkins-Smith call "policy-oriented learning." They define this as learning that is characterized by the diffusion of new beliefs and attitudinal change (1993, 42). Those seeking to spread new beliefs and change attitudes about the first-year writing course are conducting policy-oriented learning whether they are using the Outcomes Statement to train new writing teachers or to influence university-level policy concerning writing programs. This kind of learning is most successful when those attempting it have professionally recognized technical resources, and the Outcomes Statement provides exactly that.

This chapter has characterized the Outcomes Statement as an invaluable technical resource as various writing programs have lobbied for disciplinarily informed outcomes for the first-year course. The extensive vetting of Outcomes Statement drafts in a variety of disciplinary communities gave the Outcomes Statement wide publicity; the stamp of authority provided by the Council of Writing Program Administrators gave the Outcomes Statement professional credence. The widespread adaptation and adoption of the Outcomes Statement at a variety of institutions and the resulting betterment of first-year composition programs argues powerfully for the efficacy of the Outcomes Statement as a successful technical resource for policy-oriented learning. As long as the Outcomes Statement continues to reflect current best practice in composition theory and pedagogy, it will serve those shaping first-year composition programs well. But considerations of kairos and Advocacy Coalition Framework teach us that documents like the Outcomes Statement need to be timely, and policy-oriented learning must be an ongoing process. The Outcomes Statement will not remain timely if it is allowed to petrify. Those interested in first-year composition need to regularly revisit the document, and if necessary, revive the process through which it was conceived to update the document and revitalize its kairotic force. Advocacy Coalition Framework's emphasis on policy-oriented learning shows us that those directing writing programs must continue policy-oriented learning so that the project begun with the adaptation and adoption of the Outcomes Statement has lasting effects. The Outcomes Statement is not at an endpoint; it must continue to be a dynamic, ongoing effort that is regularly revisited and revitalized. We can continue to celebrate the Outcomes Statement only if we realize that our back patting must be accompanied by equal amounts of long-term effort.

PART THREE

The Outcomes Statement beyond First-Year Writing

13

WHAT THE OUTCOMES STATEMENT COULD MEAN FOR WRITING ACROSS THE CURRICULUM

Martha A. Townsend

In retrospect, I suppose I shouldn't be surprised by the dissention and controversy generated by the Outcomes Statement. My academic training in English studies as well as experience beyond academe have certainly taught me that issues surrounding language are among the most highly charged, politically sensitive matters that societies anywhere face. Witness the debates over the English Only movement, riots in French-speaking Quebec, the Oakland Ebonics debacle, and CCCC's Students' Right to Their Own Language. Nonetheless, I *am* taken aback by the range of arguments raised against compositionists' current and long overdue attempt to articulate, for ourselves primarily, what our bread-and-butter curricular staple is intended to accomplish.

I do believe that the OS framers, along with professional organizations that are asked to endorse the document, should be aware of possible pitfalls. And I do believe the OS should undergo thorough vetting by members of the field, as widely as can be done. I understand Rita Malenczyk's concern that, in light of the Boyer Commission's report, we could be subject to criticism for having produced a non-boundary-crossing, disciplinary treatise (chapter seventeen, this volume). As a longtime opponent of standardized "tests" of writing, I relate to the disquiet Mark Wiley feels at the prospect of administrators' misinterpretation of the document leading to increased pressure for quantifiable results (chapter four, this volume). And as a former teacher of developmental writers, I am sympathetic to Donald Wolff's argument that the OS oversimplifies instructors' ability to teach, and students' ability to grasp, various conventions (chapter eleven, this volume).

Thinking from the point of view of a writing across the curriculum program director, however, I don't believe these concerns, or those raised in other venues, should deter us from producing a discipline-based statement that purports to explain what higher education's most frequently required course attempts to accomplish. Maybe it's clichéd to claim this, but if professionals in the discipline can't arrive at common language to describe FYC outcomes, who can? I suspect the problem relates to our own uncertainty about what they should be as much as anything. But if the framers of the U.S. Constitution could draft a founding document for a whole nation, surely we can draft a definitional one for a population of college newcomers. I hasten to say that I believe it *is* possible to arrive at language for the OS that allows for discretion and interpretation by different types of institutions and for different levels of students, language that at the same time does not resort to meaningless, lowest common denominator definitions.

I can't help but wonder whether the central values of the academy in general and of composition studies in particular—questioning everything, "interrogating the text," inquiring critically, acknowledging differing views, privileging argument—have gotten in the way of reaching agreement on the OS. It wouldn't be the first time that intradisciplinary discord got in the way when we had the opportunity to do something worthwhile. One example of what I refer to took place in an elite setting in New York City in 1985. At the invitation of the Ford Foundation, some of the most illustrious figures in the field convened to offer their advice on a major new philanthropic initiative that Ford labeled Literacy and the Liberal Arts.[1] Occurring during a period of nationwide general education reform, the Ford grants were designed to infuse large sums of money into curricular projects that embedded composition in general education programs. Records of the meeting and participant testimonies reveal that the day-long conversation became contentious, tempers flared, and collegiality collapsed (see Townsend 1991). Astonished by what they perceived as lack of disciplinary agreement on composition theory and practice, Ford Foundation officials backed away from their initial intent and reduced the total grant program to just over one million dollars, far short of their original commitment, on the grounds that if professionals in the field couldn't agree, the foundation would be ill advised to invest what it had planned.

In citing this example, I don't necessarily wish to indict composition leaders for having cost dozens of colleges and institutions the possibility of external funds to experiment with and possibly improve their writing programs. Nor am I suggesting that hard questions be overlooked or difficult issues be sidestepped. I am suggesting that our internalized propensity to argue endlessly over virtually everything distracts us from more important matters and comes at a very high cost.

Insofar as the Outcomes Statement relates to writing across the curriculum (WAC) and writing in the disciplines (WID) programs, those matters are very real indeed. And the OS could make a difference. Having worked in WAC for some thirteen years now, I am continually surprised by the minimal contact that FYC programs, directors, and instructors have with faculty in the disciplines. Moreover, I am dismayed by the lack of trust exhibited by compositionists toward the discipline-based faculty who teach the students who have passed through FYC courses. Admittedly, the lack of trust is at times understandable. All too often, comments that filter their way back into the FYC director's office come from disgruntled teachers mumbling lines like, "Do you teach *anything* in those English classes? That student you gave an A to couldn't write his way out of a paper bag in *my* class."

With the growth of the WAC/WID movement over the past thirty years, though, fewer faculty utter such uninformed diatribes. Significant numbers of faculty have participated in faculty development workshops led by knowledgeable compositionists. Many faculty have substantially enlarged their perspectives about what writing is and how it works. Large numbers of faculty in the disciplines are teaching "writing-intensive," "writing in the major," or similarly writing-enhanced courses. At institutions that have WAC/WID graduation requirements, many faculty no longer comply by merely tacking writing artificially onto their syllabi. Some hold surprisingly enlightened views on designing assignments that directly address the pedagogical goals of their course and on using rhetorical concepts of purpose and audience to create imaginative yet relevant writing assignments that reinforce disciplinary knowledge. Many faculty have successfully adapted theoretically well-grounded ideas from sources like John Bean's *Engaging Ideas: The Professor's Guide to Integrating Writing, Critical Thinking, and Active Learning in the Classroom* (1986) to strengthen student learning.[2]

In recent years, WAC/WID advocates have discovered productive intersections and developed alliances with programs for teaching excellence. For example, former WPAs are now directing entire centers for teaching and learning at Illinois State University, Arizona State University, and Notre Dame. For better or worse, state and national constituencies have pressured higher education to pay more attention to composition's role in undergraduate teaching, as Rita Malenczyk points out in her analysis of the Boyer Commission's 1998 *Reinventing Undergraduate Education: A*

Blueprint for America's Research Universities (see also Zemsky 1989; Seymour 1995; and the Johnson Foundation 1993). Yet one more example of attention to writing beyond FYC was the recently dissolved National Educational Goals Panel in Washington, DC (its former Web site address is listed in the bibliography for those who might be able to access archived versions). Created in 1989, this body put forward goals that were signed into law in 1994. Goal 6, on adult literacy, states: "Every adult American will be literate and will possess the knowledge and skills necessary to compete in a global economy and exercise the rights and responsibilities of citizenship."[3] Unfortunately, the legislation has not been a frequent topic of discussion among compositionists, but the panel's work does have implications for WAC/WID programs in particular. For example, some six hundred faculty, employers, and policymakers participated in a study commissioned to "identify and . . . reach consensus . . . on the specific higher order communication and thinking skills that college graduates should achieve to become effective employees in the workplace and citizens in society" (Jones et al. 1995, iii). The findings have relevance for those of us designing FY and WAC/WID college composition curricula.

I see at least three sites of implication that the OS has for WAC/WID, two of which argue strongly for the statement and one which could create problems, but problems that nonetheless could be worked around. First, the OS would provide much-needed articulation of FYC's aims for faculty in the disciplines who teach WI, WAC, WID, or like courses. As WAC/WID has grown, its advocates and practitioners have come to know that every institution's program must be unique to survive, let alone thrive. These faculty are accustomed to working within their own individual institutional contexts—mission statements, fiscal resources, student demographics, administrators' philosophical understanding, campus ethos and receptivity, to name a few—to get their WAC/WID efforts off the ground and to sustain them. And they know they must evolve their own definitions of what WAC/WID means on their campuses and in their curricula. These faculty are, in other words, well versed in interpreting and adapting WAC tenets for their own needs. In doing this work, they ought to have access to a coherent statement of what the majority of the country's FYC curricula are trying to do. Faculty in the disciplines will understand that a nationally developed, discipline-based OS needs elaboration and interpretation.

Having something to start with, to work from, and to base questions on will be a good start. The OS will provide a vocabulary of words and of concepts that allows faculty in the disciplines to engage in more meaningful conversation about their own pedagogy. Given the trends in students transferring among colleges and universities, the OS will help to demythologize the curricula that many students take at disparate institutions. Various commentators who have already put the OS to use have noted that it demonstrates the commonalities that curricula hold across institutions. The OS can help faculty in the disciplines understand, at least in broad terms, what FYC does and does not do. As Donald Wolff put it in a post to WPA-L, "mostly they [school administrators, the interested public, students] want to see a document that makes common sense and mostly we [professionals in composition] want a document that makes theoretical sense. They want something readable and we want something that does not violate the complexity of teaching inexperienced readers and writers to compose effectively at the collegiate level."

Second, for writing programs that offer WAC/WID courses within the same department as FYC (e.g., sophomore- or junior-level "writing for the humanities" and "writing for the social sciences" courses, etc., taught by English instructors), the OS will help to establish baseline expectations that composition teachers can rely on as they plan and teach the subsequent material. Similar benefit will accrue to departments offering intermediate and advanced composition courses. Odd as it seems, queries appear with some regularity on WAC-L and WPA-L about how institutions define this array of courses. I'm not suggesting that the OS will, once and for all, resolve these definitions. Indeed, the conversations will continue, as they should. Minimally, though, the OS should, as above, provide a vocabulary for making the conversations more productive, the course sequences more defensible, and the course goals more discernable for students, teachers, and others.

The third, and potentially most problematic, site in which the OS is likely to intersect with WAC/WID is with administrators and state-level policymakers who may latch onto them for purposes of quantifying WAC/WID success, for either individual students or whole programs. Nonacademics who, wrongly or not, demand measureable "proof" of writing instruction may see the OS as support for their own self-interests. Interpreting OS language that others see as common or theoretically sensical, these constituencies will vex us with their misguided interpretations or even willful misuse. But this problem is by no means confined to the OS. Indeed, it already affects every other aspect of writing policy we have available. The willful misusers will be with us no matter what we do. The misguided ones can be corrected, as we now do. And perhaps they'll be a little less misguided if we produce a document that shows our desire to communicate with them, instead of wishing they'd go away.

Our best information indicates that approximately one half of all U.S. institutions of higher education have some sort of writing requirement beyond FYC. There is no doubt that the Outcomes Statement will impact this sector of writing instruction. For WAC/WID as well as other areas of the curriculum, I believe the promise inherent in the OS is high and the potential payoff is positive. David Schwalm (1999) has cautioned, "Our world is being defined for us by people who have other than educational objectives. It is time for us to stir, stop bickering among ourselves, and take charge of this accountability business. . . . The OS—in itself and in appropriate translations—is a step in this direction." It could help bring FYC in closer contact with WAC/WID practitioners. Putting the OS forward more publicly would, hopefully, move our interdisciplinary conversation forward as well. And it would demonstrate our willingness to be accountable. Let's get on with it.

14

FIRST-YEAR OUTCOMES AND UPPER-LEVEL WRITING

Susanmarie Harrington

Perhaps one of the most important components of the Outcomes Statement is its repeated assertion that first-year outcomes are only one stage in a writer's development. Other courses, other experiences, will continue to affect writing competence, and it is important for faculty in other departments and programs to consider how they can build on the work of first-year composition. Arguably no department needs this reminder more than the English department, whose advanced writing courses have typically been simply "more," "harder," or "better" first-year courses (see Haswell 1991, 319–20). Whether the OS will spur the development of better-articulated relationships among courses in English departments remains to be seen. In this essay, I explore the ways the OS specifically challenges those who teach advanced writing courses, drawing on my own department's experience with reconceiving its advanced writing courses. In so doing, I also explore some of the limitations of the Outcomes Statement in relation to advanced writing. The OS offers neat categories and clear directives about how work in other programs can continue to affect students' development. It doesn't acknowledge the jerky spiral of student development. It is advanced courses that must address the uneven ways writing skills progress, and the OS provides only partial guidance on that score.

Several years ago, contemporaneous with the national work on the OS, my colleagues and I created an outcomes grid for our department's noncreative writing courses. As we began that work, we discovered that mapping expected outcomes in advanced composition was much harder than we anticipated. We quickly learned what articles about advanced composition have reported for some time: there was very little to distinguish our first-year courses from our advanced courses, and there was no consensus on what the term *advanced composition* actually meant (see Bloom 2000 for a concise history of the term and its vagaries). As we looked at the range of our syllabi (from basic writing through senior courses in expository, business, and professional writing), all repeatedly promising to help writers build fluency, reflect on their writing styles, or master academic discourse conventions, we realized that we simply were not teaching courses that built on each other in any meaningful way. Our collected syllabi bore out a principle adopted by a CCCC working group on advanced composition in the late 1960s: advanced composition "may be [seen] as covering the range of the freshman course but in greater depth" (qtd. in Hogan 1980), an assumption that created a great degree of repetition across courses. Our local curriculum also reflected Hogan's 1980 findings: similar work was assigned across the range of courses, with essays perhaps (but not necessarily) longer, or more dependent on source texts, or written with the aid of longer or more difficult textbooks (Hogan had also found that advanced composition courses were often taught with freshman texts; that had not been our practice, although we did discover the same readings used at different course levels). The business and professional writing courses did introduce new genres to students, but the titles and course descriptions made it difficult for students (or faculty) to distinguish them. (What was the difference between Professional Writing and Business Writing? Or between Intermediate and Advanced Exposition? What was the difference between a 200-level course goal that students would explore their own writing processes and a 300-level goal that students would learn more about the writing process?) We did find much to admire in our courses, which on an individual level served students well, but on the whole, we were led to wonder just what we were teaching with the set of courses we offered.

How did we get to such a state of affairs? And more importantly, what were we going to do about it? Our habit of specializing in particular courses meant that each of us developed courses in isolation. We had little clear sense of course sequencing , and our writing major had withered in recent years, which meant that we no longer had a sense of how many students were moving through which courses in what order. Individuals may have shared syllabi or compared versions of courses, but there was no public discussion of such matters. Our weaknesses in this area were not unique. Like most writing teachers, we knew little about developmental psychology (a blind spot discussed by Haswell in this volume). It has thus been difficult for us (locally or nationally) to investigate how to meaningfully sequence writing instruction. Our curriculum was rooted in a certain faux-commonsensical notion that we could simply do "the basics" in first-year writing and then gussy them up down the line. Thus, as

Richard Fulkerson (1980) once explained, a "reasonable" oversimplification would help students function effectively:

> Perhaps freshman composition may reasonably oversimplify the world of discourse in order to assist students to gain a handhold. It may be reasonable, for example, to direct freshmen to write each essay with an explicit thesis. It may be reasonable to forbid certain developmental structures to be followed. Not on the grounds that this is all there is to real writing, but that if students master a limited number of workable techniques, they will have made major strides toward communicating clearly and efficiently in the writing situations they are most likely to encounter.
>
> If that is a reasonable—though selective—theory of freshman composition, then perhaps it is equally reasonable to regard advanced composition as helping students already skilled in selected utilitarian techniques to master the more varied and complex possibilities of real writing.

It's difficult to tell whether this perspective, penned in 1980, is common practice. *Coming of Age,* a book that has brought renewed attention to advanced writing courses and programs, regards "advanced composition as baggage left over from a period in which advanced undergraduate writing instruction was either very specialized (e.g., technical writing), an extension of the literature curriculum (the nonfiction essay), or an extension of FYC (more of the same, but harder)" (Shamoon et al. 2000, xiv). The collection makes an eloquent argument for a more expansive (not to mention more interesting) view of advanced writing, a course of study that directs students to think about writing as a career, an area of study, and an important component of civic life (the collection includes a contribution by Fulkerson, reflecting his current views on the subject of advanced composition). Administrative developments complement such scholarly developments: the number of free-standing writing programs has been growing, emphasizing the ways in which students can study writing through a sequence in a major, not simply in one or two advanced courses (see O'Neill, Crow, and Burton 2002).

Outside of writing majors, however, a broad vision of advanced writing may make only slow inroads in traditional English departments. It can be hard to move away from notions of writing that are enshrined in curricular requirements and course titles. My own department's offerings remained considerably stodgier than its faculty simply because curricular requirements outside our major drove enrollments in particular courses; it's hard to eliminate "advanced composition" from one's offerings if that's the course on the list for education students, for example, and it's hard to communicate to students or colleagues what kinds of new developments are reflected in the course as taught when the course title and description are so vague. And so we retained, far longer than we should have, a simplistic model of writing instruction: first-year composition introduced a range of rhetorical concepts, and subsequent courses repeated the same concepts, ostensibly helping students to develop more varied instances of those concepts in practice. As I drafted this chapter, I surveyed scholarship and Web sites to learn what kinds of courses other English departments offer as "advanced," and discovered an emphasis on style or audience (most articles about advanced composition referenced in ERIC in the past decade deal with teaching style or teaching in community-based programs with some form of service learning). Many courses also focus on belle-lettristic essays. Anthologies with titles like *Great Modern Essays* are popular texts. This suggests that the essayistic model of advanced composition is alive and well.

Robert Schwegler (2000) argues that the indeterminacy of advanced composition grows in part out of the belief that writing can't be taught. His historical study of curriculum development illustrates the ways reductive notions of writing as skill led to the development of isolated courses, rather than "a writing curriculum of courses designed to develop expertise and knowledge important to writers" (27). My colleagues and I realized that we had a set of courses, not a curriculum, and so our first task was to articulate what kinds of expertise and experience we were cultivating in the courses we taught. This resulted in the grid that appears in the table below.

Goals of the IUPUI's Writing Courses

Goals	100-level	200-level	300- and 400-level	Capstone
Rhetorical context	Recognize basic elements of rhetorical context: persona, purpose, audience	Develop and practice strategies for writing in varied rhetorical contexts	Expand repertoire of strategies for writing in varied rhetorical contexts	Reflect on the nature of rhetorical context
Collaboration (incl. tutoring, teaching)	Practice basic social and cognitive tools for collaboration	Increase number of collaboration tools; select tools to fit rhetorical context	Direct one's own collaboration; develop one's own collaborative tools	Reflect on nature of collaboration
Writing process	Recognize and use basic terminology of the writing process; recognize and manipulate own writing process	Sustain longer, more complex revision; practice greater control of structure	Examine reading and writing processes in relation to each other	Consider use of writing process in careers or other plans

Argument	Practice use of experience, observation, and other texts as evidence	Practice argument from experience, with increasing emphasis on observation- and text-based argument	Practice argument, integrating personal and public voices within more complex rhetorical contexts	Theorize about the nature of argument
Analysis, synthesis, evaluation	Analyze, synthesize, and evaluate reader responses, assignments, personal experiences, and texts	Analyze, synthesize, and evaluate features of one's own and other writers' texts; interpret and personalize assignments	Analyze, synthesize, and evaluate increasingly diverse rhetorical contexts, including factors such as culture and ideology	Theorize about the nature of analysis, synthesis, and evaluation
Research	Evaluate and use sources to support; use basic research strategies and MLA citation	Use research strategies for specialized purposes	Refine research strategies for specialized purposes	Reflect on research strategies
Style, conventions, language awareness	Correct major surface errors; recognize basic conventions and styles; recognize and manipulate own style; appreciate variety	Increase appreciation of styles; expand stylistic repertoire; understand conventions of specific discourse communities	Recognize relativity of conventions; increase awareness of language varieties	Master editing and style; reflect on diversity of conventions
Genres	Recognize and use basic academic genres	Expand repertoire of academic and workplace genres	Master increasingly diverse academic and workplace genres	Reflect on the nature of genre

We identified eight key terms: rhetorical context; collaboration; writing process; argument; analysis, synthesis, and evaluation; research; style, conventions, and language awareness; genre. We chose these terms because they emerged from our conversations about our courses, and they were the terms in use as we debated what we meant by "fluency" or "peer review" at different levels. Had the Outcomes Statement been available to us at the time, we likely would have used more of the OS language, but as it stands our terms map well onto the Outcomes Statement. We can easily take our grid and rearrange it into groupings reflective of the Outcomes Statement: Rhetorical Knowledge (for our terms rhetorical context); Critical Thinking, Reading, and Writing (for our terms research, analysis, synthesis, and evaluation); Processes (for our terms collaboration, writing process), and Knowledge of Conventions (for our terms style, conventions, and language awareness), and future work with our grid will likely make such a move. Using these categories, we teased out some differences among courses that were hidden by similarities of terms. And we started dreaming of ways to distinguish our courses, so that we could create distinctions where before none had existed. (We realized we needed to create additional research opportunities at the upper levels, for instance.)

In a sense, then, our grid expanded the Outcomes Statement, laying out more particular lists of outcomes over time. Like the Outcomes Statement, it doesn't specify standards; each teacher needs to decide exactly how a given course will work with what array of expectations. It's a flexible document that guides application. And like the Outcomes Statement, our grid is open to the critiques Haswell and Elbow offer in this volume. It ignores important dimensions of writing, such as voice, curiosity, adventurousness, risk taking. And it risks reducing writing to a set of objective skills that has little or nothing to do with content or meaning making. Under argument, for instance, we identified three levels of "practice" for students, all of which involve technique (the use of experience or texts for evidence, primarily). In our class activities, we link the use of evidence to understandings of context and audience, and we share a commitment to the notion that a good research question born of curiosity is the first step in any extended project, but the grid doesn't capture that. The verbs we use in our grid are similarly vexed: students will "recognize" issues of rhetorical context in their first year; "practice" argument techniques throughout; they will "theorize" in the capstone course, although it's not clear just what that term means. These terms don't capture the excitement of creating meaning, interpreting evidence in order to develop ideas and communicate with an audience. We could return to the grid and clarify several of its cells; a small group of my colleagues is doing just that as they investigate relationships among two new advanced courses, our introductory composition sequence, and our campus general education goals.

Despite—or perhaps because of—the attendant complications in any outcomes statement, our grid was a powerful motivator. The process of constructing it illustrated that our course "sequence" lacked a coherent rationale. That linear grid didn't describe a sequence of courses in a way that explains to students why the courses are sequenced as they are, or what they all add up to. Why bother "practicing argument" from year to year? What kinds of specialized purposes are hinted at? No one writes to practice; we write because we have something to say. But how to describe this to students? We realized that we could not communicate this to students with the course offerings we had on the books. And this illuminates a potential limitation of the Outcomes Statement itself: to the extent that the OS describes first-year composition, it functions in the realm of general education outcomes. Its terms are necessarily general, so that they can be connected to a host of disciplinary (and extradisciplinary) arenas. Even though the OS draws on the discipline of rhetoric and composition for its terminology, as we describe advanced programs in writing, we must expand the language we use and move beyond linear notions of sequence. To use the Outcomes Statement as a starting point for advanced writing is to define the specific contexts in which rhetorical outcomes will occur. This moves us closer to defining specific realms of expertise for our courses of study. Looking at outcomes is important, but considering outcomes necessarily shifts our focus back to our course sequences: where are these outcomes developed?

Richard Haswell's masterful *Gaining Ground in College Writing* argues that the development of writing abilities is complex, involving forward and seemingly backward movement, interpretation, growth, and discovery. This has complicated ramifications for curriculum designers. As he notes: "The multiplex writing competency of an undergraduate writer has not progressed in the past nor will it progress in the future uniformly, all of a block in military parade formation. . . . fluency battles thought, syntax battles flow, vocabulary battles fluency. To enrich a conclusion may be to impoverish an introduction, to sharpen an introduction may be to dull the logical organization, to enliven the organization may be to weaken the support, to shore up convincing particulars may be to undermine a pointed conclusion" (1991, 339).

A writing sequence needs to make room for this complicated, uneven, sometimes contradictory development. Haswell's own discussion of sequencing (described fully in *Gaining Ground*'s chapter 13, "A Curriculum") centers on a two-semester sequence, one in the first year, which would focus on "organizing and generating college ideas" (320) and the second in the junior year, which would focus on "flow, syntax, and diction (in that order) and in meta-linguistic analysis of the relationship of language to reality and to audience (in that order)" (321). As *Coming of Age* (Shamoon et al. 2000) reminds us, though, we are at a point in our field's development where we can look beyond a simple two-course sequence and begin to design whole courses of undergraduate study. As we do so, we must bear in mind that the messiness of human development simply precludes any simple representation of a writing sequence. In part, this very messiness requires us to consider calls for "standards" and "excellence" in a new light. Given that abilities develop in a jerky spiral, at best, we cannot construct grids that will neatly describe student texts—and we cannot develop courses that will fit together in lockstep.

Rather, our courses must acknowledge both students' growth over time and their progress (remembering that progress in one area may seemingly come at the expense of progress in another—comma splices will probably increase as final free modification does, too; spelling errors may increase as students move into a broader vocabulary; or specific examples may fall as more complicated ideas are nurtured). Simple grids that look for the presence or absence of features (optimistically assuming forward progress from year to year) may not communicate to students the developmental nature of their progress. And courses that assume that everything learned in one course will be manifested at the same level in a subsequent course are doomed to failure. Rather, advanced composition programs should offer students many chances to learn in ways that take advantage of their development. More specialized courses later in their careers are appropriate vehicles for developing a much more specific set of competencies, tied to writing in particular situations. Advanced writing courses that look toward working writing situations—group writing tasks, professional writing tasks, writing tasks grounded in a major program— would allow students to grow into assignments that ask them to reflect on the ways language shapes their experiences. This is the challenge of the Outcomes Statement: we must define the writing situations that will them- selves define the specific outcomes we seek. Those outcomes should con- nect back to the expectations from first-year composition; the Outcomes Statement is an initial step in that definition. But our advanced outcomes should encompass and surpass those first-year expectations.

So what should a writing curriculum look like after first-year composi- tion? My own department's answer to this question is found in this chap- ter's appendix. Considering outcomes led us to redesign our major (a step we were able to take in part because the entire department was of a mind to revise the major, and in part because Indiana was of a mind to revise its requirements for teaching certification). We didn't leave our grid behind, but we didn't use it to map our major, either. Rather, we considered what specific expertise and experiences we wanted our students to have, and this led us to embed those general outcomes in specific courses. We didn't start by looking at what our courses had in common; we started by asking what we thought graduates who specialized in writing and literacy should know and be able to do. We debated how important various technological experiences are, and how important literary study is for a writing major.

The revised major maps writing and literacy as terrain to be studied, with the following major landmarks: a gateway course on literacy and public life; a course on language, focusing on social elements of language use and development; a course on the history and theories of language; and four courses on writing in different genres. Only the gateway course to the concentration is required of every student, but our requirements highlight elements of writing and literacy study that we feel are essential for productive workers and citizens. It was not easy to agree that every student should take a course in history and theory and a course on language; for a time (mirroring the history of the Outcomes Statement), we had a requirement that every student take a course addressing technology and literacy. We had to determine our collective professional priorities, and then decide what courses we could offer regularly enough to meet the requirements we envisioned. It was long but exciting work.

The Outcomes Statement created our framework, in that it encouraged us to move from an area where we had common goals and outcomes (our first-year writing courses) into a terrain that had, until then, remained uncharted. Our new concentration doesn't suggest a linear developmental model for students. Its weakness is arguably in its sequencing; we still don't have a good mechanism for ensuring that students take some courses before others (generally, students take the capstone shortly before graduation, but other than that, course sequences are largely determined by students' working schedules on our commuter campus). This is a developmental hurdle with which many commuter campuses struggle. And perhaps, on such campuses, there is a large element of mythology involved with course sequencing. We can be sure that most students will take most of their 300- and 400-level courses after taking their 100- and 200- level courses, but we can also be sure that some transfer students will arrive needing more earlier courses than later. We can also be sure that some students who can only take courses at night, or only on Tuesdays and Thursdays, will find themselves taking some advanced courses sooner than we imagine and some lower-level courses later. The mixed nature of the student body on our campus is one of its signal delights, and the real-life constraints on students' course choices mean that our best sequences will never be fully realized.

We are aware, as we roll out our newly created courses, that we still have more work to do as we coordinate our new offerings. Yet we have designed a concentration that highlights realms of experience and expertise. To use Schwegler's terms, it provides "grounds for curricular presence and space," showing students how their studies connect to theories of language, professional options, and community events (2000, 29). And this structure gives us added clarity when we turn again to our outcomes grid. We can look at collaboration, for example, as something that students should experience across these realms, and we can now begin the work of assessing how we teach collaborative techniques in what portions of the major. Through such conversations, we will return to our grid, revising and adding to it as necessary. (We will also consider making connections between our departmental grid and the OS more explicit, in order to set our major in the disciplinary context represented by the OS.)

Toward the end of *Gaining Ground*, Haswell moves among metaphors, problematizing the military, medical, and culinary metaphors he had used to describe writing instruction in earlier portions of the text. Haswell settles, in the end, on a diagnostic metaphor: the teacher as "the coach, the decorator, the plumber, the tuner—those craft-wise fixers who can not only tell you what's wrong or what's going to go wrong but also suggest what to do about it. Isn't this really what students bring their writing to us for?" (1991, 349). Real diagnosis, Haswell suggests, is forward looking. It *proposes*, Haswell says, "via future-directed theory or hypothesis" (338), honestly asking what future developments could do better, given the needs of the text, the personality of the student, the situation of the reader/teacher, and other factors. The Outcomes Statement pushes us toward diagnosis in this sense. It asks us to consider what our own curriculum can do better in each of its domains, and it challenges us to consider the specific situations of our departments, our missions, our students. It challenges us to define environments in which critical reading, writing, and thinking interact, as well as those in which complicated processes can be staged. Such conversations are among the most important we can have with each other, and they will enable us to communicate with our students more effectively. What better way to show students and colleagues what we value than by determining common frameworks and outcomes?

Appendix

IUPUI'S CONCENTRATION IN WRITING AND LITERACY (FALL 2002)

GATEWAY COURSE (3 CREDITS)

An introduction to the uses of literacy in public and civic discourse, with connections made to theories of writing and professional prospects for writers.

- W210 Literacy and Public Life

LANGUAGE (3 CREDITS)

Introduces students to the formal study of the social/cultural dimensions of language use.

- G204 Rhetorical Issues in Grammar and Usage
- G310 Social Speech Patterns
- ANTH L300 Language and Culture
- ANTH L401 Language, Power, and Gender
- W390 Topics in Writing

HISTORY AND THEORIES OF LANGUAGE (3 CREDITS)

Provides a foundation for analysis rooted in history, culture, and theory.

- G301 History of the English Language
- W310 Language and the Study of Writing
- W396 Writing Fellows Seminar
- W400 Issues in the Teaching of Writing
- W412 Technology and Literacy
- Comm Studies R350 Womenspeak: American Feminist Rhetoric
- Comm Studies R310 Rhetoric, Society, and Culture
- W390 Topics in Writing (as appropriate)

WRITING IN DIFFERENT GENRES (12 CREDITS COVERING AT LEAST TWO AREAS)

This requirement explores a range of literacy practices and texts, including how texts are produced, used, and interpreted by writers and readers in particular contexts

Business and Organizational Writing

- W231 Professional Writing Skills
- W315 Writing for the Web
- W331 Business and Administrative Writing
- W365 Theory and Practice of Editing
- W390 Topics in Writing (as appropriate)
- TCM 320 Written Communication in Science and Industry
- TCM 340 Correspondence in Business and Industry
- TCM 350 Visual Elements of Technical Documents
- E398 Internship in English

Nonfiction Writing

- W290 Writing in the Arts and Sciences
- W305 Writing Creative Nonfiction
- W313 The Art of Fact: Writing Nonfiction Prose
- W390 Topics in Writing (as appropriate)

Creative Writing

- W301 Writing Fiction
- W302 Screen Writing
- W303 Writing Poetry
- W401 Advanced Fiction Writing
- W403 Advanced Poetry Writing

DISTRIBUTION COURSES (9 CREDITS)

One three-credit course, at the 200-level or above, in three additional English subfields.

CAPSTONE COURSE (3 CREDITS)

15

USING THE OUTCOMES STATEMENT FOR TECHNICAL COMMUNICATION

Barry M. Maid

During the whole development of the Outcomes Statement, one of the driving forces was the overwhelming need to keep the document flexible. There were several reasons for the need for flexibility. Clearly, if the Outcomes Statement were to be accepted and have an impact, it must necessarily serve the needs of diverse programs located in diverse institutions. The original thought was that these diverse programs would be the wide range of first-year composition programs. Yet, even in its beginning stages, there was the notion that the Outcomes Statement might also serve beyond first-year composition.

Indeed, the last paragraph of the introduction to the Outcomes Statement speaks to this very point:

> These statements describe only what we expect to find at the end of first-year composition, at most schools a required general education course or sequence of courses. As writers move beyond first-year composition, their writing abilities do not merely improve. Rather, students' abilities not only diversify along disciplinary and professional lines but also move into whole new levels where expected outcomes expand, multiply, and diverge. For this reason, each statement of outcomes for first-year composition is followed by suggestions for further work that builds on these outcomes.

We can see the Outcomes Statement lays the groundwork for movement beyond first-year composition in the bulleted lists that begin, "Faculty in all programs and departments can build . . ." Therefore, the Outcomes Statement directly invites, and I think even challenges, faculty who teach courses other than first-year composition (whether they be other writing courses, writing-intensive courses, or courses where writing is only a small component) to engage the Outcomes Statement and, by building upon it through appropriate disciplinary means, metamorphose it into something they can call their own.

As a result, when I was faced with developing a new program in multimedia writing and technical communication for Arizona State University East, my several years as a member of the Outcomes group quite naturally led me to think about including programmatic outcomes that could be used for program assessment. Like so many others involved in the process of creating it, I was drawn to the Outcomes Statement. However, though cognizant of the potential springboard effect built into the Outcomes Statement, I was very well aware that it was originally conceived for first-year composition programs. I was creating an undergraduate degree, and a postbaccalaureate certificate in multimedia writing and technical communication. What surprised me, someone who had been involved in the Outcomes process for several years, was how little I had to tweak the first-year Outcomes Statement to make it appropriate for my program.

In retrospect, there were good reasons for this. While perhaps it should have been evident to me during the process, the Outcomes Statement was developed based on the premise of how writers really work and what writers really need to know, as opposed to some narrow focus of how writers are supposed to work or about developing one and only one kind of writing. Kathleen Blake Yancey makes this observation in her "Response" to the initial publication of the Outcomes Statement in the *WPA Journal.* There she makes what may be the most insightful comment of all about the Outcomes Statement: "It talks about the more non-controversial of our practices in first-year composition, writing process and rhetorical knowledge, for instance, and it doesn't prescribe. Let me break that line out so we don't miss it: it doesn't prescribe" (Yancey 1999).

Since my program is designed to train students who will write in the workplace, working in fields (if my previous experience in technical communication programs is any indicator) as wide ranging as information technology to life sciences to manufacturing to telecommunications, with a wide smattering of nonprofits and government agencies thrown in for good measure. In order to meet the needs of a definition of technical communication I would prefer to see as "all-encompassing" rather than generic, I found the generic Outcomes Statement most appropriate to my program's needs. As I mentioned above, I was able to make just minor changes, title the document "Course Evaluation Criteria," and then distribute it with every course in our program.

A UNIQUE SITUATION

When faculty work on curricular issues such as modifying the Outcomes Statement for local needs, the process usually involves a committee of appropriate people getting together and working things out. When I came to Arizona State University East to start the program in multimedia writing and technical communication, there wasn't really a faculty in place to form a committee. There was one other full-time faculty member in technical communication. As a result, the process we used to develop our programmatic version of the Outcomes Statement was for me to submit drafts to her for review. We then met and agreed upon the document. That document (appendix A, p. 146) served the program from the time we offered our first classes in spring 2001 to the start of the fall 2003 semester. As of fall 2003, we implemented a new version (appendix B, p. 148).

The intention was always that our Outcomes Statement was to continue to be fluid. We fully expected that we would modify it when more full-time faculty were hired. What has happened is the present economic climate has prevented us from hiring needed full-time faculty. Even without new faculty, by receiving feedback from one of our part-time faculty and from several other faculty whose students take courses in our program as service courses, we were in the fall 2003 semester able to move into our second iteration of our Outcomes Statement. What follows is how the two versions emerged.

PHASE ONE: THE SIMILARITIES

I was able to use the last three categories (Critical Thinking, Reading, and Writing; Processes; and Knowledge of Conventions) as originally written because of small details in the Outcomes Statement. For example, in the knowledge of conventions section, the Outcomes Statement only mentions "appropriate means of documenting their work." In a program where students are as likely to be using IEEE (Institute of Electrical and Electronic Engineers), CSE (Council of Scientific Editors), or MMS (*Microsoft Manual of Style*) rather than CMS (*Chicago Manual of Style*), APA (American Psychological Association), and especially not MLA (Modern Language Association), the flexibility expressed in the original Outcomes Statement not only opens the door to having students use alternative documentation styles but, perhaps even more importantly, helps to create an environment where we can talk about what an "appropriate documentation style" means in any particular context—whether defined by industry, organizational, or other standards. Likewise, in the Critical Thinking, Reading, and Writing section, the outcome "understand the relationships among language, knowledge, and power" serves very nicely as we work with our students to help them understand what their role, as writers, will be within an organizational structure—especially as that role often calls for them to mediate, in writing, between subject matter expert and end user. Clearly, the impetus of the Outcomes group to ensure flexibility within the Outcomes Statement in order to allow it to be appropriate to use in very different educational environments also invites it to be used beyond first-year composition.

PHASE ONE: THE CHANGES

The only place I felt a need to make changes in the Outcomes Statement to make it more appropriate for my program was in the first section, Rhetorical Knowledge. The first changes were very specific and based on the structure of the program. They had to do with the issue of genre. In technical communication, understanding the nature of genre, and the conventions that govern genres, is a crucial issue. It is paramount to understand that conventions for a proposal, for example, are markedly different from conventions for a software manual. Knowing this, I made slight changes to two of the outcomes in the Rhetorical Knowledge section. I changed the simple "write in several genres" to "write in multiple genres." While both "several" and "multiple" are vague adjectives, my reasoning was that "multiple" implied not only more than "several" but also a level of consciousness on the part of writers that would enable them to perhaps create the same document in more than one genre. I also slightly changed the outcome "understand how genres shape reading and writing" to "understand how each genre helps to shape the writing and how readers respond to it." Once again, from a technical communication perspective, I felt our students needed to understand more about genre and its rhetorical role. What we see here may be one of the real strengths of the Outcomes Statement. Minor changes, a word here and there, can make the Outcomes Statement appropriate for courses and programs other than first-year composition.

THE HEART OF THE MATTER

Finally, I decided I needed to add one additional outcome to the Rhetorical Knowledge section: "choose the appropriate technology for the genre and audience." At first glance, this may not seem to be a major issue. Understanding which technology to use, and as a corollary which medium, is clearly a rhetorical decision that our students need to be able to make. Yet, considering my own history with the Outcomes group, adding a new outcome that specifically speaks to technology issues is important. I was one of a small group who, from the beginning, argued against including what became known as the "technology plank" in the Outcomes Statement. Yet, here, when I develop my own version for my own program, I not only keep the outcome "use a variety of technologies to address a range of audience" in the Processes section but create a second technology-based outcome.

No, I haven't changed my mind. I think we are looking at two very different contexts that in fact help to underscore my original argument for not including a technology plank. My argument was simple. Writing has always been a function of technology. The technologies simply keep on changing. We are presently living in a time of frequent technological change. To tie any kind of outcomes or writing instruction to a particular technology is dangerous. (We may even see it as being prescriptive—the very opposite of what Kathi Yancey says is at the heart of the Outcomes Statement.) The technology might become outmoded before the outcome is even approved or made public. Second, the original Outcomes Statement was geared toward first-year composition. In a way I see emphasizing technology in a first-year composition course as a bit like emphasizing penmanship. My view of the first-year composition course is one where students learn about the intellectual processes involved with writing, not a place where they are trained in the technology of writing tools—whether those tools be fountain pens or word processors. Ultimately, teachers of writing, especially in first-year composition, need to work in an environment where technology is seamless and transparent—where the focus is on teaching writing—not teaching technology.

This is not to say that I wish to downplay or denigrate the issue known as the "digital divide." I am well aware that there are serious social and educational issues that are a function of access, or the lack of access, to segments of the population. In fact Cindy Selfe (1999) addresses those issues most eloquently in *Technology and Literacy in the Twenty-First Century: The Importance of Paying Attention.* Though I am very conscious of the fact that Selfe strongly supported the technology plank in the Outcomes Statement, I think her book is a better place to confront the issue than in the first-year composition Outcomes Statement.

That being said, I also think that a degree program in technical communication is different from a first-year composition program. Frankly, if I thought students in my program could expect to work as writers who only used standard word processing software, I would have hesitated to include the technology outcome in my revised criteria. However, since my students will be expected to work not only in multiple genres but in multiple media, the issue of understanding the rhetorical choice and effect of technology becomes crucial. I see a substantive difference in a technology outcome that is present in the Rhetorical Knowledge section and one in the Processes section.

PHASE TWO: INFORMATION LITERACY

Like many other programs ours relies heavily on part-time faculty. In the late spring of 2003, one of our part-time faculty, Barbara D'Angelo, who is a full-time reference librarian at ASU East and who has developed and teaches two courses in our program, InfoGlut and Information Architecture, suggested we make changes in the program's Outcomes Statement to include concerns about information literacy. We followed a similar process to our original outcomes. Only this time it was D'Angelo who did the drafting, which was then reviewed and negotiated to come up with our current Outcomes Statement.

I think anyone looking at the original WPA Outcomes Statement, viewing our first slightly modified version, and now our latest version will see a natural progression. Ensuring that our students will be able to work with information as part of their research/writing process is something that writing teachers sometimes take for granted. However, working with a librarian, we were able to more closely articulate the specific information literacy skills we expect from our students. We also found it to be relatively easy to integrate these skills into our version of the Outcomes Statement.

PHASE TWO: THE SIGNIFICANT CHANGES

Our latest version of the Outcomes Statement shows some changes to all four sections. However, the changes to the Rhetorical Knowledge and the Processes sections are minor. They can be found in the last two outcomes in the Rhetorical Knowledge section and the last outcome in the Processes section. We made more substantial changes to the Critical Thinking, Reading, and Writing and the Knowledge of Conventions sections.

The major addition to the Knowledge of Conventions section is in the inclusion, in several of the outcomes, of the idea of intellectual property, copyright, and the ethical implications of following the appropriate conventions. Clearly, this is hinted at in the initial outcome that speaks of proper documentation. However, looking at the outcomes through an information literacy lens, we realized this needed to be expanded—

especially since the ethical use of intellectual property and copyright is already integrated into our entire curriculum. In addition, since many of our students work in electronic environments, we added a section where we can expect them to understand about the issues of accessibility and the conventions surrounding it.

We also engaged in significant revisions in the Critical Thinking, Reading, and Writing section. The crux of our revisions lay in D'Angelo's observation that the way the outcomes were written it appeared as though research and writing were two separate, parallel processes. Indeed, I think, too often they're taught in that way. What we have now are outcomes that emphasize that research and writing are one integrated process.

CONCLUSION

In a previous draft of this chapter, I wrote the following concluding paragraph:

> Whether anyone agrees with my view of the placement and inclusion or exclusion of a "technology outcome," finally, seems to me to be less of an issue than the understanding that I was able to take the first-year composition program Outcomes Statement, and with just minor revisions, turn it into a statement that can effectively be used for evaluation in an undergraduate technical communication program. From my perspective, that speaks volumes about the potential, the breadth, and the effectiveness of the Outcomes Statement.

Now, having revised the revision, I am even more convinced of the document's strength, flexibility, and dynamic nature.

Appendix A

SPRING 2001 VERSION

RHETORICAL KNOWLEDGE

Students will show they can

- Focus on a defined purpose
- Respond to the need of the appropriate audience
- Respond appropriately to different rhetorical situations
- Use conventions of format and structure appropriate to the rhetorical situation
- Adopt appropriate voice, tone, and level of formality
- Understand how each genre helps to shape the writing and how readers respond to it
- Write in multiple genres
- Choose the appropriate technology for the genre and audience

CRITICAL THINKING, READING, AND WRITING

Students will show they can

- Use writing and reading for inquiry, learning, thinking, and communicating
- Understand a writing assignment as a series of tasks, including finding, evaluating, analyzing, and synthesizing appropriate primary and secondary sources
- Integrate their own ideas with those of others
- Understand the relationships among language, knowledge, and power

PROCESSES

Students will show they can

- Be aware that is usually takes multiple drafts to create and complete a successful text
- Develop flexible strategies for generating, revising, editing, and proofreading
- Understand writing as an open process that permits writers to use later invention and rethinking to revise their work

- Understand the collaborative and social aspects of writing processes
- Learn to critique their own and others' works
- Learn to balance the advantages of relying on others with the responsibility of doing their part
- Use a variety of technologies to address a range of audiences

KNOWLEDGE OF CONVENTIONS

Students will show they can

- Learn common formats for different genres
- Develop knowledge of genre conventions ranging from structure and paragraphing to tone and mechanics
- Practice appropriate means of documenting their work
- Control such surface features as syntax, grammar, punctuation, and spelling

Appendix B

FALL 2003 VERSION

RHETORICAL KNOWLEDGE

Students will show they can

- Identify, articulate, and focus on a defined purpose
- Respond to the need of the appropriate audience
- Respond appropriately to different rhetorical situations
- Use conventions of format and structure appropriate to the rhetorical situation
- Adopt appropriate voice, tone, and level of formality
- Understand how each genre helps to shape the writing and how readers respond to it
- Write in multiple genres
- Understand the role of a variety of technologies in communicating information
- Use appropriate technologies to communicate information to address a range of audiences, purposes, and genres

CRITICAL THINKING, READING, AND WRITING

Students will show they can

- Use information, writing, and reading for inquiry, learning, thinking, and communicating
- Understand that research, like writing, is a series of tasks, including accessing, retrieving, evaluating, analyzing, and synthesizing appropriate information from sources that vary in content, format, structure, and scope
- Understand the relationships among language, knowledge, and power, including social, cultural, historical, and economic issues related to information, writing, and technology
- Recognize, understand, and analyze the context within which language, information, and knowledge are communicated and presented
- Integrate previously held beliefs, assumptions, and knowledge with new information and the ideas of others to come to a conclusion, make a decision, or design a product

PROCESSES

Students will show they can

- Be aware that it usually takes multiple drafts to create and complete a successful text
- Develop flexible strategies for generating, revising, editing, and proofreading
- Understand writing as an open process that permits writers to use later invention and rethinking to revise their work
- Understand the collaborative and social aspects of writing processes
- Learn to critique their own and others' works
- Learn to balance the advantages of relying on others with the responsibility of doing their part
- Use appropriate technologies to manage information collected or generated for future use

KNOWLEDGE OF CONVENTIONS

Students will show they can

- Learn common formats for different genres
- Learn and apply appropriate standards, laws, policies, and accepted practices for the use of a variety of technologies
- Develop knowledge of genre conventions ranging from structure and paragraphing to tone and mechanics
- Apply appropriate means of documenting their work
- Control such surface features as syntax, grammar, punctuation, and spelling
- Understand and apply legal and ethical uses of information and technology, including copyright and intellectual property
- Understand and apply appropriate standards for use of technology, including accessibility

16

USING WRITING OUTCOMES TO ENHANCE TEACHING AND LEARNING
Alverno College's Experience

Robert O'Brien Hokanson

The WPA Outcomes Statement expresses a shared understanding of what students should know and be able to do as writers, written both to make expectations for first-year composition more public and to foster continuing discussion of what those expectations should be and how faculty and programs can help students meet them. Alverno College has a thirty-year history of teaching and assessing for outcomes in writing and other abilities, and the lessons we've learned can inform both the continuing conversation about outcomes and the use of the Outcomes Statement on other campuses. Rather than describing a direct "application" of the Outcomes Statement, then, I'm writing as a critical friend to the Outcomes Statement and the commitment to improving the teaching and learning of writing it represents. It is my hope that the story of outcomes for writing at Alverno will lead to more informed use of the Outcomes Statement and help stimulate campus-specific conversations about expectations for writing.[1]

Alverno's experience with outcome-based approaches to writing and other abilities demonstrates the fundamental ways in which outcomes can contribute to improved teaching and learning. When developed and used in ways that are meaningful to faculty and students, outcomes statements can be much more than the bureaucratic exercise they too often become. Well-crafted outcomes linked to the curriculum constitute a common language that clarifies what we mean by effective performance. This shared frame of reference benefits everyone involved in the learning process: for students, clearly defined outcomes help promote understanding of course expectations and their own performance and development over time; for faculty, outcomes not only provide a basis for coherent curriculum design and informed pedagogy but also promote a continuing conversation within and across the disciplines about our goals and expectations as educators; and, of course, outcomes provide a means by which faculty and administrators can assess the progress of their program toward meeting institutional goals—and a means of expressing that progress in terms that are understandable to various publics. (For more information on Alverno's approach to teaching and assessing for outcomes, see Alverno College Faculty 1994; Loacker 2000.)

So, how does Alverno's experience with outcomes for writing relate to the Outcomes Statement? As we'll see, the moral of this story has more to do with the process of developing and maintaining a language of outcomes than with the particulars of the language itself. First and foremost, perhaps, making a commitment to teaching and assessing for outcomes means making a commitment to a process of ongoing review and revision of your outcomes (and, in our case, the criteria that support them). Just as the Outcomes Statement grew out of a discussion that has continued beyond its publication date, those who would bring the idea of writing outcomes to a program or campus should expect that they are opening a conversation rather than settling something once and for all. Second, meaningful outcomes are tailored to the particulars of the institutional setting (as the other chapters in parts two and three of this volume illustrate). The language of the Outcomes Statement provides a baseline, but programs and campuses should consider how site-specific concerns such as student needs (level of preparation, personal/professional aspirations, etc.), faculty judgment, program goals, and institutional mission may affect their expectations for student writing. Third, to be genuinely effective across the curriculum, the language of outcomes must strike a balance between the perspectives of specialists in writing and communication and the perspectives of other disciplines. Outcomes are also more likely to be effective to the extent that they can promote coherence in courses and programs without mandating sameness in pedagogy and curriculum. Finally, opening a conversation about outcomes for first-year writing can and should lead to wider conversations about college-level learning, a point stressed in the parts of the statement addressed to faculty in other programs and departments. For example: What are (or should be) the expectations for writing beyond first-year composition? How can and should writing relate to the development of the full range of knowledge and abilities that constitute general education? In the pages that follow I will summarize our story and some of the lessons we've learned about using outcomes as a common language for the teaching and assessment of writing.

THE ALVERNO CONTEXT

Alverno began its work with outcomes in 1973, when the college shifted its educational paradigm to a program based on the development and demonstration of learning outcomes or abilities rather than traditional course requirements and grades. Effective communication was one of the first abilities identified as a learning outcome for all graduates, and we define communication broadly, to include listening, reading, speaking, and computer and quantitative literacy as well as writing. Just as our understanding of communication developed and deepened over time, the scope of the learning outcomes we expect all graduates to demonstrate has grown to include eight abilities: communication, analysis, problem solving, valuing in decision making, social interaction, developing a global perspective, effective citizenship, and aesthetic engagement.

Having identified learning outcomes in terms of abilities to be demonstrated across the curriculum, the college needed to develop standards by which faculty (and students themselves) would be able to assess demonstration of abilities in student performance. Our commitment to the development of our students as individual learners also meant that we would not be satisfied with limiting our assessment of their abilities to selected samples or aggregated data. Rather, Alverno faculty worked to embed assessment of learning outcomes into the teaching-learning process itself. Faculty and academic staff from across the disciplines collaborated to articulate criteria that could be used in assessing student development and demonstration of abilities within courses and across the curriculum. Instructors use these criteria not only to make judgments about student performance in their courses but also as a means of articulating the relationship between the abilities and the disciplines. A structure of "ability departments" charged with maintaining and developing our understanding of the abilities as a fundamental element of the curriculum evolved over time. The faculty and academic staff from across the disciplines who serve in an ability department take responsibility for being the campus specialists in that area—reviewing and revising collegewide criteria, coordinating faculty and staff development in teaching and assessing the ability, and setting policy on curriculum and assessment related to the ability.

As with each of the eight collegewide abilities, Alverno's criteria for effective writing (and other modes of communication) were articulated by faculty and staff from across the disciplines, and they continue to be discussed, revised, and refined through the work of the communication ability department. These criteria provide the basis for student self-assessment and faculty judgment of student performance in communication courses and across the curriculum. Unlike a grading scale, the criteria define what for us are the key aspects of effective writing and provide a developmental picture of the college's expectations for student performance as writers from entry through graduation. Instructors use the criteria as a guide to what they expect from students (on particular writing assignments and in terms of their development throughout a course) and how they can best prepare students for their future learning.

The membership of the communication ability department currently includes specialists in listening, reading, speaking, and writing from the disciplines of English and professional communication as well as colleagues from disciplines like computer science, education, mathematics, nursing, and physical science. This cross-disciplinary group engages in ongoing discussion of what we, as a college, mean by effective writing and communication generally both with each other and with colleagues across campus. In addition to this conceptual leadership, the communication ability department supports communication across the curriculum by overseeing the college's placement assessment in communication, coordinating the required communication courses in the general education curriculum, and offering faculty and staff development programs in teaching and assessing for communication.

WRITING OUTCOMES AS AN ONGOING PROCESS

The "Criteria for Effective Writing" sheet that Alverno students receive in their beginning communication courses and that faculty use in designing and responding to writing assignments across the curriculum bears a series of copyright dates: 1977, 1980, 1982, 1984, 1988, 1993, and 1998. (See this chapter's appendix, p. 161, for selections from the 1998 "Criteria for Effective Writing.") This list of dates demonstrates how our developing sense of what "effective writing" means has led to fairly regular revisions of the document over time. The changes in the document have included moving from a list of twenty-three separate items to criteria organized in relation to seven key components of effective writing and articulated in terms of developmental levels for each component. We have also refined the language of our criteria, condensing or expanding on our descriptive statements based on our developing knowledge of the ability and our experience in the classroom. For example, our description of effective structure in first-year writing has evolved from "shows general sense of structure" (1981) to "establishes and maintains focus on a clear purpose, providing transitions to clarify relationships between most points of development" (1998) in order to provide students and faculty with a fuller sense of what "purposeful structure" means (see Alverno College Communication Ability Department 1981, 1998 for the full explanation of our criteria). Revisions like these reflect the way in which statements of outcomes can and should be adapted to respond to our developing understanding of the ability as teachers and scholars in the field, changes in our students and their needs as learners, and changes in the way communication works in the world around us.

At Alverno, our understanding of writing as an ability has led us to define developmental criteria for progress toward becoming an effective writer and communicator. This means, for example, that our expectations for how a student supports a position or develops an idea become more rigorous as she progresses in the curriculum. At the beginning level, we expect that a student will show "ability to use examples and/or evidence meaningful to audience"; as a student completes her general education and moves into advanced-level work, we expect that her writing will exhibit "development of appropriate length and variety and of sufficient interest to convince audience of worth of message" (1998). What "appropriate" and "sufficient" mean here is determined by the course and disciplinary/professional context. Such criteria capture the qualitative difference between what we expect from students as they begin their degree program and where we expect them to be as they move into the major. In addition to describing increasing sophistication in engaging and persuading readers, the criteria for development of ideas also reinforce the extent to which effective performance is determined in the context of the course and discipline or professional area. What counts as "appropriate" length and "sufficient" interest can and should vary across assignments and courses, and part of what we aim to teach our students is the ability to respond successfully to a variety of rhetorical situations within and across the disciplines. This kind of attention to varied audiences and writing in disciplinary contexts is consistent with the Outcomes Statement, but we have also tried to articulate what it means for student writers to become increasingly sophisticated in the ways they support a position or develop an idea as they move from first-year communication courses through the general education curriculum.

In addition to refining our understanding of what it means for students to develop as writers over the course of their studies, we have also attempted to refine our criteria in response to our changing sense of the nature of writing, particularly in terms of how writing relates to other modes of communication. We have defined "effective communication" broadly over time, and in addition to writing it has come to include listening, reading, and speaking as well as quantitative and computer literacy. Yet even as we have developed and refined discrete criteria for each of these aspects of communication, we have also increasingly recognized the integrative nature of effective communication, particularly at more advanced levels of performance. As a result, we have worked with instructors to help them teach and assess writing both discretely and as part of an integrated performance, using discussion and/or oral presentations as part of a writing process, for example, or designing assignments that combine oral and written performance. We also continue to be challenged by such "new" literacies as information, media, and visual literacy, and the communication ability department is currently considering how to adapt our criteria in order to convey more explicitly what we expect of students (and faculty) in these areas. Though writing will always be with us, departments or programs that embrace outcomes for writing should be prepared to embrace the changing nature of communication and commit themselves to ongoing reevaluation of their expectations for what constitutes effective student writing.

LOCAL DIALECTS IN THE LANGUAGE OF OUTCOMES

Another important lesson about outcomes for writing is that they need to be site-specific. A generic statement like the Outcomes Statement is a valuable benchmark and point of departure, but statements of outcomes should also reflect the particular needs and concerns of the program or campus from which they come. At Alverno, for example, the nature of our student population, the college's mission, and the professional judgment of our faculty and staff have led us to define our expectations for effective writing in the way we have. Our writing outcomes are generally consistent with the Outcomes Statement, but the way they are expressed reflects the particular place and role of writing on our campus as well as our best sense of what our students will benefit from as developing communicators. For example, the Outcomes Statement says students should "understand the relationships among language, knowledge, and power." At Alverno, we would endorse this idea, and we think our students do develop and demonstrate such understanding over the course of their studies, but we haven't explicitly articulated this kind of critical literacy as part of our outcomes for communication. Rather, we see the communication abilities our students develop as a necessary element of the critical awareness of self and world promoted by the college curriculum as a whole. Our outcomes also differ from the Outcomes Statement in terms of the place and role of genre in the teaching and assessment of writing. The Outcomes Statement say students should "understand how genres shape reading and writing" and "write in several genres" by the end of first-year composition. Here, too, we would accept this position but haven't articulated it as a part of our outcomes. Our students work in a variety of genres in order to address varied audiences or meet the demands of different disciplinary contexts rather than studying genre as a concept unto itself.

Alverno's ability-based curriculum as a whole informs how we think about writing. Since effective communication is one of eight learning outcomes expected of all graduates, writing and effective communication haven't had to be all things to all people. We expect our students to develop and demonstrate critical thinking, social awareness, aesthetic engagement, and reflective learning through writing, but we don't have to feel it's up to the writing program alone to ensure that this happens. Likewise, the value and practice of self-assessment and reflection is something students learn across the curriculum—not just when they're prompted to analyze and reflect on their performance in a communication course. At Alverno, the ability departments for analysis, problem solving, social interaction, valuing in decision making, developing a global perspective, effective citizenship, and aesthetic engagement promote the development of abilities that writing programs often see as part of their mission and purpose. Even if no comprehensive approach to learning outcomes is on the horizon at your campus, it still makes sense to consider whether and how elements of your outcomes for writing are also being addressed by other programs on campus, both to build on meaningful connections and to weed out unnecessary redundancy that may blur your focus and frustrate your students. Conversely, your outcomes should highlight what is truly distinctive about your approach to writing, such as the citizenship values of a writing program with a strong service-learning component.

Within the larger curricular context for writing at Alverno, we have been able to concentrate on what we think our students will benefit from the most as developing communicators. Alverno is an urban women's college serving a student population that is diverse by age, race, ethnicity, and academic preparation. Given our students and our mission of promoting the personal and professional development of women, we have primarily envisioned writing and communication as instrumental—providing the means to both personal empowerment and economic independence. As a result, we have defined our outcomes and criteria for writing in terms of the communication skills we think our students will need for success in college and beyond. For us, however, these essential skills encompass much more than just "back-to-basics" correctness or slick presentation. The central concept in our criteria for effective communication is audience, and each dimension of effective writing we have defined is stated in terms of how it connects with audience. The ability to understand and respond to the needs of your audience, together with the ability to analyze and reflect on your own performance, are the touchstones of what we mean by effective communication at Alverno. These are the tools we think our students will need to continue to develop and succeed as communicators and lifelong learners.

OUTCOMES AT WORK—AND IN PLAY

In addition to capturing the local dialect of its institutional setting, the language of outcomes for writing should express a balance (or at least a creative tension) among the multiple interests involved in any effort at promoting writing across the curriculum. Well-crafted outcomes aim to promote coherence in curriculum and pedagogy without mandating sameness in practice. They are shaped by the expertise of writing specialists in dialogue with the disciplines, professional areas, and the various publics with which the institution is engaged. At their best, statements of outcomes can be used to define a range of theory and practice that constitutes a working consensus on what writing means on a campus. Such a rough consensus will never be absolute or entirely settled, but the continuing dialogue that outcomes statements should represent can help maintain awareness and develop understanding of the role of writing (and effective writing instruction) in college-level learning—both for newer faculty and on a continuing basis.

At Alverno, this creative tension among various interests and perspectives plays out in a number of ways that may sound familiar to writing program administrators and others involved in writing across the curriculum. Even after twenty-five years of using collegewide criteria for effective writing, questions about what we expect our students to know and be able to do as writers are very much alive on our campus. In recent years our discussions have centered on such issues as the nature and role of research in effective communication, our expectations related to students' computer literacy, and, of course, the perennial issue of responding to student error in the conventions of written English.

The outcomes embodied in our college criteria for effective communication helped focus our most recent conversations about the role of research and computer literacy in communication across the curriculum—particularly in the first year. Our outcomes for first-year communication have long included the ability to distinguish one's own thoughts from those of others and to support one's generalizations with examples and evidence, but we have not mandated that a research paper be part of the first-year curriculum in our integrated communication seminars. We address research skills and strategies more explicitly and thoroughly in the final course in our three-course sequence of integrated communication seminars, which most students take in their third semester. From the perspective of the communication ability department, this made sense in terms of how our students develop as communicators and in terms of the college curriculum. We offer students instruction in research after they have mastered basic skills and strategies in listening, reading, speaking, writing, and computer literacy and at a point in the curriculum where they are beginning to do research in discipline-based courses.

At the same time, however, we became increasingly aware that our image of the first year didn't completely match the reality. Faculty teaching our integrated communication seminars and other first-year courses in the disciplines reported that our criteria (and related curriculum) didn't necessarily fit student needs. For example, whether we communication specialists liked it or not, many first-year students were being required to do research (particularly using the Internet) or were pursuing such research on their own. At the same time, first-year students with little computer experience or limited access to computers were being asked to use information technology in ways they hadn't been taught. Members of the communication ability department worked with colleagues in the disciplines and relevant administrative departments to address this issue. The results were better understanding of why research is a priority for some but not all first-year general education courses, an improved process for assessing beginning students' computer literacy and delivering the right instruction to the students who need it most, and a revision of our college criteria for computer and information literacy to reflect our current expectations and pedagogical practice in the first year. In cases like these, outcomes for writing and communication don't solve the problem in themselves, but they represent a shared commitment to addressing such concerns across the curriculum and a means for articulating and disseminating solutions.

The ongoing conversation about responding to error in student writing on our campus is another example of how the language of outcomes and criteria provides a means for addressing concerns about student writing. Our collegewide criteria for effective writing have been intentionally ambiguous when it comes to what we call the use of "appropriate" conventions (usage, spelling, punctuation, capitalization, sentence structure, format). Our expectation for first-year students is that they "consistently" follow appropriate conventions, and we have left it up to faculty to define what "consistently" means in the context of their course and discipline. The Outcomes Statement language on knowledge of conventions is similarly open to contextual definition. It refers to "control of conventions" but leaves it up to faculty to determine exactly what control of conventions means. On our campus, such language allows us to express what we can agree on when it comes to conventions, and it has helped generate continuing discussion of how to both teach and respond to this aspect of writing.

One constructive result of the way our outcomes for writing address the issue of error in conventions has been ongoing dialogue between communication specialists and faculty from across the disciplines about why our criteria take the form that they do. The category of appropriate conventions is one of seven dimensions of writing we address in our criteria, reinforcing the idea that the use of conventions is important but not the sum total of effective writing. Similarly, the general language of the criteria for conventions itself reflects the degree to which judgments about the appropriate use of conventions are contextual rather than absolute. Through department meetings and faculty in-services we have been able to talk with colleagues about the research that demonstrates the limitations of direct instruction in "grammar." We also offer faculty ideas for communicating with students about their expectations for the use of conventions and strategies for identifying and addressing patterns of error in student writing. These efforts have not and will not end every complaint about what our students don't seem to know or be able to do as writers, but our outcomes for writing have helped us explain that our approach to error in conventions is an informed one—and not merely a sign of neglect or grammatical relativism.

Finally, our work with outcomes for writing and effective communication has consistently shown us that an outcome-based approach shouldn't begin and end with first-year writing. Our criteria for effective writing express our expectations through general education and into the major, and they reinforce the message that developing students' writing ability is a collegewide commitment. The language in the Outcomes Statement about how faculty across the disciplines can build on the outcomes for first-year composition is a useful step toward this kind of collective commitment. What remains is for departments and programs to maintain conversations about where and how faculty across the curriculum can follow through on this commitment. Alverno began reinventing its curriculum with a paradigm shift that put a set of learning outcomes at the heart of the teaching and learning process, and we continue to see how we must address more than just writing and the first-year experience in order for our students to reach their full potential as learners. We continue to grapple with how to (re)define what it means to be an effective communicator as our understanding of the ability and of the world in which our students communicate continues to evolve, and we continue to talk with our colleagues across the disciplines about how we can better understand and address our students' needs as writers and learners. Writing outcomes, as a process and a product, represent a shared commitment to this ongoing inquiry.

Appendix

ALVERNO OUTCOMES FOR FIRST-YEAR WRITING

Connects with audience by:

- Giving audience full sense of purpose and focus, distinguishing own thoughts from those of others
- Using language that shows general awareness of appropriate word choice/style/tone
- Consistently following appropriate conventions
- Establishing and maintaining focus on a clear purpose, providing transitions to clarify relationships between most points of development
- Supporting most generalizations with examples and/or evidence meaningful to audience
- Demonstrating appropriate application of designated or selected ideas

In relation to self-assessment:

- Shows some understanding of development in one's own writing ability, based on criteria

(Source: "Alverno College Criteria for Effective Writing at Level 2")

17

WHAT THE OUTCOMES STATEMENT IS NOT

A Reading of the Boyer Commission Report

Rita Malenczyk

The exodus of the Outcomes Statement from the loving home of its birth parents (see Rhodes et al., chapter two in this volume) foregrounds the following question: What pitfalls do the writers of the statement—and the Council of Writing Program Administrators—need to be aware of as the statement is circulated and used? This essay will consider that question in light of the recent push toward general education reform as exemplified in a report issued in 1998 by the Boyer Commission. What implication does general education reform, which is usually driven by high-level administrators, have for the reception of the Outcomes Statement? What difference does the thinking behind such reform make to those of us who would like to see the statement become a respected, widely used document?

The Boyer Commission report—which seems to me representative of the thinking behind general education reform—is, in many respects, terrific. Titled *Reinventing Undergraduate Education: A Blueprint for America's Research Universities*, it addresses—and calls for redress of—the grievances both students and faculty have filed, metaphorically speaking, against large research institutions in this country. According to the writers of the report, students at such institutions typically find their educational experiences disjointed and impersonal: from day one, they take a series of courses that are circumscribed by the boundaries of disciplines and therefore compartmentalized ("writing goes here, and history in *here*, and math . . ."). The connections between these seemingly discrete subjects could be made clearer by caring faculty members who were willing to spend time with students; yet students have limited contact with any faculty at all, in large part because the reward system of research institutions privileges research over teaching and classroom time over office-hour time. The end result is that faculty who enjoy talking and working with students see their morale, if not their jobs, eventually disappear;

faculty who see students as a mere distraction from their research are awarded promotion and tenure; a new crop of soon-to-be-disaffected freshmen enters the university; and the cycle begins all over again (Boyer Commission 1998). The cycle is, of course, a result of the historical evolution of the American university, a process that began in the 1870s with the importation of the German research-institution model and the splitting of the formerly well-integrated, classical-curriculum-based college into specialized departments with separate disciplinary cultures and expectations (see, for instance, Brereton 1995, 4–11).

The Boyer Commission report calls for stopping the cycle, in part by reconceiving both the way faculty think of research and the way they are rewarded for research and teaching. Universities, the authors of the report suggest, should give faculty more time to spend one-on-one with students, helping students with research as part of their course load. Those who evaluate teaching should be encouraged to seek new ways of measuring the success of teaching, not simply to rely—as has traditionally been done—on research and publication as an index of productivity. The report also calls for other teaching reforms, including more explicit connections among courses: the freshman year should provide a strong foundation for the kind of academic work that is to follow in all disciplines, and the sophomore, junior, and senior curriculum should build on that foundation. Departments should restructure courses at the upper levels to rely less heavily on the traditional lecture mode of instruction and allow students opportunities to do the kind of hands-on research, using primary sources, that their professors typically do. Throughout the research process, professors should provide students with one-on-one mentoring and establish long-term relationships with them, thereby increasing each undergraduate's sense of belonging to an intellectual community (Boyer Commission 1998).

It seems to me that these recommendations would elicit a sympathetic response from most compositionists, particularly WPAs, for whom the departmental and curricular structure—and, consequently, reward system—of the traditional research university have historically presented problems. Ernest Boyer's *Scholarship Reconsidered* (1990) and *Scholarship Assessed* (Glassick, Huber, and Maeroff 1997) are frequently cited on the WPA-L listserv when questions arise about how to convince committees and administrators of one's worthiness for promotion and tenure; they are also referenced in the Council of Writing Program Administrators' document "Evaluating the Intellectual Work of Writing

Program Administration" (1998). They inform the thinking of the Boyer Commission report as well (though it is, I think, important to note that Ernest Boyer himself was only a marginal member of the commission, having died well before it completed its work). Furthermore, if one takes the Outcomes Statement as representative of WPA thinking about teaching, the OS and the report are to some degree simpatico. Both encourage the integration of theory and practice; both call on faculty across the disciplines, those teaching upper-division courses, to build on what students learn in the freshman year. Both advocate—though the OS does this only implicitly—the crossing of disciplinary boundaries.

However, the report raises, for me, a troubling issue. The Outcomes Statement is, crossing of boundaries notwithstanding, a disciplinary document: its virtue, and its reason for being, is that it is a statement about what people within the field of composition and rhetoric think first-year writing courses should do. The Boyer Commission report, on the other hand, critiques the very idea of disciplinarity, chiding academic departments—where disciplinary expertise presently resides—for being too insular, too concerned with maintaining their own political power within universities at the expense of "change":

> University budgets are now based on the principle of departmental hegemony; as a result, important innovations . . . are often doomed for lack of departmental sponsorship. Departments necessarily think in terms of protecting and advancing their own interests. . . . Initiatives for change coming from sources outside departments are viewed as threats rather than opportunities. New decisions on distributing resources must be carried out at the highest levels in the university, and they can be expected to meet little enthusiasm from those whose interests are protected by existing systems. (Boyer Commission 1998)

The report's critique of disciplinary faculty is encoded, more deeply in some places than in others, within its language. Here the encoding is not particularly deep. Taken in the larger context of the report, this passage implies that students are the ones who suffer for what would appear to be faculty members' natural tendency to think only of themselves; administrators, who are charged with a higher calling, need to withhold resources from selfish faculty in order to benefit the students.

Those of us who have run writing across the curriculum workshops can understand this view of disciplinary expertise—and departmental hegemony—to some extent. Most of us have experienced resistance from faculty who refuse to incorporate new ways of teaching into their courses because to rethink teaching would (1) take too much time from their research; (2) take too much time from content coverage; or (3) violate their academic freedom. WPAs with degrees in rhetoric and composition are also aware of the history and evolution of composition as a discipline: the division of the university into the majors our programs "serve" has had, as we know, a huge hand in creating composition's lower-class status and its relegation to the proverbial basement. WAC workshops occasionally bring those historical facts—and the resentment they have engendered in us—into sharp focus.

However, if we think back on those same workshops, we can also probably remember the faculty member from history who, following the workshop, created the informal writing assignment we used as a model in our *next* workshop; the computer science prof who figured out how to sequence writing assignments in a more beneficial way; the psychologist who finally decided to spend more class time conferencing with students about their writing. A vision of faculty within departments as *only* resistant to change, as *only* protecting their own interests, is reductive and inaccurate.

Particularly when such a vision is applied to us. In the section of the Boyer Commission report charging universities to "link communication skills and course work," the authors proclaim: "The failure of research universities seems most serious in conferring degrees upon inarticulate students. Every university graduate should understand that no idea is fully formed until it can be communicated, and that the organization required for writing and speaking is part of the thought process that enables one to understand the material fully."

The section concludes by calling on faculty across the disciplines to evaluate students by "both mastery of content and ability to convey content"; to emphasize "writing 'down' to an audience who needs information, to prepare students directly for professional work"; and to "reinforce communication skills" across the curriculum "by routinely asking for written and oral exercises." Graduate courses should also include "an emphasis on writing and speaking." The section also calls on "the freshman composition course" to "relate to other classes taken simultaneously and be given serious intellectual content, or . . . be abolished in favor of an integrated writing program in all courses. The course should emphasize explanation, analysis, and persuasion, and should develop the skills of brevity and clarity." The report goes on to cite the "Little Red Schoolhouse" at the University of Chicago as an example of graduate students, faculty, and undergraduate students working together on integrating writing across the curriculum.

The drafters of the Outcomes Statement would not necessarily disagree with everything the writers of the report say here about the teaching of writing. Elsewhere in this section, the report states: "Unfortunately, today's students too often think of composition as a boring English requirement rather than a life skill. . . . Faculty too often think of composition as a task the English or composition department does badly, rather than understanding that an essential component of all faculty members' responsibility is making sure that their students have ample practice in writing."

Many WPAs would agree, I think, that writing should take place across the curriculum; that writers should learn to write for a variety of audiences, not simply the professor; that writing should be seen as a "life skill"; that being able to write well when you graduate from college is good; that the Little Red Schoolhouse is an exemplary program. (The Outcomes Statement, in fact, makes many of these claims both implicitly and explicitly.) However, from a disciplinary perspective, the report's judgment of what it means to write, and to teach writing, is in many respects—like that vision of faculty mentioned earlier—reductive and inaccurate. Why divorce style from content? Why is writing only a matter of communicative performance? Why emphasize writing "down" to audiences? Why is the goal of writing instruction to induct students into the professional class? Why are brevity and clarity absolute values in writing? And—above all—why are compositionists seen to be teaching badly? It seems that a disciplinary statement of what writing courses should do is sorely needed to deepen and complicate the view of writing, and how writing is learned, expressed here. One worries, however, that in an institutional and political atmosphere increasingly hostile to disciplinarity itself, the idea of a disciplinary statement of what writing courses should do might be received as simply another means by which "specialists" protect their turf—particularly when nonspecialists seem to know perfectly well what it is to be able to write.

So, as the Outcomes Statement makes its way into the cold cruel world of general education and other types of reform, what might those responsible for its development and dissemination do to ease the way for its reception? How might we position ourselves within reform debates so that we are listened to, even as we try to maintain our disciplinary integrity?

I would suggest that our discipline itself has prepared us to answer this question, since another way of phrasing it is "How can we deploy rhetoric to our advantage?" Rhetoric is, after all, at the heart of what WPAs do, as Edward M. White (1995) has pointed out ; unfortunately, we fail to use it as often or as skillfully as we might. There are some good reasons why. If we think, for example, of the rhetorical strategies that are often required to convince faculty to give WAC techniques a try, some of those strategies feel a lot like selling out. One has, for example, to deploy a sympathetic ethos ("I feel your pain" or "Yes, you are right—those students don't always write very well") just to get people to listen to us, even though we might be squirming inside. One might argue, however, that using such rhetoric is akin to teaching writing center tutors not to say "We don't proofread" straight out, if only to keep students coming back so they can get to the real work the writing center might do. The work of Barbara Walvoord and her colleagues also suggests that not only is temporary compromise potentially effective, it is necessary to any ethical and realistic view of faculty change. In *In the Long Run*, Walvoord et al. write that most WAC studies—and therefore the minds of many WAC directors—adhere to "the Pilgrim's Progress model of faculty change," in which the researcher (or workshop presenter, or whoever is trying to "convert" the faculty to WAC) sets the standards to which the faculty are supposed to conform (1997, 13). "Researcher-defined good practice" they note, is at odds with more expansive definitions of good teaching; some studies suggest that innovative teachers are willing to try new techniques even before those techniques have been proven successful, and that WAC is only one peda-gogical movement competing for the attention of those teachers (6–7). Ironically, then, the very thing that makes WAC pedagogies attractive to innovators—their effectiveness—also plays into the innovators' desire to move beyond them.

Furthermore, at least one study notes that teaching careers are not sim-ply moves that one goes through, but a complicated and deep process of self-development: "The process of teacher development has to be under-stood in relation to personal sources, influences, issues and contexts. While changes in status and institutional mandates provide both pos-sibilities for, and limitations to, . . . development, there is also a deeper, more personal struggle. . . . Professional development is, in this sense, an enactment of a long process of creating *self,* of making and living out the consequences of a biography" (Raymond, Butt, and Townsend, qtd. in Walvoord et al. 1997, 12).

So, too, I would argue that the professional selves of those who drive general education reform—whether trustees, deans, or college presidents—are built over the long term, and we may need to think rhetorically with that fact in mind, so that we can find some way to get to the common ground our disciplinary outcomes statement shares with other movements.

And we should remember that, to some extent, we've already come pretty far. In chapter 13 of this volume, Martha Townsend reflects on the benefits the OS can provide for WAC/WID programs, reminding us along the way that there are already many programs in this country that encourage faculty to reach beyond the bounds of their own disciplines, even while helping students be more capable writers and thinkers within those disciplines. The Boyer Commission report does seem, to some extent, to overlook the breadth and scope the WAC movement has gained over the last thirty years. Of course—as Townsend's essay suggests—that oversight may be our own fault: it's taken the field of composition a long time to jump, with a formal Outcomes Statement, into a game in which it had already been a player for a very, very long time.

PART FOUR

Theorizing Outcomes

18

THE OUTCOMES STATEMENT AS THEORIZING POTENTIAL
Through a Looking Glass

Ruth Overman Fischer

The Outcomes Statement is now artifact; the process that produced it exists in memory. Approved by the WPA Executive Board and published both online and in print, the OS now stands as an object of study subject to local revision. Even as Irvin Peckham (unpublished) characterized the statement as "a valuable quasi-end product" (meaning that it should look like an end product but it should never come to closure), the fact remains that the Outcomes Statement as a published document is static, a status that obscures its informing theories.

I was not an "insider" in framing the Outcomes Statement. I became involved in the Outcomes project in the spring of 1998 when I joined the Outcomes-related listserv. A new WPA, I wanted to keep up with current issues regarding first-year composition. That summer at the WPA conference in Tucson, I attended the WPA Executive Board meeting when the statement was discussed to offer moral support. I also attended the presentation on the Outcomes Statement and gave my input to the document. During the discussion of this book, I commented that a section on the theories/theorizing that influenced the framers in constructing the document might be helpful. I was asked if I would like to take on the task—and here I am.

This essay is not the one I had envisioned when I began. In my original plan, I would query the framers online about the theory/ies that had informed their work in general and their participation in the Outcomes project. I would then provide a synopsis of this electronic communication. However, the silence to my e-mail query was, as they say, deafening. Not deafening, perhaps, but muted. Out of the responses I did receive the list included such theoretical perspectives as the semiotics and pragmatism of Peirce, expressivism, writing to learn, process theory, writing across the curriculum, social constructionism, and constructivism—an interesting list, but not what I had been expecting. I had hoped for a more outcome-by-outcome relation to particular theories.

However, such articulation was more difficult than I had first naively imagined. One difficulty may have been the "complicated rhetorical situation" of the Outcomes Statement "for a complicated set of readers . . . with no recognized authors . . . , by authors who are and aren't there for readers who definitely will be" (Peckham, unpublished). A second may have been differentiating the "theories of how we go about explaining our own work rather than theories of how students write" (Rhodes 2000). Also, Wiley (1999b) noted the different aspects of theory—linguistic, rhetorical, hermeneutical, sociological, political, and ethical—within which the framers individually worked. In addition, we have the nature of composition as a field itself: "no mainstream theory . . . dominat[es] Composition Studies. . . . Theories are intertwined, and theoretical perspectives overlap" (Kennedy 1998, x).

Perhaps I was asking the wrong question. Wolff (1999) echoed my thinking: "the Statement itself is not intended to lay out the theoretical grounds. . . . Rather, the Outcomes Statement is for a broader audience [school administrators, the interested public, students], which 'simply' needs to know that we have theoretical and practical grounds for suggesting these particular outcomes for FYC (actually, they'd be happier than usual if they thought we had outcomes at all)." He went on to note that "the suggestions which have led to the current Statement are themselves the products of wide reading in theory—too wide to begin to document in the Outcomes Statement—and a wide variety of approaches—too wide to essentialize and inevitably various. . . . It is the theory that they have read, lived through and taught by, leavened by encounters with countless students, that informs the Statement."

Why am I hung up on theory anyway? First, as a compositionist who finds tremendous potential in first-year composition, I am sensitive to the ways in which FYC teachers are negatively characterized as practitioners within a field often viewed by "outsiders" (to include colleagues in other subdisciplines of English studies) as atheoretical. Indeed, Gordon Grant (1996) voiced the same concern about colleagues outside of composition who had been tasked with writing objectives for FYC but who "either refuse[d] or [were] unable to acknowledge that a body of scholarship guides our work, . . . relying on their own prejudices and memory of their own current-traditional experiences." And so, I wanted to make explicit the theories implicit in the statement in order to lend credibility to the document and its development and to demonstrate its validity based on a robust intellectual exchange, both online and face-to-face.

In addition, as a "big picture" person with a preference for clarity and order, I need the rationale underlying claims I see made. Once the introduction to the Outcomes Statement asserted that the "following statement articulate[d] what composition teachers nationwide have learned from practice, research, and theory," my immediate reaction was what practice? what research? what theory? Teaching FYC clearly has a pragmatic focus. But what we do in the classroom has to be based on more than a "what works" mentality. Underlying our best laid plans has to be some kind of rationale, whether we articulate its points or not, that helps us assess what works—but even more important, what has happened when what once worked no longer does. And since the generative processing was essentially over by the time I joined the Outcomes listserv, I was curious about how the composition scholars who had framed the statement might talk about their rationales.

My initial plan was not to be realized. However, Wolff's earlier comments initiated an "Aha!" moment. If the theory that has informed the statement is indeed "theory that [the framers] have read, lived through and taught by, *leavened by encounters with countless students*" (emphasis added), then what we have here is the theorizing—the coming to a situated theory through one's own reading and reflected practice—that belies my "laundry list" approach to theory/ies in the statement.

The issue, then, is not *which* theories influenced the framers but *that* theory shaped the Outcomes Statement. What ultimately matters are the practices/research/theories, the context of the praxis, that readers and potential participants in the local instantiation of the statement bring to their readings of the document. Readers ultimately "see" which ones are present—or absent—through their own theoretical frames.

Indeed, it may even be better if we allow ourselves to theorize off of/ through the Outcomes Statement. To the extent that we claim agency as educators in literacy, each of us is—or should be—a theorist, not in the "big T" use of the term but as reflective practitioners. Bizzell defines theorizing as "thinking about what one is doing—reflecting on practice—but thinking about it in a systematic way, trying to take as much as possible into account, and using the ideas of other thinkers wherever they may be useful. Theorizing might then lead not to laws but to rules of thumb, which enable us not to predict outcomes infallibly but at least to speculate about what is more or less probable . . . not [to] dictate practice but [to] guide it" (1997, 2–3).

Moreover, "theoretical frameworks help us organize our observations in useful ways, and classroom experience pushes us to build or restructure these frameworks" (McLeod 1997, 23). And to some extent, "Theory is autobiography . . . a form of intelligibility that the theorist tries to give to personal dilemmas, deeply felt . . . a way to make sense of life. . . . In composition, theory is irrevocably committed to practice: begins there and returns there in recursive loops" (Phelps 1988, vii–viii).

As I considered my situation in writing this essay, I have found the process to be a walk down the memory lane of my evolution as a teacher over the past thirty years (almost forty, if you count my experience as an apprentice marksmanship instructor in the National Rifle Association in the late 1950s). Along the way, I recalled not only influential names and ideas but personal and student learning experiences and the ways that both these theoretical influences and reflected practice have intertwined into my own informed theoretical eclectic.

Following my earlier teaching experiences in the upper elementary grades in the late 1960s, I stepped out of the classroom in the early 1970s to focus on raising two daughters—three years apart in age and light years apart in personality and learning style—until our family went to the Republic of Korea in the late 1970s. There I began teaching English as a foreign language. Upon our return to the United States, I entered graduate school in English linguistics in the early 1980s. My reading in second-language acquisition led me to teachers/researchers who, while not claiming to be theorists, were certainly theorizers in their quest for understanding how language users learn to communicate in their first and subsequent languages.

I came upon Corder and his appreciation of the inevitable mistakes learners make in their language learning, Selinker and his concept of interlanguage to explain the naturally evolving grammars of language learners toward the target language (and the processes that can inhibit a successful approximation), Gardner and Lambert and their distinction between integrative and instrumental motivation, Krashen and his monitor model, which added the affective aspect of language learning into my evolving theoretical frame. As a teaching assistant tutoring in a writing center for our ESL students, I was introduced to the theorizers in composition at that time—which, based on my earlier study, seemed a natural extension into written language. I first heard about writing process pedagogy. I was influenced by the ideas of Shaughnessy; Elbow, Murray, and Macrorie (the so-called expressivists); Emig, Perl, and the fluency/effectiveness/control model of Kirby and Liner ("getting it down"—"getting it right"—"checking it out").

During my early years of teaching first-year composition for both non-native and native speakers of English in the mid-1980s, I moved from the "pure" process model of Fulwiler and others, which allowed students to shape their own writing projects over the term, to a more rhetorically focused approach. I discovered that my students could not make the transition from the personal writing prompted solely by personal interests and experiences to the kinds of writing they would be asked to do beyond FYC. I began to focus more overtly on rhetorical modes, but always with the caveat that the mode serves the message, not the other way around.

In my professional reading I came upon social construction, the genre analysis of Swales (from the applied linguistics perspective) and Kress (from the sociopolitical perspective), and Jungian personality theory as enacted in the Meyers Briggs Type Indicator and its effects on writing behaviors. As part of my doctoral studies in the early 1990s, I met Vygotsky, Bakhtin, and Freire. I also started teaching FYC in a linked setting with a service-learning component (which included an ethnographic component) and so became part of the service-learning and learning communities discussion. And long before the so-called "post process" movement materialized, I recognized that all writers, students and otherwise, already write within a process. And while the typical "write it at the last minute because I work better under pressure" process may not always have served the student well, still it worked often enough. My task was opening students up to other processing possibilities—inventing, composing, revisioning—on which they could draw.

Out of this mix (among other influences) has come my informed theoretical eclectic, which leads me to a particular reading of the Outcomes Statement and a particular assessment of its implications in my local situation both as teacher and as writing program administrator. I appreciate the intellectual work that went into the statement to "write it short." Although its brevity has been cited as one of its weaknesses, this distillation makes it more amenable to local discussion. To a certain extent, it has the elegance of parsimony that characterizes a tightly constructed formula in math.

From my perspective, then, I see nothing in the Outcomes Statement that counters what I hold valid in the teaching of reading/writing/critical thinking in FYC. And I find particular resonances with the outcomes that focus on the rhetorical situation, such as:

- Focus on the aspects of rhetorical situations (audience, purpose, language, e.g., tone, diction)
- Focus on the relationship of effects of different genres on reading and writing

I also find the "focus on respect for writing as 'an open process'" to be consistent with my thinking.

As sites of expansion at my local level, I see the outcomes about "writing and reading for inquiry, learning, thinking, and communicating," "understand[ing] the relationships among language, knowledge, and power," "the collaborative and social aspects of the writing process," and the recognition of the need for a variety of technologies to address a range of audiences to be most useful.

I experience the greatest dissonance with the Outcomes Statement in what is not said; rather than asserting that students "should be able to," I would insert the phrase "should have demonstrated the ability to." Such a change recognizes more overtly the developmental nature of student readers/writers/critical thinkers. As Sternglass and Haswell so ably point out in their chapters below, students cannot be expected to have full command of any of these outcomes by the end of the course. However, they should have demonstrated some level of ability at some point(s) along the way—and with the assistance of faculty across the curriculum will have continued opportunities to develop in these areas.

Each of the invited authors in this section has perused the Outcomes Statement through his or her own theoretical frame. Marilyn Sternglass uses the findings of her award-winning longitudinal investigation of the development of the reading and writing competencies of students who began in basic writing and regular first-year composition courses at the City College of City University of New York from 1989 to 1995 to interrogate the Outcomes Statement for its failure to more overtly note the importance of development through practice over time. Setting the Outcomes Statement against lifespan development theory, Richard Haswell takes the statement to task for failing to recognize the variances in student development that would make the attainment of different outcomes difficult, if not impossible, because of their personal course of development. Peter Elbow offers an attitude for reformulating the statement in ways that bring students into the discussion and that clarify more specifically what we expect student writers to demonstrate in their writing.

19

A FRIENDLY CHALLENGE TO PUSH THE OUTCOMES STATEMENT FURTHER

Peter Elbow

I should "situate myself" and say a word about the history I bring to the Outcomes Statement. In the 1970s I spent three years in a research project with six others looking closely at seven experiments in outcome-based ("competence-based") higher education. We each studied our own site for three years—interviewing and observing and eventually writing a case study. But the whole group paid a visit to each site at least once for additional interviewing and observing so that we could provide each other with "triangulation" or additional perspectives. (Sites varied from single courses to programs to entire institutions. Alverno College is perhaps the best-known institution we studied and reported on.)

Each of us also wrote a second essay about an issue or dimension of outcomes-based education. In my essay, "Trying to Teach while Thinking about the End" (1979), I struggled to understand how an outcomes approach affected the teaching process. I say "struggled" because I felt my whole temperament to be at odds with an outcomes approach. Just as I have always valued writing as a voyage of discovery toward an unknown direction rather than toward an outcome or outline specified in advance, so I value teaching as a similar voyage. I don't like destinations specified too much in advance. But in my three years of observing various programs and in my lengthy process of working through to my conclusions about outcomes-based teaching, I ended up with high respect for the specification of outcomes. I want to summarize here two of my conclusions.

First, even though my temperament and personal goals in teaching seemed inimical to an outcomes approach (goals like growth, intellectual integrity, curiosity, the ability to question), I finally concluded that in fact there is no conflict here. I concluded that *anything* you are trying for in teaching may be specified as a goal or an outcome or even a competence—as long as you go about specifying it in a sufficiently careful and sophisticated manner. I conceded that the outcomes folks were right: it's all a matter of forcing yourself to figure out and admit what you really want. Second, the issue of whether to specify outcomes turns out to be interestingly tangled up with issues of class. The resistance to outcomes tends to come with elitist attitudes and elitist institutions: "No one is going to force me to specify my goals. I'm the expert. They wouldn't understand."

So I arrive at the WPA Outcomes Statement for first-year writing respectful but wary—since of course we also saw how an outcomes approach could be used badly in various ways (sometimes mechanistically, unthoughtfully, unreflectively). And I was suspicious of the WPA Outcomes Statement because I didn't see any evidence that the authors had consulted or were even aware of the *extensive* experimentation and literature on outcomes-based or competence-based education at all levels of curriculum—including higher education.[1]

I end up admiring the Outcomes Statement. The framers have done something important, useful, and very difficult. They took one of the most chaotic realms in all of higher education—first-year composition— and broke it down into clear goals. Perhaps more striking, they managed to attain remarkable agreement among a very disparate but important group of leaders in the field.

Still, I'm not satisfied and I offer this essay as a friendly challenge. I promise to join in on further work if invited. The framers of the WPA statement have gone a long distance but I want to push further. In this essay I will offer three challenges.

THE SHIP

Consider this thought experiment. It's one I like to use when I—or new teachers I work with—begin to feel slightly or even very troubled:

> Imagine your first-year writing course as a ship—as Jonah's ship tossed on hurricane-driven waves and in great danger of sinking. Your class is not working well at all. Students are resisting you, they don't seem to be learning, you are suffering. Like the mariners on Jonah's ship, your only hope of making it to port is to jettison cargo. Imagine, then, that you have to jettison *almost everything* on your Good Ship ENG 101. What *few* things would you cling to and not throw overboard? What do you care about most? If you could only accomplish one or two things in your writing course, what would you try for?

I love this question for the way it forces us to figure out our priorities. (I also like the way it invites us to be frank about a feeling many of us more than occasionally have: fear that our class is in trouble.)

This thought experiment gives me a troubling perspective on the outcomes on the WPA list. I'm not troubled that I'll have to throw overboard many of their outcomes; that's how it is with storms. What's troubling is that I can't find on their list any of the outcomes I most want to hang onto. I'm talking about the outcomes that I feel are most central and writerly for a first-year writing course: getting students to *experience* themselves as writers and to *function* like writers. The last piece of cargo I would jettison before my ship sank to the bottom of the sea would be a clump of practical and writerly outcomes like these:

- The ability to get lots of words and lots of ideas down on paper or on the screen without too much struggle. This general statement implies two very practical corollary outcomes: the ability to get started in writing something without too much harmful delay or procrastination, and the ability to keep on writing even when you are tired or discouraged. I like to phrase this in the strongest way as the ability to *enjoy* writing. Face it, the only way that students will get good at writing is to continue writing when no one is holding a gun to their heads.
- But I'm not talking about just any words. Rather, my central goal for the course is the ability to put down words and ideas that match one's felt meaning or intention—that produce a click of grateful recognition where you say, "Yes, that's what I mean, that's what I want to say."
- Also, the ability to write *past* what you "had in mind" when you sat down, so that you know how to discover words and thoughts that feel new—that you *didn't* have in mind or at least that you didn't know you had in mind.

Why did the framers so utterly neglect this practical, nitty-gritty, behavioral dimension of writing? Did they assume that our first-year students can *already* write without too much struggle and procrastination—and find words that match their existing meanings and intentions as well as new words and thoughts? Yet any teacher of first-year writing who knows what's really going on with the students as they write knows that many of them cannot wield words in this way.

Perhaps the framers felt they "covered" the abilities I've just mentioned when they specified the ability to "use writing and reading for inquiry, learning, thinking, and communicating." But this is unhelpfully vague and doesn't get at the nitty-gritty abilities I'm talking about. Insofar as the Outcomes Statement treats invention at all (and mostly it doesn't), it treats it more as a matter of finding and responding to material in readings. I see no awareness of the root ability to find thoughts and topics of your own—to write as an initiator and agent rather than as a responder.

I think the problem is that the framers were too preoccupied with another goal—one that is of course equally important and that Mark Wiley sums up with this phrase: "help them develop into rhetorically savvy, critically aware, versatile writers" (1999a, 67). The framers seem to me to stress this goal to the point of redundancy: the ability to suit your words to various audiences, to various purposes, to various genres, and to various situations.

In effect I am calling attention to two very large or general goals: invention (finding lots of words and thoughts and getting them out) and rhetorical savvyness (critical awareness of audience, purpose, genre, situation). It is common to feel that these two goals or emphases are in conflict with each other; people tend to assume an either/or attitude toward them: naive vs. sophisticated, being careless vs. exercising care, doing it with pleasure and satisfaction vs. doing it right.

It's this kind of thinking that is the problem: the sense that one has to choose one or the other. That's exactly what the framers seem to have done. In effect, they opted for what felt like "sophistication"—but I would call it an unsophisticated or crude decision. For in truth both these goals can reasonably and effectively be pursued—indeed they must be pursued if we want to help produce well-equipped writers. If the only goal is invention and fertility, we lose critical awareness and rhetorical savvy. But—and here is the problem with the WPA list—if teachers emphasize only critical awareness and rhetorical savvy, this functions as an *impediment* to students' mastering what I would call the prior or foundational competences of finding lots of words that match their felt intention—and thus getting intrinsic satisfaction from the act of writing. This one-sidedness is precisely the condition that leads to so much wooden, thoughtless, uninvested writing from first-year students.

Throughout most of my work on writing, I have emphasized this problem of the seeming conflict between the generative and the critical. I've emphasized that, in practice, *time* is the key: we can do justice to both dimensions if we give dedicated time to each. The framers do allude to this crucial and writerly ability to strategize in the deployment of time: they specify the ability "to save extensive editing for after invention and development work has been done very completely." Yet amazingly, they don't include this central aspect of the writing process as an outcome for the first-year writing course itself but rather only in the list of outcomes that teachers in *other* disciplines *might* adopt!

The framers' unconscious preoccupation with rhetorical awareness of audience/genre/purpose led them in fact into an unsophisticated blindness to an audience/genre/purpose that is central for most writers—and one that is a foundational ability that I would also cling to in a terrible storm:

- The ability to explore a topic for yourself, on your own, because *you* are interested—even when others are not interested. This is the ability to keep on writing when there's no feedback or when the feedback is negative. Putting it differently, here is the ability to *like* your own writing so you care about it enough to really work further on it when others ignore it or don't like it.

Because the framers were so preoccupied with critical awareness, their only way of imagining peer response was as "critique." They totally neglect:

- The ability to give *supportive* responses to others, to suit your response to the needs of the writer
- Nor do they mention the crucial abilities that *writers* need in soliciting response: figuring out what response *you* need for your draft, and learning to get readers to give it to you—rather than what is inappropriate or unhelpful.

I think their preoccupation with rhetorical theory makes them neglect the central experiences of writers in peer groups. So they leave out one of the hardest but most important skills for freshmen (not to mention full professors):

- The ability to listen well to feedback from others—hear it and take it seriously yet not be hamstrung by it

The WPA members' unconscious emphasis on "critical" also leads them to neglect a basic skill in good persuasion and argumentation. Though they talk about "critical thinking, reading, and writing," they don't mention:

- The ability to understand and write with respect (and even sympathy) for points of view different from your own (the believing game)

Am I just reacting like so many reviewers of anthologies who write, "Those selections you chose are all very well, but you left out some of my old favorites"? No, it's more than that. I'm troubled by a serious tilt toward *knowledge about* the principles of rhetoric, and a tilt away from *knowing how* to be a writer: learning how to function as and experience oneself as a writer.

KNOWING HOW

If I wanted to make fun of the list, I could propose a scary thought experiment. Consider a hard-assed, skeptical, high-level administrator or legislator who thinks that teaching first-year writing is too expensive—and who wants more money for large-scale assessment. He might take this list and say, "Good work! At last these vague, wishy-washy English teachers have shown a spark of efficiency and spelled out exactly what they are trying to teach. With this list, we can now teach what needs to be taught by means of a large lecture course with a machine-graded exam at the end." I fear that the outcomes list lends itself to this perversion because so much of it is "knowledge" that students could gain by reading and listening to lectures, and that they could demonstrate on machine-graded exams. To use a distinction from philosophy, there is too much "knowing that" and not enough "knowing how." Let me illustrate.

Consider the following clump of outcomes—all taken from the first two sections of the Outcomes Statement (Rhetorical Knowledge and Critical Thinking/Reading/Writing):

- Recognize different audiences and their needs
- Recognize differences in communicative situations
- Have a sense of what genres are and how they differ
- Learn the steps necessary to carry out writing
- Investigate, report, and document existing knowledge

We could teach these outcomes with lectures and readings, and attentive students could give correct answers on an exam—even a sophisticated multiple-choice exam.

The third section of the Outcomes Statement is Processes, and here is where we would expect the most emphasis on "knowing how" rather than "knowing that." And yet under Processes, we are told that students should *be aware that* it usually takes multiple drafts and *understand* that writing is an ongoing process and *understand* the collaborative and social aspects . . . and so on (my emphasis). These too could be taught in lectures and tested on an exam. The fourth section of the Outcomes Statement comprises Knowledge of Conventions: this knowledge can obviously be taught be *entirely* with workbooks and tested with machine-graded exams.

Needless to say, my reading is satirically hostile. No one but a mean-spirited, cost-cutting administrator would fail to realize that the framers of the outcomes did not intend for them to be used in this way. And half of the outcomes ask for "knowing how" (but half isn't really very many): *use* conventions of format, *adopt* appropriate voice, *write in* several genres, *use* writing and reading for inquiry, *develop* strategies for generating, and even *practice* means of documenting, and so on.

Still, the issue I raise is far from trivial. Not only do we live in a time when institutions are desperate to cut costs and frame learning into outcomes that can be inexpensively assessed; in addition, the whole point of an outcomes statement is to help us be more sophisticated about the nature of knowing—and thus to avoid getting mixed up about the difference between knowing that and knowing how.

My dissatisfaction feels substantial, but in a sense it is a minor one, for it was pretty much cured by a revision of the Outcomes Statement prepared by Irv Peckham (Outcomes Statement Steering Committee 1998–2003). (Unfortunately, it's no longer available at the Outcomes Statement archives.) It did an admirable job of framing outcomes in terms of knowing how, and this made the outcomes much clearer and crisper than in the main document.

WHAT ARE YOU LOOKING FOR?

It seems to me that any further discussion of outcomes needs to benefit from the lively experimentation and extensive scholarship on competence-based education in the 1970s. The movement was frankly democratic, egalitarian, and liberatory. Let me try to spell out my sense of the central premises that I saw driving it.

- Poor teaching in colleges and universities often stems from faculty being characteristically inept at giving clear and concrete answers to their students (and often to themselves and to the public) when asked the direct question, "What are you actually trying to teach?" In a sense the competence-based movement could be summed up as a concerted insistence that we take seriously that pesky question that students like to ask and teachers like to duck: "What are you looking for?" The movement seemed to me driven by an irritation if not downright anger at teachers who answer in effect, "Don't ask. Keep your mind on higher things. Besides, you wouldn't understand. I'm the expert here. Only I understand the criteria; only I can be the judge of what constitutes, [say], good writing." People in the movement argued that teachers don't deserve their jobs unless they

can answer the question clearly and concretely enough that the student
and teachers will agree about whether or not the student has learned that
particular skill or ability.

- Outcomes should be "validated." That is, faculties and educational institutions have an obligation to consult with people *outside* the academy in
deciding what knowledge, skills, and abilities students should achieve.
(The WPA framers explicitly declined to open this can of worms—asking
various constituencies what they see as good writing or a competent writer.
The competence-based folk insisted it was a cop-out not to open it.)

- Colleges typically mystify the relationship between teaching and assessing or certifying. Curricular structures often tacitly legislate that learning
doesn't count or deserve credit unless it occurs while enrolled in a course.
It was a central premise that structures should be set up so that students
could get credit for things they learn without having to undergo instruction. Constantly we felt the theme that students should not have to be
so dependent upon teachers for learning. A major goal was to clarify the
relationship between the teaching functions and the assessing or certifying
functions of education in such a way as to empower students. The competence movement yielded some very sophisticated insights about assessment that are particularly needed today.

- Most assessment is problematic because it assumes a "norm-based model"
of assessment; we need instead a "criterion-based" model. Norm-based
assessment treats *time* as the constant and *learning* as the variable: thus
the normal constant is a semester or sixty minutes, and the variable is the
degree of learning—and thus the range of scores or grades that students
get. Criterion-based assessment, in contrast, treats *learning* as the constant
and *time* as the variable: the constant should be a set of specific abilities
or skills that all students must attain, and the variable will then be the
amount of time that different students will require. The central pedagogical and ideological point is this: if we articulate outcomes in more
concrete detail, we can ask that *all* students master them (the term *mastery
learning* was sometimes used). We mustn't write off the ability of certain
students to achieve the important outcomes just because it takes them longer. (*Slow* is a euphemism for *stupid.*) Thus the norm-based model tends
to emphasize difference and competition (the IQ "intelligence" test is the
paradigm of norm-based assessment), whereas the criterion-based model
emphasizes the expectation that all students can learn—as long as we provide good conditions and flexibility of time. (See McClelland's 1973 foundational essay for the movement: "Testing for Competence Rather Than
for Intelligence.")

- Finally, by insisting on clearer outcomes, we can increase learning in yet another fashion, namely, by helping students themselves understand more concretely the skills and abilities we are attempting to impart—thereby increasing their ability to teach themselves and to assess themselves about whether they learned. In short, for the competence-based movement, the key to improved learning and student empowerment is meta-awareness: the ability to notice, monitor, and take control of one's own learning process.

I was troubled when I started observing and writing about outcomes-based learning: its adherents are so committed to meta-awareness and self-consciousness whereas I am so committed to intuitive processes like freewriting where you turn off critical awareness and control. But I gradually learned that I didn't need to fear their approach (though too few of them understood the value of the intuitive—sometimes using "intuitive" as a bad word). That is, I figured out that I could do a better job of fostering *my* attempts to make use of intuitive and non-self-conscious processes if I learned from the competence folks to be more critically aware of these as goals—goals that I need to be better at articulating. I learned how to say things like this: "If our ultimate goal is deeper and more connected thinking—and even rhetorical savvyness—we can get there better if we consciously set aside periods where we explicitly engage in *non-goal-oriented* writing behavior. There are certain goals that we attain better when we take time to set those goals aside."

If the WPA framers had explored the literature from the competence-based movement of the 1970s, they would have found it helpful and sympathetic. But they would have learned two important principles that I would argue for strenuously in a revision. Yet I think I'm asking for no more than the next logical steps in a journey on which the framers have already gone the hardest distance.

TAKE STUDENTS INTO OUR CONFIDENCE WHEN WE ARTICULATE OUTCOMES

Another thought experiment. Imagine we were professional mountain guides leading a party of amateur climbers—we would do well to get our destinations and goals very clear among ourselves. Where are we headed and what do we need to do to get there? Clearly the WPA framers took this sensible step in formulating outcomes. But we wouldn't stop there if we were thinking hard about outcomes. We'd realize that our mountain expedition would have a much better chance of getting to its destination if the guides took care to ensure that *those we are trying to lead* also know the destinations and goals.

This analogy seems to me particularly apt for teaching. Students will get much more from our teaching if they know where we are trying to lead them and thus can help us get there. Most of us have experienced this truth in an unfortunately negative form: we notice that if students don't understand or share our goals, they can prevent learning no matter what we do.

I think I understand why the WPA framers decided not to talk to students (declaring, "We expect the main audience for this document to be well-prepared college writing teachers and college writing program administrators. We have chosen to write in their professional language"). Sometimes I too can't figure something out about my teaching if I have to talk it out publicly with my students or with parents or the public. Yet given the good work the framers have already done, they are now in a good position to take the second step and articulate these outcomes in such a way as to address students too. This is not just a "rhetorical" choice of audience in the trivial sense of "rhetorical"; it's rhetorical in the deeper sense. That is, decisions about how to frame or articulate knowledge are always deployments of power. The Outcomes Statement as we now have it constitutes an insistence on retaining power to ourselves as professional experts—and refusing to invite power and participation by the student learner *or* the outside world. I'd call it professionalism in the bad sense.

Am I too harsh in charging the WPA framers with hiding behind their professional expertise? I'm importing a flavor of harshness that I felt from leading figures in the competence-based movement of the 1970s—often aimed at arrogant faculty members and elite institutions that pretended to educate when they were really just rewarding students for the training and talent they already possessed before they came to college or enrolled in the course. (There's no need to be clear and explicit with students if those students are already in good shape to learn what you are teaching.) Of course the community of composition scholars and teachers is anything but an elitist bastion of power and authority (though WPAs do in fact have nontrivial authority). Still I'm troubled when I consult the version of the outcomes that the WPA group *does* provide for students (again on a link from the main statement). I think it's a version that most students would experience as condescending and obfuscatory—a piece of rhetoric that says, in effect, "You wouldn't understand us if we really tried to explain these outcomes to you, so we'll just give you vague hip slang." Let me reiterate the premise of the competence-based movement: if we want to improve teaching and learning by articulating outcomes, the job is not done till we take the students into our confidence. We need to be smart enough to spell out what we are looking for so clearly that students can see as well as we can whether they have attained any particular skill or ability.

On one of my visits to a site, I was sitting in on a dreadful lecture—rambling, disorganized, dull. I was starting to tune out in a mood of strong irritation when gradually I noticed how differently all the students were reacting. They didn't look absent or annoyed, and they were busily absorbed in taking notes with great focus. When I talked to some of them afterward, they told me that of course they knew it was a pretty bad lecture, but they knew what they had to get from it—and they could indeed get it. When we explain outcomes clearly to students, they can get good benefits from bad teaching.

People with portfolio assessment programs are discovering the same thing. When students know ahead of time what skills or abilities they need to display in their portfolios, they can be more active and intellectually aware as they try to *produce in themselves* the learning needed to get those skills and abilities visible in their portfolios. Notice the difference between these two statements to students:

- Give me your portfolio and I, in my professional wisdom, will judge it and reveal to you whether you pass or fail.
- Here's what your portfolio will have to demonstrate to readers: . . . I probably can't teach all those things brilliantly in fourteen weeks, but if you will try to *learn* them while I'm trying to teach them, you have a much better chance of success.

And remember: as students try to get their portfolios to demonstrate the required abilities, they will be trying out, testing, and confirming their *conceptual* or *theoretical* knowledge of these sometimes difficult, subtle, or fuzzy rhetorical outcomes. In short, this route addresses both "knowing how" and "knowing that."

MAKE OUTCOMES AS CLEAR AND DOWN TO EARTH AS POSSIBLE

In a way, this principle follows from deciding to take students as audience. Of course some competence-based enthusiasts went much too far toward micro "behavioral objectives," but I came to respect a general push in the movement toward being down to earth. Outcomes folks insisted on a simple but productive two-step sequence of thinking. First they ask, "What are you trying to teach?" but then they always go on to ask, "So how will we know this skill or ability or piece of knowledge when we see it? What does it look like in the flesh—on the hoof?"

Thus, I could have framed the whole opening section of this essay in terms of a neglect of the traditional and basic rhetorical skill of *invention*. But this is abstract and it is general. It's crucial to talk instead about things that every student will recognize and appreciate as a worthwhile goal: "getting lots of words down without too much struggle" or "learning to avoid unproductive procrastination."

It's interesting and perplexing to me that the framers worked so hard to avoid talking in terms of texts. They wrote outcomes like, "focus on a purpose and address audience needs," instead of "produce a *portfolio* that shows you can focus on a purpose and address audience needs." This may sound like semantic quibbling, but my reformulation will be clearer and more productive for students and lead to fewer arguments. (The extensive work on portfolio assessment in the last couple of decades will prove enormously useful here—especially where experimenters and researchers have begun to specify extremely interesting and sometimes subtle writing outcomes.)

But if the framers had opened the door to the concreteness of text, they would surely have made a huge change—and one that strikes me as desirable. That is, even though they were willing to talk about textual features like "control of spelling and grammar" (what does "control" really mean?) and "use of appropriate voice and register," for some reason they ran away from talking about many of the textual features that turn up most prominently in teachers' mouths and written comments: clear sentences, coherent paragraphs, and effective structures. Perhaps the framers felt that these textual features were not sufficiently "rhetorical" and smacked too much of "Platonic-good-writing-in-the-abstract." But these sorts of textual features are just the kind that *must* be specified if we want to give honest answers to that central question that an outcomes approach invites: "*What are you looking for?*"

Furthermore, these textual outcomes do not exclude the rhetorical dimension—indeed, they are very problematic unless formulated in a rhetorical manner:

- The ability to create openings that bring readers in satisfactorily, and endings that give a satisfying sense of closure

- The ability to structure essays so that readers have an appropriate sense of where they are being led—so they don't get lost
- The ability to create sentences and paragraphs that are clear for the kind of readers and genre addressed

Note how this rhetorical formulation avoids the trap of rigid formulas such as insisting that there is only one right way to open or close or structure an essay.

The framers stay at a similar level of generality when they speak merely of "critical thinking." No doubt they didn't want their list too long, but the term strikes me as useless on its own. We need enough concrete clarity that students and teachers could agree about whether so-called "critical thinking"—or certain dimensions of it—has been demonstrated. This means listing outcomes of the following sort. In writing essays, students should be able:

- To work at both the general and specific level and to move clearly and comfortably between levels
- To create a movement of thinking and not just reiterate a static "position"
- To do some justice to points of view other than their own

Of course the framers wanted to avoid getting into issues of grading—of defining "standards or levels of ability." Rightly so. But the rhetorically formulated textual outcomes I've just named don't fall into that trap. A piece of writing could lack or be significantly weak in some of these outcomes and still manage to be very good indeed. Yet nevertheless, these are textual outcomes that most teachers are indeed looking for—and they are the features most helpful to specify if we want students to *help* us move toward the destination we are trying to reach in our teaching.

For a while now, I've been hearing a voice:

> But Peter, you've misunderstood us. We were trying for outcomes to help plan programs and classrooms, not to assess individual students. Your "nitty-gritty" outcomes will just reinforce the push for large-scale assessments.

But it strikes me that you miss the benefits of outcomes—and indeed the very meaning of the word—if you run away from saying what your outcomes look like in students and in texts. Large-scale assessments are upon us, and I think outcomes of this sort can make them less harmful. Plenty of the process outcomes I suggested earlier (such as the ability to avoid procrastination, to write past what's on your mind, and to balance the use of others and reliance on self) can only be assessed by students themselves—but that doesn't make them less important.

One of the many goals of the competence movement was to create new structures for teaching and learning. Adherents argued that if we specified more clearly and concretely what we are teaching and how we know when students have learned it, we wouldn't be so unthinkingly stuck with the standard structures like the "course" and the collection-of-courses adding up to a degree. Surely, first-year writing is unhelpfully stuck in the model of the standard course: fifteen to thirty students and one teacher meeting in one room for ten to fifteen weeks. It was my experience with the competence movement that led me to propose experimenting with what I called the "yogurt model" for first-year writing.[2]

To conclude, let me say again that I'm not so much arguing *against* outcomes in the WPA statement as arguing for others in addition and for some reformulation. I think the framers did a good and a difficult job in bringing the statement as far as they did. If invited, I would be happy to join in a revision process.

20

OUTCOMES AND THE DEVELOPING LEARNER

Richard H. Haswell

On our quick'st decrees
The inaudible and noiseless foot of Time
Steals ere we can effect them.

Shakespeare, *All's Well That Ends Well*

My topic of lifespan development and the Outcomes Statement bridges two different academic disciplines, psychology and composition. In the past the bridge has proven shaky. Min-Zhan Lu remarks, accurately, that "composition studies have long questioned the function of the developmental frame, especially the plot line of 'you have to . . . before you can'" (1999, 341). But whose plot line is this? It is true that sequence is the benchmark of the developmental survey of human lives, but the great majority of developmental theories posit no "have to." Instead they record the "did" of individuals, the "tend to" of cultural groups, the "ought to" of human value systems, and the "required to" of institutional programs. Lu, for instance, is warning specifically against the expectation that minority and second-language writing students need to learn the majority language before they can assume their own voice. Yet that is hardly an expectation one will find among developmentalists, who customarily defend the cogency and legitimacy of each individual's voice at whatever point in life.

These notions of sequence and voice mark just two of many disconnects between the field of composition and the field of personal development, a topic that I will return to at the end of this commentary. But first I should attend to my main question. How do theories of adult or lifespan development critique, illuminate, and perhaps suggest improvements to the Outcomes Statement? Voice, it will be remembered, is an explicit outcome in the statement ("students should adopt appropriate voice, tone, and level of formality"). Sequence, it may not be noticed, is missing from the statement. Is the statement's inclusion of the one and exclusion of the other countenanced by developmental thinking? What else of this careful decree—had Shakespeare seen its authoring, he would hardly call it "quickest" of foot—does developmental theory countenance?

THE DEVELOPMENTAL FRAME

Actually, since there is not one theory of lifespan development but rather a cloud of theories, it might be better to drop in elevation. I will adopt Lu's terminology and talk about the "developmental frame," the customary way the discipline of personal development looks at persons. It is, of course, hard to find any knowledge frame more intuitive and universal than that of lifelong development. Children yearn to be grown up, grownups compulsively write and rewrite the story of their growth since childhood. Childhood, adolescence, majority, maturity, senility are massive cultural constructs backed with the authority of personal change, social expediency, and legal code, and preoccupied with the important stuff of our lives: sex, cars, marriage, alcohol, nicotine, ownership of property, military service, retirement, etc. In every culture around the world, the story of growing up and growing old is an ur-narrative in the sense that it underlies many other stories and few if any underlie it.

But formal study has broken down this folk ur-narrative into a number of elements (or Lu's "plot lines"). Sequence is only one aspect of a complex of notions widely assumed by lifespan developmentalists. (1) Eras of a person's life form structured wholes, organizations of the self that make sense and, for the person, make sense of the world. (2) Major changes then, reorganizations of the self, are not "quantitative" but "qualitative," defined not by the accumulation of new knowledge or skill but by the acquisition of a new mode of understanding that allows new knowledge or skill. (3) Life changes correlate with age and event but do not depend on age and event. (4) However, life changes form sequences, normative in terms of and usually across class, sex, and culture. (5) The sequences are directional in the sense that they grow in "complexity," one step laying a foundation for the next. (6) Life changes involve all aspects of the person—physiological, psychological, intellectual, emotional, spiritual, social, historical. (7) Aspects are not deterministic but "plastic." People, as in Shakespeare, shape their own ends. (8) Aspects are interdependent or "embedded"—changing at different rates, with one aspect often exerting a pull upon another.

Admittedly, there may be chasms between some of these assumptions and folk understanding of life growth. Reorganization of self, for instance, is not something that any of us can recall as we do a wrenched knee, even though such reorganization may be demonstrated when we read a book with distaste that years earlier we read with captivation, or appreciate one we once read and thought stupid. For evidence of these assumptions, look to the developmentalists, whose plentiful studies of lifespan change are characterized by rigor, scope, and intelligence. For this essay I will not question the lifespan developmental frame but instead ask what light it casts upon the Outcomes Statement. Four of the components seem especially pertinent: *sequence, complexity, plasticity,* and *embeddedness.* In the end, however, the disjunct between the fields of composition and personal development needs to be addressed, because it casts its own light on a decree that has arisen very much from the center of the composition field.

Sequence

It goes without saying that if your preoccupation is temporal sequence, then your basic unit of observation has to be no fewer than two points in time. To do otherwise would be like trying to infer direction of movement from a single photograph. The first thing a developmentalist would note about the Outcomes Statement is that it rather insistently frames itself as a snapshot taken at only one point in time ("By the end of first-year composition, students should . . ."). Sequence then has to be either inferred from the statement or imposed upon it. A developmentalist would ask, Where should students be at the *beginning* of first-year composition? Where should they be at graduation? In short, where should this poised state at the end of first-year instruction have taken and be taking students? Depending upon the answer, every item in the statement can be read in radically different ways. Should students "adopt appropriate voice" so later they can switch, integrate, or hide their own distinctive voice? Clearly, different sequences, and the authority for different sequences, will make quite different sense of the statement's end-of-course goals.

Notions of adult development authorize their sequences from a variety of sources. The most obvious are those life steps ideologically set and materially enforced by our culture: schooling before self-support, self-support before marriage, marriage before children, etc. For college students, the dominating sequence is the way education is expected to lead to work (Havighurst 1973). There is ample evidence (e.g., Astin 1993) that college students' attitudes and achievements take a developmental leap when they see themselves not just as learners-at-large but as apprentice professionals, usually with the taking on of upper-division work within a major. The way the writing of students, and their view of writing, takes qualitative jumps at that point has also been recorded (Light 1993; Sternglass 1997). It is within this compelling social sequence more than any other that the Outcomes Statement explicitly lodges itself, most noticeably in the way it recommends that subsequent-year instructors "build on" first-year outcomes by teaching competencies associated with professional fields.

A second source for sequence—and the one with the longest tradition in developmental study—is simply the lives of individuals. An instance is the way students shift in their conception of authorship during college. Longitudinal studies have found first-year students with a weak awareness that textbooks are authored by live people. Only gradually do they read with a sense that the words on the page emerge from the limited experience and perspective of individual writers (Haas 1994; Haswell 1994; Wineberg 1991). Here it will be noted that the statement isolates no outcomes connected with this reading ability. In fact, under Rhetorical Knowledge, the recommendation that students should "understand how genres shape reading and writing" might be taken as an outcome that would block students from making that critical step. A developmental rewriting of the Outcomes Statement might well add a new "build-on" to this section, recommending that faculty can help students learn that while genres shape reading and writing, genres may also imbue writers with false authority that needs to be deconstructed. Generally the "build-on" sections of the statement picture a nonproblematic continuation of outcomes, while life-story studies of individuals picture a conflicted transformation of positions. Both the statement and lifespan studies cheer us on, but the cry of the one is *Allons, enfants* and of the other is *Reculer pour mieux sauter.*

A third source for developmental sequences, group comparisons, suggests another way the statement might be written more usefully. Normative change in language competency can be mapped by comparing different college classes at the same time or the same group at different years, using the same prompts and measures. Rarely is change smooth. The maps show periods of focus, laissez-faire, and concession. Vocabulary is a case in point. College undergraduates show rapid increase in their working vocabulary (e.g., Haswell 2000; Newberry 1967), but the change seems to be largely in the area of formal vocabulary, especially technical jargon, and so probably means some regression in the kind of plain diction promoted by writing handbooks. The statement recommends the teaching of "specialized vocabulary," an advance that students are making on their own, but wouldn't it be better to teach students to recenter that advance?

Essentially, sequence is a refinement of succession. To its credit, the statement recognizes that first-year achievements are parts of a succession, are moments in a moving stream: "As writers move beyond first-year composition, their writing abilities do not merely improve. Rather, students' abilities . . . move into whole new levels where expected outcomes expand, multiply, and diverge." This takes a strong developmental stance. But it also declines a fine developmental opportunity. How much more meaningful should the statement describe its "knowledges" and "processes" as a sequence, that is, with predicted and meaningful changes at more than one academic level—say, at entry, end of first year, and end of second year.

Complexity

A fourth source of developmental sequence is internal logic. The basic assumption is that developmental sequences will tend to evolve from less to more complex—more complex in the sense that the new structuring is based logically or pragmatically on the previous structuring. A first position of trust in "durable categories" (the assumption that what holds for one person holds for everyone) is entailed in a later position of "cross categories" (the assumption that some principles connect differing individual viewpoints) (Kegan 1994), or an ability to handle problems cognitively (knowing *how* to compute figures) is entailed in an ability to handle problems metacognitively (understanding *when* figures should be computed) (Kitchener 1983). Such internal logic might raise compositionists' fear of "you have to . . . before you can," but only if we accept the highly unlikely rule that people always take the logical way as they live out their lives. Alas, people who ought to know better—though probably for cogent developmental reasons—sometimes act as though everyone else sees categorically as they do, or sometimes discover they need to compute in a way they never learned or have forgotten.

Among its various "outcomes," the statement does not distinguish degrees of complexity. Sometimes the result is a little unreal. Under Critical Thinking, Reading, and Writing, the statement expects first-year students to "Understand a writing assignment as a series of tasks," a narrative-order or "second-order consciousness" outcome that we reasonably might look for in schoolchildren, and to "Understand the relationships among language, knowledge, and power," a trans-system or "fifth-order consciousness" outcome found only in a minute portion of college graduates (the terms are from Kegan 1994). A widespread developmental finding is that reflective or metaconscious understanding aids qualitative advance in learning only when it is directed to knowledge or skills already learned and somehow felt inadequate. Reflexivity is a step, for example, that takes one from a position of apprentice to practitioner (Schön 1987) or from a passive agent to an active agent in one's emotional life (Bearison and Zimiles 1986). When the statement asks students to reflect, it makes more developmental sense when the target is audience needs, and less when the target is professional genres, in which first-year students are unlikely to have had the working skills, goals, privileges, and disappointments that would make metathinking profitable. Does it profit to "Understand the relationships among language, knowledge, and power" if one does not have the power or does not doubt the knowledge?

Imagine a first-year outcomes statement that would sort writing processes, skills, knowledge, and metaknowledge into four categories: already internalized, in acquisition, in doubt, and for the future. It would be a much more contentious decree, but more realistic from a developmental perspective.

Plasticity and Embeddedness

For sequence developmentalists also draw upon value systems, upon not only what does happen but also upon what could or should happen. Of course, none of the sequences already mentioned take the form of pure biological imperative. Instead they draw a picture of individuals slowing down and speeding up, hesitating forward and circling back, a picture not of mechanical drive but of human "plasticity" (e.g., Gollin 1981).[1] Any one of the sequences could be altered with changes in society and schooling. Students, for instance, could arrive at college with a much stronger awareness of textbook authorship had they been thoroughly exercised in the kind of author role-playing described by Graves and Hansen (1983). To a certain degree, all the sequences assume human plasticity, the ability to change direction, and thus are idealized or value laden (Bruner 1986b).

Consider gender "crossover," the postadolescent sequence distinguished by males gravitating toward culturally defined feminine positions and females toward masculine positions. Sometimes crossover is presented as a cultural effect (e.g., Giele 1980), sometimes as a postsecondary educational effect (e.g., Baxter-Magolda 1992), sometimes as a literacy effect (e.g., Peterson 1991). Other times, though, it much more takes the shape of a moral ideal. Labouvie-Vief (1994), for instance, offers the sequence as a healthy personal life-course choice but one that today is countercultural, a new turn in the way Western civilization has developed since the classic Greeks. The Outcomes Statement is gender washed, of course—a choice that might surprise many developmentalists, who would find it hard to believe that all these outcomes are pertinent or proactive for first-year college males and females equally.

Or that both males and females will stress all outcomes equally. Can we expect or want all students to achieve all of this spectrum of writerly outcomes across the board? Everything that is known about development argues strongly that such is not the way people learn. With a skill as complex as writing, individuals progress on only a few subskills at once, and since subskills interact, then advance of the others is characteristically uneven (Feldman 1980 is a now-classic description of this "embedded" process).

All in all, the general developmental judgment on the Outcomes Statement is mixed. The statement accords best where it implies that the outcomes stand as a way station in the middle of an ongoing journey (as with the "build-on" sections), not as a terminal sufficient for the rest of an educational career. As criterial points, made explicit for students and teachers to consider and use, the outcomes serve a general developmental purpose of making things metaconscious—a step that often helps a developmental cycle spiral on to a new level (Bruner 1986a). In terms of particular well-documented adult developmental sequences, some of the outcomes fit well enough, others do not. But where the Outcomes Statement most transgresses developmental lore, it does as a whole, not part by part. To the degree that the Outcomes Statement mirrors the all-angles-covered format of a rhetoric textbook or of a professionally sanctioned program, it departs most deeply from the developmental frame.

OUTCOMES AND HUMAN CONTEXTS

In response, the Outcomes Statement argues that these developmental concerns lie beyond its purview. Its job is to "describe *only* what we expect to find at the end of first-year experience" (my emphasis). It just lays out certain educational "results" at one curricular moment. In college at thirty semester hours students should "focus on a purpose" in their writing. If they don't, they are simply not where the curriculum expects them to be. In *our* frame, the statement would argue, these students are unlearned. In *your* frame they are remedial or "developmental." To "focus on a purpose" is a learning outcome; the before and after is a development outcome, if you wish.

The developmentalist's counter response is twofold. First, to separate learning and development evokes a false distinction. They are the same. Any developmental change is an act of learning; any act of true learning is developmental. That is why developmentalists, in fact, dislike the term *developmental* as applied to students who happen not to have learned what educators expect them to have learned at the start of a particular course. That is why a developmentalist would do a double take on reading the title of this commentary. The "developing learner"? What other kind is there? To "focus on a purpose" is also and always a developmental outcome, and to term it a "learning outcome" will not erase the before-and-after that is part of its nature. All it takes to realize that before-and-after nature is to imagine the possibility that the great majority of students could demonstrate all the statement's outcomes on the first day of first-year composition. Then the statement has no reason to exist.

Second, the nature of an outcome such as "to focus on a purpose" is even more radically developmental. To call it a learning outcome puts it in a particular semantic box, but *not* to call it a developmental reality is to help make the box meaningless. It strips it of one of the contexts without which the words are little more than empty placeholders.

I want to clarify this important point by looking at a single developmental study. Practically any recent investigation might make the same basic point, but the piece is especially instructive because it deals with a kind of language performance that glosses the terms of my example from the statement, "focus" and "purpose." The study was undertaken by Carol Feldman, Jerome Bruner, David Kalmar, and Bobbi Renderer and published in 1993 as "Plot, Plight, and Dramatism: Interpretation at Three Ages." The researchers read aloud the same short story to individuals who formed three participant groups: children aged ten to twelve, adolescents aged fifteen to nineteen, and adults aged twenty-six to forty-nine. Each participant was asked questions at fixed points during the reading, and finally asked to retell the story and to give the gist of it. The story, "Truth and Consequences" by Brendan Gill, about a young man caught between romance, seminary, and his mother's wishes, is easy to follow but open to interpretation.

The basic finding of the study is clear cut. The way participants recounted the events differed little across age groups, but the way groups *interpreted* the events, the narrative model by which they made sense of the story as a whole, changed consistently.[2] The children looked for *plot*, simple motives leading directly to action by characters identified as occupying categorical roles: "He says he can't because he is a priest." The adolescents looked for *plight*, characters with a time-bound inner being whose past inexorably leads through current circumstances to a future that remains poorly understood: "To go out into the world, he would have to break ties with his mother." Adults looked for *dramatism* (in Kenneth Burke's sense), a situation composed of different factors (agents, actions, scenes, motives, etc.) whose clashes create tension and irresolvability: "He's trying to do the right thing without really knowing why he's trying to do it." On hearing the same language artifact, the groups shape it into different cultural stories. The adolescents write a narrative of people driven by uncontrollable inner forces, a de Maupassant tale of fatalism. The adults write a psychosocial drama, a troubled situation in which conflicting elements struggle, a Chekhov play with comic and ironic undertones.

What happens when we read the Outcomes Statement in light of "Plot, Plight, and Dramatism: Interpretation at Three Ages"? The implications are not minor. First, the statement will be seen as a document whose every item will probably be interpreted differently by students and teachers or administrators. To first-year students, "focus on a purpose" may mean to write a paper supporting a point that the teacher believes in, to upper-division students it may mean to ape the topics and conventions of the professional field, to teachers it may mean to find and maintain a position that surprises or challenges the reader. So too with the Outcomes Statement as a whole. Students are likely to envision, plightwise, a series of unavoidable hurdles en route to some undefined future state. Teachers are likely to envision a set of overlapping constraints and goals promoted by different constituents with conflicting motives (chairs, deans, politicians, public, past teachers, present students, etc.). In sum, the Outcomes Statement does not exist outside of the interpretation of it, and, as Feldman et al. put it, interpretation itself—that fundamental human condition—appears "to undergo interesting and rather systematic reorganization with age and development" (1993, 340).

Second, it is the same for all the fundamentals of human behavior. Lifespan study has always focused on fundamentals because they are always on the move; they are life-changes in the parameters of perception, in the organizations of thought, in the structures and impulses of sex, in the shaping power of emotions, in the schemas of discourse, in the mechanisms of the drive to learn—life-changes, perforce, in the primary motives and motivations for writing that lie more deeply than the epiphenomena listed in the Outcomes Statement. They lie more deeply because they lie as deeply as the givens of home, experience, age, ethnicity, class, sex, and culture—givens that are the "master statuses . . . that must be implicated in the process by which identities form and change" (Stryker 1987, 100), and whose combinations guarantee that no two students will perform their way through the statement's outcomes—universal as they would like to appear—at the same rate, from the same time and place, with the same understanding, via the same route, and to the same effect.

In a word, all the human contexts by which the statement will be realized show developmental change throughout our lives on this planet. As Feldman et al. say, how students will understand and deal with the outcomes is "a matter not only of cognitive but also of cultural development, the two being inextricably connected in the act of interpretation" (1993, 336). The irony is that developmental theory has been questioned or ignored by compositionists supposedly because it does not "directly acknowledge the social aspects of writing" (Jameison and David 1998, 31).[3] Yet in the light of lifespan studies it is the Outcomes Statement that seems to neglect social context, and it is the developmental frame that could rescue a vital part of the human context needed to help give the outcomes meaning and function. Maybe here is why development has so often been questioned within composition circles. Might it not be the field of composition that still cannot absorb the fact of contextualism and that brackets the temporal developmental frame because it brings with it contexts more powerful, or at least more basic, than temporary programmatic decrees?

21

PRACTICE
The Road to the Outcomes over Time

Marilyn S. Sternglass

The introduction to the Outcomes Statement states its most important principle: "Learning to write is a complex process, both individual and social, that takes place *over time* with continued practice and informed guidance" (emphasis added). In light of that observation, it seems critical to distinguish between outcomes at the end of first-year composition courses and outcomes over the college years. The notion of *continued practice over time* is one that I emphasized strongly in my book, *Time to Know Them* (1997), by recounting the experiences of students who started at basic writing levels and in the regular freshman composition course at the City College of City University of New York in 1989, following them to graduation in 1995. Through assignments, both in composition courses and discipline-area courses, *over the years*, that stressed critical reading, critical writing, and practice with the processes of analysis and synthesis, these students learned to undertake the complex writing tasks demanded of them. Simultaneously, students with second-dialect and second-language backgrounds were gradually able to improve their control of the conventions of academic writing. All of these processes required instructional support that emphasized conceptual development while encouraging and facilitating the grammatical forms that enhanced the expression of the students' ideas.

Critical reading is the primary skill that students must acquire in their first year of college and it can best be learned through demands for critical writing. In the first-year composition courses, students benefit most when they are challenged to investigate a variety of topics analytically, while simultaneously being encouraged to incorporate or modify their own worldviews as the Outcomes Statement proposes. Rather than expecting full competence, instructors of first-year composition courses should see their role as giving students the opportunity to *practice* the processes of analysis and synthesis, which the students will develop further in upper-level courses.

Writing as a means of learning has frequently been described as having three stages: (1) as recall (primarily of facts); (2) as the ability to organize and synthesize information; and (3) as the ability to apply information to create new knowledge (Sternglass 1997, 19–20). The Outcomes Statement says that by the end of first-year composition students should be able to analyze and synthesize appropriate primary and secondary sources. While this is an admirable goal, this competence cannot be seen to be universal in regard to all readings since the ability to respond in this way is dependent on background knowledge brought to the assigned readings. When complex cognitive processes are examined through a longitudinal lens, it is possible to see that the ability to handle them is not always linear in that students may be responding to one task at one level and to another task at a different level. This can be accounted for by considering the prior knowledge the student has in relation to a particular task and to the student's commitment to that task (Sternglass 1986).

While the Outcomes Statement proposes "using writing and reading for inquiry, learning, thinking, and communication," it does not address the potential difficulties for students from a range of backgrounds who may differ markedly in the prior knowledge they bring to an assigned reading. The importance of prior knowledge has been a fundamental tenet of the psycholinguistic model of reading (see Goodman 1967; Smith 1978). Whether students read at a literal or an interpretive level is heavily dependent on what they know about the subject being introduced in the reading. That knowledge may be factually based or based on the students' prior experiences and worldview. An important consideration for instructors of first-year writing is to select reading materials that will challenge their students but not frustrate them. When students bring adequate background knowledge to a reading, they will be prepared to go beyond using writing as a means of simply "retelling" a story or "recounting" the information they have been exposed to. To stimulate the process of analysis, it is essential to encourage students to incorporate their prior knowledge and their worldviews into writings about topics that they create, thus fostering an environment in which they see that their viewpoints are respected and valued. Writing combined with reading in this way provides opportunities for students to try out their perspectives and gain from critical responses by their instructors and their peers. It is precisely this continuous practice that must start in the first-year writing courses with the understanding that students may not master the ability to analyze all materials effectively at first. But by being given opportunities to increase their knowledge base and to practice analyzing increasingly complex materials, they will be preparing themselves for the still more difficult materials they will encounter in their discipline-area courses.

The importance of prior knowledge is stressed by researchers who describe transactional models of reading (see Rosenblatt 1978; Bleich 1978; Petrosky 1982; Harste 1984). For Harste, the combination of prior knowledge and text results in a shift from information transfer to transaction. Instead of the primary focus being on the transfer of information, the reader constructs a new meaning in this transaction that results in "a new event, larger than the sum of its parts." In the writing that is produced in response to this "new event" in their reading, writers have the opportunity to create a text that will bring original perspectives to their own readers.

This opportunity to create original perspectives is especially important for students who come from backgrounds where their perspectives have not always been acknowledged or valued. The students in my longitudinal study, of primarily African American, Latino, and Asian backgrounds, brought sensitive responses to readings that would have been unarticulated by students from middle-class European backgrounds. For example, Chandra, an African American communications major, wrote a paper titled, "The Media Image of Black Women: Mammies, Sapphires, and Jezebels." In this paper, she argued that "television perpetuates and reinforces cultural stereotypes. Thus, viewers must become critical thinkers and decoders of this information that we are force-fed every day." Then she went on to ask: "But who controls what we see?" Arguing that television programming is controlled by "white males," she questions how "black women are portrayed in situation comedies." Seen as "Mammies" (servants responsible for domestic duties and rearing children), "Sapphires" (talkative and sassy), or "Jezebels" (shapely seductresses who use their sexuality to get their way), "blacks were locked into stereotypes" as the only way of even being included. Citing the research of others, Chandra noted that television has "evolved from just being a tool for escapism to become the myth makers, the story teller and the passer of old cultural ideas." She also argued that "television's unspoken motive was to sell the 'American dream,' a white way of life and values to the American public." We see in this passage an example of Chandra bringing an analytical stance to television programming that has been created by a combination of her research and her life experiences (Sternglass 1997, 88).

Prior knowledge is also a factor in discerning the conceptual level an individual has attained in attempting a particular task. The difficulty in assigning a particular conceptual level becomes apparent when we consider the ways that writing is used in learning: recall, analysis and synthesis, and creation of new knowledge. Each of these ways of using writing would be assigned a different conceptual level, but students may respond to different reading/writing tasks depending on what knowledge was brought to that task. It is likely that students will merely regurgitate information from a text in responding to a writing assignment if there is no prior knowledge of the subject and no ability to transform that information into something personally meaningful. Instead of relegating students to a lower level of cognitive development, it is essential to consider that the students are unable at that point in their knowledge level to put the ideas into their own language. That step is an important cognitive move, but it becomes possible only when the students know enough about the subject to perform that operation.

Even seeing the improvement in analytic writing as a pure developmental process is muddied by what actually happens in different instructional settings, especially when the amount of prior knowledge differs so greatly. The difficulty in making generalizations about cognitive level can be seen in the responses a student in a basic writing class in my longitudinal study made to two different tasks in the same semester. In her second semester at the college, after having completed the second level of basic writing, Delores, who had come to the United States from the Dominican Republic four years before starting her college studies, wrote a paper for an introductory philosophy course, explaining the philosophy of Henry James:

> In his piece, "Pragmatism," William James discusses the truth of ideas. In his work, James made a mere distinction between pragmatists and intellectualists view about the truth of an idea. For intellectualists, as James describes, the truth of an idea is an inert and at the same time stationary property of an idea. Intellectualists supposition is that once an individual has reached the truth of anything the process of searching for the truth is discontinued. (Sternglass 1997, 44)

I do not wish to assert here that Delores did not understand James's ideas, but it is clear that she has stayed so close to the language of the source text that it is clearly an example of "information transfer."

In a paper that Delores wrote that same semester for her freshman composition course, she ventured further into an analytic stance. In writing about Orwell's "Shooting an Elephant," she offered her own interpretation of the effects of subjugating others on the "tyrant" himself:

> Orwell says, "A tyrant needs to wear a mask." Orwell in his essay, "Shooting an elephant" is referring to the kind of behavior that the tyrant must display in front of people they oppress. Even through they might as well behave differently following their own feelings, they have to behave as expected by the people. Even though tyrants subjugate the people, in some way or another they are also subjugating themselves by having to let feeling [be] suppress. And at the same time robbing themselves.

Although she was not yet deeply involved in her major of psychology, Delores was given an opportunity in this paper to express a compassionate sense of understanding the impact of certain behaviors on the individuals involved in such acts. And in a composition setting in which the primary readings were literary ones, critical interpretations of such texts were highly valued. Since this reading did not require complex prior knowledge to provide avenues for interpretation, Delores' ability to perform at an analytic level would certainly be judged at a higher cognitive level than in the preceding example during the same semester (Sternglass 1997, 44–45).

Further conceptual development occurred as Delores continued in her psychology major, demonstrating her ability to both analyze and synthesize ideas from complex readings. Toward the end of her third year at the college, Delores wrote a lengthy paper on the role of social support groups in the individual's life in which she explored the roles of race and gender on an individual's ability to function in the society:

> Thus far, we have seen the influence our immediate social support groups have on our health (Psychological and physiological health). But it is not only our immediate social support group influencing our health, the group to which we hold membership and the status in which our group is regarded by society also influences important [aspects] of our lives. Our membership in groups which are regarded as high" status" or "low," "inferior" or "superior," influences the way we feel about ourselves and by the same token influences our health.

In this excerpt, we see the combination of the knowledge Delores has gained from her readings in the field of psychology and the worldview she has internalized from her background, which she has described as being a "proud Black, Latino woman" (Sternglass 1997, 45).

As stated before, the Outcomes Statement calls for students to use "writing and reading for inquiry, learning, thinking, and communication." If the notion of "inquiry" can be thought of as including the idea of "questioning," than such an outcome would carry students into the essential factor to be derived from a college education, the ability to challenge the assumptions of the society when they feel it is appropriate to do so. Some of the questioning may seem lighthearted, but even then, more serious concerns can be seen to be addressed. In a psychology class, Ricardo, a Latino student who came to the United States from Puerto Rico as a young adult, wrote a paper in which he asserted his confidence in himself as a complex, autonomous person, even as he presented an analysis of what some might consider a trivial topic, the color of the umbrella he carried:

> In the last month as the winter waned away and spring began to entice in its spell an interesting event kept repeating itself every time I used my colorful bright umbrella. I received from fellow students, friends, and acquaintances a very similar comment, they all asked if I took my wife's umbrella. I gave the same answer to all of them and that was that it was indeed my umbrella. That is not your umbrella! or they said, That is a woman's umbrella, not a man's umbrella! I was shock by their response to my colorful umbrella and I decide to give it some thought.
>
> I began to question what made my umbrella men or a woman umbrella? So began a little search for some ideas about what they thought? I began with a young female student who said, those colors are not man colors they are woman colors. She was referring to the bright yellow, greens, blues and red colors over a white background on my umbrella. I ask her why I couldn't have those colors on my umbrella at that moment a fellow student (who happens to be gay) told me, those bright colors are saying to the world, look I'm here and I'm gay! I answered that I like my umbrella because those colors make me feel good in a cloudy/gray rainy day. It was to no avail. They all have a prejudice against my poor little umbrella. (Sternglass 1997. 93–94)

As this excerpt reveals, Ricardo was not threatened by the views of those who critiqued his individualism, and although he was married, he clearly felt no constraint about being identified with men who were gay. He asserted his right to be a nonconformist both in his dress and in his actions.

Another student in the longitudinal study, Donald, who was placed directly into the freshman composition course, wrote a paper for that course comparing the discrimination against minorities with that leveled against immigrants in the field of higher education. Drawing on his own experiences as an African American, he described the advice given to him and other minority students by his high school guidance counselor:

> Under personal experience in high school, my guidance counselor many times tried to discourage minorities from applying to well-known and respected colleges. Even with an acceptable grade point average, they were told it would be impossible to be accepted. After this belief from my counselor was issued many went on their own and applied. And to their surprise, they were; well many were accepted. And to our surprise many non-minorities with poor grade point averages were encouraged [to apply].

Although Donald's voice was muted in this discussion, his sense of personal outrage at this type of treatment is apparent. Furthermore, his experience provides just a small window into the obstacles that many minority students face as they attempt to negotiate the "system," which is often closed to them (Sternglass 1997, 78).

As these two excerpts reveal, questioning the accepted mores of society is an essential component leading to the kind of learning, thinking, and communicating that fosters responsible values in individuals. Writing is the means by which students are encouraged to grapple more deeply with the important issues of their time.

Just as the ability to read more complex materials and to handle more complex writing tasks through the processes of analysis and synthesis develops over time, so does the ability to gain control over the surface features of writing such as syntax, grammar, punctuation, and spelling. Absolute control of these conventions cannot be expected of all students by the end of first-year composition, nor should it be. If instructors become too fixated on these forms, they are likely to pay less attention to the content of the student writing, a characteristic already frequently noted when students are evaluated in timed, impromptu writing tests that are used for placement into the varying levels of composition offered at a particular institution. Minority students with second-dialect language features or immigrant students with second-language backgrounds are the ones most often penalized, but the same difficulty applies to other native speakers who produce nonstandard features in their writing. Second-language users who have the least expertise in academic English are often placed in English as a Second Language (ESL) classes until they have acquired enough proficiency to be placed into composition classes.

But, as for many of the students in my study, those who do not produce a great many grammatical features that identify them as second-language users may be placed into basic writing classes. The problem is not that students who use nonstandard features in their writing may not benefit from an additional semester of composition, but that they continue to be discriminated against even when they are enrolled in the freshman composition course and upper-level required core courses and their majors. Such students may have their work evaluated on the correctness of the forms rather than the sophistication of their ideas.

The Outcomes Statement is somewhat contradictory on the handling of conventions in writing. On the one hand, it states that by the end of first-year composition, "students should *control* such surface features as syntax, grammar, punctuation, and spelling" (emphasis added). But then the statement goes on: "Faculty in all programs and departments can build on this preparation by helping students learn 'strategies through which better control of conventions can be achieved.'" Since the latter statement acknowledges correctly that full control cannot be expected to be achieved by the end of the first-year composition courses, the first statement should be modified to indicate that by the end of first-year composition, students should have been *practicing* the conventions of syntax, grammar, punctuation, and spelling, *working toward full control.* In this way, the emphasis on mastering these conventions would be continued, but unrealistic and unfair expectations would not be generated.

Composition teachers and upper-level instructors must learn the sequences of development in language features so that, for example, an Asian student who omits articles in a piece of writing or an African American student who omits some past tense verb markers is not condemned for carelessness or heavily penalized. It is likely the case that each student is aware of the expected grammatical form, but does not control the particular form *automatically.* In such cases, instructors must be knowledgeable about *patterns* of language use so that they can see when students are still erratic about one or two instances of a pattern that is otherwise well controlled.

Placement and exit exams for composition courses are insidious in providing hazards for students with second-dialect or second-language backgrounds. In the case of the first, the placement exam, the student is confronted with a timed, impromptu test demanding essentially all the components of writing required for entrance into the regular composition course, requirements that are probably not too different from the outcomes required to complete the course. Students who fail to demonstrate such competence are then placed either into basic writing sections or into ESL programs. The instruction in these courses deliberately teaches the students to write drafts and later edit their texts, including the formal conventions of writing. But when these students confront the exit examinations, again timed, impromptu writing is demanded and no time for editing is available. Thus, the instruction has set the students up for likely failure, when they lack the time to edit their writing. Another difficulty faced by second-language students in particular is their potential unfamiliarity with the cultural aspects of the topics they are asked to write about in these placement and exit tests (Gleason 1997).

Instead of demanding control of these surface features by the end of first-year composition courses, instructors should focus on making students familiar with the patterns they are having difficulty in controlling. By pointing out such features, instructors can assist students in differentiating between those patterns they control automatically and those that still require specific attention. A particularly dramatic example of a student having difficulty with one particular feature in his writing appeared in a piece of writing produced by a Latino student for a communications course. In the paper, Ricardo was very critical of what he called the "media stereotypes" in Spike Lee's film *Do the Right Thing:*

> A Teleologist *would examined* the consequences brought by the uses of stereotypes and he or she *would not justified* the use of them. They will argue that the use of stereotypes encourages prejudice and discrimination upon any ethnic group and that the consequences will always be harmful to those groups which are being portrayed.
>
> A theorist using Aristotles Golden Means theory *cannot justified* them either. Their decision is based upon the analysis that *did not presented* diversity or I should say, he *did not presented* a range of characters within those ethnic groups. He just presented the groups as one. [emphasis added]

Although the instructor carefully marked each inappropriate verb form, there was no comment about the patterns of verb endings, each incorrect one being attached to a modal or negative auxiliary verb. It is clear that Ricardo had overgeneralized the past tense forms of regular verbs, but without his attention being called to this pattern, he would be likely to continue using these forms, seeing only discrete verb forms marked by his instructor (Sternglass 1999).

As is apparent from the discussion presented here, the Outcomes Statement posits many important processes that must ultimately be mastered by college students. My recommendation would be that the statement be read as one that identifies the processes that students should be *practicing* throughout the college years and that the assumption should not be made that students have *mastered* all these processes by the end of the first-year writing courses. Students will be starting their freshman year with a dizzying array of different backgrounds, academically, culturally, and personally. First-year composition courses should provide them with the basis of developing the skills necessary to undertake the academic and professional tasks that await them. If students are shown *how* to approach a variety of tasks, as the outcomes listings already suggest, then students will be able to demonstrate greater competency over time. Instead of saying, "by the end of first-year composition, students *should be able to do*" the following, I believe the statement should say, "By the end of first-year composition, students *should be prepared to do*" the following. Such a change in wording would emphasize the developmental aspects of learning to read critically and write critically. As potential athletes and musicians are often told, the way to achieve success is to practice, practice, practice.

Afterword

BOWLING TOGETHER
Developing, Distributing, and Using the WPA Outcomes Statement—and Making Cultural Change

Kathleen Blake Yancey

What's left for an afterword to do?
Anne Gere

The WPA Outcomes Statement has succeeded: we know this. Patti Ericsson's research has documented this claim, and we have lists of (many kinds of) schools— from Johnson Community College and UC Santa Barbara to Arizona State and Xavier University and the *entire* Virginia Community College system—that have used it in a fundamental way, to help *shape* composition curricula: through using its concepts and vocabulary to write the composition curriculum, through designing activities that lead to demonstration of the WPA outcomes, through creating assessments that link these activities and outcomes. We also know that other institutions not on the "Ericsson" list have used it as well: Hawkeye Community College, for example, and UNC Greensboro.[1] In addition, we know that at many institutions the statement has been applied in achieving *other* purposes related to the delivery of first-year composition: helping to professionalize teaching assistants, for instance, and inviting students to assess their own work in the specific language of the outcomes as part of their own development.

Moreover, assisting such efforts—and perhaps commodifying them, depending on your perspective—textbook authors and publishers have used the WPA Outcomes Statement not only as a marketing tool to sell books (such as the well-regarded and best-selling *Call to Write*) intended for use in composition classrooms, but also as means of demonstrating that the approach used in the text is congruent with the principles espoused in the statement. (This point is worth repeating: the statement is informing the textbooks, even if after the fact, and not the reverse, as is historically the case.) And we know that the authors and publishers of books intended to "train" teachers of composition also want to locate their appeal, in part at least, in the WPA Outcomes Statement.

One small claim, then, is that the Outcomes Statement has been fundamental in changing the first-year composition course at many institutions.

BEYOND THE INITIAL CLAIM, SOME RESERVATION(IST)S, AND A COMP THAT MATTERS

A second claim is that the WPA Outcomes Statement has been used in writing and learning contexts beyond first-year composition, in contexts students participate in both before they enroll in first-year comp—and after. It has been used with teachers in high schools, for example, not to script their practice, but to facilitate articulation between the two contexts, to see what vocabulary and concepts college and high school writing curricula *share* as well as to see how these contexts for learning are (appropriately) *differentiated*. The statement has also been used, in the postsecondary setting, as part of review and reform of general education—at the University of North Carolina at Chapel Hill, at the University of Wyoming, and at Clemson University, to name three such locations. It has been highlighted nationally at conferences hosted by the two major professional organizations representing higher education: in 2000, the Outcomes Statement was part of a plenary session of the American Association of Colleges and Universities (AAC&U); in 2003, it was part of a keynote session of the American Association of Higher Education's (AAHE) Assessment Conference (Yancey 2003a). Given that the most important point of influence is the student, and given that the student takes with him or her the experience of first-year comp, the WPA Outcomes Statement would necessarily exert influence beyond the composition classroom: we understood that. What's interesting is that such influence has been extended more formally and structurally, through making curricular connections with those who work with our students both *before* they become our students and *afterward*.

More generally, then, it's fair to say that the Outcomes Statement has spoken to numerous stakeholders—students, teaching assistants, faculty teaching first-year comp and faculty administering programs, colleagues in other disciplines, the leaders of major organizations seeking to reinvigorate undergraduate education. Which, however, is not to say that the statement has met with unqualified endorsement, even within composition studies.

In our field, we have to assume, I think, that many if not most teachers of first-year composition are only vaguely aware of the statement, *if*
they are aware of it at all. Certainly, most of our colleagues across campus
are happily ignorant of it, as demonstrated by the fall 2003 writing-the-
matized issue of AAC&U's *Peer Review*, whose articles discussing current
writing programs cite the WPA Outcomes Statement not once. And of
those who are aware, some are not amused—or gratified. Derek Soles,
for instance, responded to the publication of the statement in *College
English* with concern that it did not include an endorsement of specific
philosophies of composition, from expressionism with its "self-hyphen-
ated words" (2002, 378) to the "radical agenda[s]" (377) of feminism and
Marxism, nor, he (rightly) said, did it seek to whet the appetites of upper-
level administrators for student "academic and career success" (378). His
point: the individual teacher's composition philosophy should trump the
curricular commonality of the Outcomes Statement.[2] James Zebroski, in
"Composition and Rhetoric, Inc.," complained about the same issue, but
from another perspective. In discussing the role of knowledge making in
composition, he refers readers to the "recent[ly] vetted" WPA statement
endorsing a "limited notion of knowledge in composition and rhetoric"
(2002, 179). Although the point is not elaborated, one inference of
Zebroski's critique is a concern that in trying to speak to such a broad
mandate and set of conditions, the authors of the statement have diluted
the substantive purposes of first-year composition unacceptably.

Still. Still. *Still.* What's remarkable is that *anyone* is paying attention at
all.[3] In other words, to paraphrase Shirley Logan's 2003 CCCC address
and Doug Hesse's 2004 CCCC conference theme, a lot of someones
(finally) seem to know that we are here—and that we is the we of the WPA
Outcomes Statement, and not the we of grammar, as is so often the case,
nor the we of a benighted elite seeking to corrupt students through a
radical agenda, which is how we are often presented to the public at large,
as we see in the case of UT Austin. Which itself leads to a simple question:
Why? Why is it that the Outcomes Statement has exerted—and continues
to exert—such influence?

THE TECHNOLOGY OF DISSEMINATION, THE RHETORICAL
MOMENT, AND COMMUNITIES OF PRACTICE

A cynical answer to the question of why the Outcomes Statement has been
so successful might be that since it promises much but costs little, it's an
easy statement to endorse. In other words, were we to in fact abide by the

recommendations of other, like-minded reform documents—and I take the Outcomes Statement to be a reform document—it would be trickier and certainly more expensive, which in turn may be why some of our sister documents have not wielded more influence. If the recommendations made in the CCCC Position Statement on Assessment were followed, for example, institutions would need to abandon all indirect measures of writing—especially standardized tests on grammar and usage—in favor of assessments, like portfolios, that enhance learning. Even apart from the administrative costs, this would be an expensive—although useful—transition for many schools. The Wyoming Resolution, if followed, would be even more expensive since it requires faculty to be paid a living wage, with benefits. By way of contrast, the Outcomes Statement neither requires new practices for students nor mandates any structural change, and thus it incurs no new costs. By way of contrast, it's easy to endorse.

Another quick explanation accounting for the statement's success might also be considered instrumental: the distribution of the document. In this case, however, the distribution was means and method both and substantive as well. Several points about its early distribution are worth noting. First, from the very beginning of the effort, the document was as widely distributed as possible, *even as it was being developed.* Making it available from the start permitted people both to try it out as we went forward *and* to speak back to it. Second, because the document was widely distributed—to high school teachers as well as to college faculty, for instance—thinking about the document occurred in many different sites; it was thus developed in a multicontextual environment. Third, the statement-in-process was made available in several media: first, of course, as a draft document, used in person at conferences and workshops; *and* delivered as a draft in the pages of *WPA: Writing Program Administration; and* made available to anyone and all on the Web. Fourth, the point of the distribution wasn't to announce only (although that was certainly its purpose in part), but to solicit response as well. In other words, getting the statement "out there" also constituted an invitation to participate in its formation.

Once adopted by the WPA, the statement was again made available in several venues: on the WPA Web site; in the pages of *College English,* when editor Jeanne Gunner invited its publication; reprinted in various program handouts and conference presentations across the country. Not long after the statement's adoption, WPA received requests from textbook authors and publishers to reprint it. Put generally, then, one reason that the Outcomes Statement has succeeded is that it was widely distributed, and that its distribution was understood as a means of development. As important is the fact that the statement was distributed by the *technology of the discipline* rather than only by the technology of an organization: conference presentations and workshops of various kinds, including WPA, CCCC, and NCTE; the Web sites, the journals, the textbook industry, and now, of course, this volume. That technology, in turn, fed the technologies of higher education, both on local campuses in their larger reform efforts and in professional organizations like AAHE.

From a Bitzerian perspective, the process of the document's development, as well as the way that development was managed, was highly unusual, and this too has played a role in the success of the statement. Ordinarily, as the history of composition reform documents suggests, such documents are "commissioned" by a professional organization. The WPA's document on WPA Work as Intellectual Work exemplifies this observation, as does the CCCC Committee on Learning, Teaching, and Assessing in Digital Environment, a group I am currently chairing and whose sole purpose is to develop a position paper on these topics. In each case, the leaders of the organization, sometimes acting on their own and sometimes responding as well to specific calls from the memberships, charge an organization's subgroup to create the document. The amount of oversight of the document's development varies (according to the nature of the topic, the timeline, the temperamental disposition of the leaders, and so on), but at the end of the day, the organization itself—ordinarily through the commissioning, oversight, and approval process of its executive committee or board—plays a role in authoring the document. By way of contrast and, again, as articulated in this volume, the WPA Outcomes Statement developed quite differently: there was no organizational charge; there was no oversight; there were suggestions for revision, but there was adoption rather than approval.

The exigence for the Outcomes Statement, although not framed in this language at the time, was identified by a grassroots movement as doubled. Seen from one vantage point, one exigence was a frustration with the panoply of composition courses and approaches used in various programs and a sense that this seeming incoherence (1) made composition programs vulnerable; and (2) wasn't necessary, could be addressed. One Bitzerian response, then, was to create the document that would speak to and resolve this frustration. From a second vantage point, a second and related exigence has to do with a question: *Could such a document be written?* It was, as I said in the introduction to its publication in *College English,* the first time such a curricular statement had even been *attempted* (Outcomes Statement Steering Committee 2001). The effort, then, was twofold: to explore the *possibility* of creating a coherent set of outcomes for students at all kinds of schools and, if possible, to articulate such a curriculum as well.

The Bitzerian response, of course, occurred within an immediate context, that of the WPA listserv, which itself deserves note. In the language of today, we would say that this listserv is a virtual *community of practice,* a major concept currently informing educational reform, especially at the national level. Such communities, be they virtual or face-to-face, are "groups who interact regularly in order to explore common problems, build new ideas, develop relationships and address shared interests" (Wenger et al. 2002). *Interacting* is the key piece: it is the interacting through which both community and knowledge are made. Moreover, the interacting is highly ritualized, either explicitly or implicitly, often focused on a particular goal or outcome, guided by rituals that occur within a collective activity that is *ongoing.* Although they may be linked to or sponsored by a formal group, such communities often have a voluntary dimension to them. And such communities, according to Wenger and others, have been highly successful in achieving their goals. The participants in creating the Outcomes Statement seem to constitute a community of practice.[4] We had a goal; because of the electronic medium, we interacted very frequently, and we mixed that interaction with f2f meetings, presentations, and workshops. We saw ourselves as an ongoing group, and indeed we accomplished our goal.

Before we had developed the language to identify who we were, we were already members of a community of practice.

FIVE CRITICAL DECISIONS

Although many factors explain the success of the Outcomes Statement, in retrospect, five critical decisions seem especially important:

- Deciding to separate the statement's outcomes from standards that might apply
- Deciding that the statement should be a "living" text, such that even the outcomes written into the statement should be changed as local needs recommended
- Deciding that a chief purpose of the statement was to assist with faculty development

- Deciding to use a vocabulary that might appear unfamiliar to many but that was the vocabulary of the discipline
- Deciding to use a "gateway in" approach—one focused on the exit point of the curriculum, regardless of where that might be—in locating the outcomes

Each of these merits some explanation.

Deciding to separate the statement's outcomes from standards that might apply. The (first) genius of the statement stems from the ways it parsed the relationship between and among outcomes, standards, national, and local. The statement itself would be national in scope, would seek to speak to every (kind of) first-year composition curriculum in every (kind of) institution. At the same time, each of these institutions would have the "right" to set its own standards, which was a neat way of accommodating the very clear differences that define campuses. This ability to straddle both the local and the national, indeed, is a key feature of the statement. And a quick review of how the statement has been used demonstrates that, indeed, campuses with very different programs have used it in some of these anticipated ways.

Deciding that the statement should be a "living" text, such that even the outcomes written into the statement should be changed as local needs recommended. Just as the progression of the document's development was underprescribed, so too were admonitions about its use. The assumption, in fact, was that it would be used, it would be used variously (given different campuses and their still-different needs), and that we would learn from those differences. In general, then, it's probably fair to say that campuses were encouraged to adapt the statement to serve their students, which they have.

Deciding that a chief purpose of the statement was to assist with faculty development. As Barbara Walvoord (1996) has argued, various writing programs, particularly WAC programs, have succeeded because they have targeted faculty development as the means of making change. We worked similarly, in the process creating a document that could speak to the faculty audience as well as the student audience, and creating the idea that such a document and such an approach would be useful for any institution engaging in curricular reform. In other words, in adopting this approach, the writers of the WPA Outcomes Statement also modeled one of its uses.

Deciding to use a vocabulary that might appear unfamiliar to many but that was the vocabulary of the discipline. As Derek Soles (2002) suggests, the vocabulary of the discipline is a plural vocabulary: *critique* is a key term for a cultural studies approach, *collaboration* for many focused on active learning. At the same time, the purpose of the document itself was not to document the key terms of different approaches; we did not define this task as an accumulation of different key terms, nor did we target specific pedagogies. Rather, we tried to find a common frame that would be inclusive without being prescriptive. Given this task definition, one obvious approach might have been to revert to "standard" language that readers would recognize, to terms like *thesis* and *correctness.* Such an approach might also allow the widest possible readership and thus the greatest adoption. Another goal, however, was to write a statement that was congruent with current theory in the field, and this goal could not be satisfied with the current-traditional language of thesis and support. Ironically perhaps, the most current theory is also the oldest: rhetorical theory. Accordingly, an articulation of a composition curriculum used *rhetoric* as its principal frame, which led us to expressions like *rhetorical situation* (and the category Rhetorical Knowledge) that are not commonly understood, even in the twenty-first century. At the end of the day, however, we included many discipline-specific concepts, but the statement also includes terms like *conventions, format,* and *audience* that are familiar to nearly anyone who has taken a writing course . In this practice, the beauty of the statement is in its use of familiarity to contextualize the new and thus signal that this is a new curriculum (which is not your father's composition). As important, through this vocabulary—particularly in terms like *rhetoric* and *genre*—a new construct of writing is created, and though that, good assessment—that is, assessment of what it is that we really want—is also made possible. Or: vocabulary matters.

Deciding to use a "gateway in" approach—one focused on the exit point of the curriculum, regardless of where that might be—in locating the outcomes. Another decision that participants needed to make was how to define writing programs in the first year. Could they be thematically focused writing seminars as at Harvard? Were they computer/writing classes? Were they taught by a special group of instructors? Given basic writing, at what point did they begin, and at what point did they end? To focus our efforts, we took the end of the first-year composition program (be it course, courses, seminar) as the common point for all first-year programs. Even if students opted out, they too would demonstrate these outcomes. That decision, like many program decisions, was wise, in part because it's oriented to the gateway in rather than to gatekeeping (students out). Let me explain.

Too often, writing programs have been used, willingly or otherwise, to gatekeep, to keep students *out*. Even so, today 49 percent of all students matriculate in college. Unfortunately, too few of them complete their programs at either two-year or four-year institutions. Nationally, only 28 percent of all adults have a BS or BA degree. At 10 percent for African Americans and 1.7 percent for Latinos/Latinas (and even lower for Native Americans), the figures shrink for minority populations. And yet, as the research of Richard Light (2001) shows, writing helps keep students in school and assists them as they become professionals. The research provided by the National Survey of Student Engagement echoes this phenomenon, only from the perspective of students; students' satisfaction with postsecondary education is keyed to the frequency with which they write *across* the years of their college experience. The WPA Outcomes Statement is likewise oriented to moving students into the college experience and helping them succeed there. It is, then, oriented not to the moment of entry, but to the gateway into *the rest of the curriculum*. From an assessment perspective, this is equally important. As I have argued elsewhere (Yancey 1999), when tests do take a benign form, one of the reasons is that the test is seen, as in the case of the AP test, as a measure of a curriculum. It is linked *to* the test. In citing a negative exemplar of the same point, Mary Trachsal (1992) demonstrates that once curriculum is separated from assessment—as it has been historically in the gatekeeping moment of entry—those responsible for curriculum tend to be discounted, which of course is what we see in tests like the SAT. What the WPA Outcomes Statement does is work toward the gateway moment, thus keeping alive the hope of linking curriculum and (appropriate) assessment.

FORWARDING THE AFTERWORD

As we go forward, there are several issues we will need to consider. Among these, I'd like to highlight four.

- In *Bowling Alone*, Robert Putnam (2001) makes the case that in late-twentieth-century America, we have lost a sense of community that had previously defined America, and he further suggests that the social capital we create through community is necessary for a healthy community. Located inside the humanities, we have ordinarily constructed our work as individuals—individual teachers, separate students. Certainly, those of us interested in programs engage in a competing impulse, as we see in the

collective activity surrounding the WPA Outcomes Statement.
Nonetheless, there is more we might do. Question: In a time when
research on enhancing student development is sorely needed, how might
we engage the outcomes stipulated here? In other words, separate institutions—as the cases here identified attest—have made wonderful strides.
What if we worked together cross-institutionally with our students as we
did in creating the document? What kind of change might we make then?

- There is a small line of research indicating that asking students to work
  explicitly with the language of outcomes as they assess their own work—
  that is, to assess their own work in the language of specific outcomes—
  enhances student learning and improves the products of that learning.
  Washington State University, for instance, has developed a sophisticated
  set of criteria for critical thinking and has invited faculty to work with it
  in their classes. Some of those faculty have required students to evaluate
  their own work and to do so in the language of the criteria. Although
  the effort is young and the classes involved few, so far the student work,
  rated by independent scorers, is better than that of students who have
  not engaged in this activity. A similar finding characterizes a portfolio
  program at Portland State University, where students are asked to evaluate their writing in the language of the course, and this finding is also
  connected to significantly increased rates of student retention. Question:
  What might be the effect on student writing if several institutions tried
  such an approach with the WPA Outcomes Statement?

- One of the questions that has vexed compositionists since the modern
  iteration of composition is the *content* of composition: what is it? It's not
  uncommon, as Derek Soles (2002) attests, to think of composition as an
  almost empty vessel, eager to be filled with any number of studies, from
  cultural to queer to critical and liberation pedagogy to literacy. Indeed, as
  cogently outlined by David Bartholomae in his 1989 CCCC chair's address,
  composition's interdisciplinary quality is both charm and strength. In
  reviewing the language of the WPA outcomes, however, I have to wonder
  if what is articulated there isn't already a curriculum. Genre and language
  and rhetorical situation: they *are* the curriculum. Question: What would
  happen if we took this idea seriously and understood that we are a discipline after all, that *composition is the content of (any) composition* class and
  program? How much change might we see in student learning?

- As explained in this volume, one of the critical decisions that was made
  exempted technology as a critical component of composition. As Dennis
  Baron (1999) argues, this can make sense: the technology of composing is
  subordinate, not substantive. And it's fair to note that historically, writing

for print has played a central role in the development of students intellectually and socially; it has been placed at the heart of education institutionally as well. This document speaks to that history and to that role. At the same time, however, in school and out, on the street and in the classroom, we have already migrated to the screen and to multimedia. And there are those who would claim, myself among them, that while composition is not about technology, it *is* about the media, plural. Question: If we continue to elect to focus exclusively on print, without explicitly including the literacy of the screen, will we prepare our students for that gateway into the completion of college—and beyond? Will we endanger the relevance and even survival of our own field?

In calling our students and ourselves to what's visionary, we created new outcomes for all of us. In creating a foundation for students, we created one for programs as well.

Given the promise of the WPA Outcomes Statement that has already been realized, it's critical that this legacy be carried forward. To do otherwise would be both tragic and ironic indeed.

NOTES

CHAPTER 2 (RHODES, PECKHAM, BERGMANN, AND CONDON)

1. This became: "we expect the primary audience for this document to be well-prepared college writing teachers and college writing program administrators. In some places we have chosen to write in their professional language. . . . While we have also aimed at writing a document that the general public can understand, in limited cases we have aimed first at communicating effectively with expert writing teachers and writing program administrators."

2. This became: "As writers move beyond first-year composition, their writing abilities do not merely improve. Rather, students' abilities not only diversify along disciplinary and professional lines but also move into whole new levels where expected outcomes expand, multiply, and diverge."

CHAPTER 5 (SELFE AND ERICSSON)

1. We offer here, as a suggestion, the term CPAs (composition program administrators) rather than WPAs, as a way of acknowledging the changing nature of composition in an age and culture that is increasingly electronic and that has made what Gunter Kress (1999) calls the "turn to the visual." We use composition to accommodate the practice of creating texts that may well exceed the alphabetic—and the sociocultural values and beliefs associated with such texts. In this use, we are informed by the work of the New London Group (Cope and Kalantzis 2000), which has explored similar practices and values under the rubrics of multimodal literacies or multiliteracies.

2. A term used by Manuel Castells (1996) to refer to the era generated by the "converging set of technologies in microelectronics, computing (machines and software), telecommunications/broadcasting, and optoelectronics" (30) and the "networked society" (21) that has transformed "all domains of human activity" (31).

3. By *literacy*, we mean the practices of reading, composing, communicating, and the complex set of cultural and individual values and formations associated with these practices. By emerging literacies, we mean those literacies associated with making meaning in new kinds of electronic composing environments. Many of these literacies are visually based and not alphabetically dependent. By fading literacies, we refer to those literacies associated with making meaning in composing environments that are less frequently used now than they have been in former points in history—for instance, writing letters by hand.

4. The term *cultural ecology* we borrow, in part, from work in communication undertaken by Ronald Deibert and other scholars in that field whose work has to do with the emergence and "fitness" (Deibert 1997, 31) of communication media in historical, social, cultural, and educational contexts (Bruce and Hogan 1998; Cooper 1986). To us, however, the notion of a cultural ecology also suggests a "duality of structuring" between social systems and literacy practices that comes through more clearly in the work of Anthony Giddens (1984) and Manuel Castells (1996, 1997, 1998). In combination, the work of these scholars indicate to us that literacies emerge, compete, flourish, and fade because they share a "fitness" with the cultural ecology of a given time and place. This ecology both structures, and is structured by, human beings who use literacy as a means of strategic social action.

CHAPTER 9 (LITTLE LIU)

1. I refer here to the thousands of individuals teaching college writing courses across the country whose preparation and scholarly interests do not include composition theory, and to the similarly situated faculty still running first-year writing "programs" at hundreds of colleges and universities around the country. Those of us who are a part of the community of composition scholars, and work with colleagues like ourselves, can easily be misled into believing that our situation is the norm, but I daresay it is not.

2. To the credit of the Outcomes group, they were apparently aware of the potential misunderstandings this wording might cause. Rita Malenczyk provided me with logs of several of the MOO sessions in which the Outcomes Steering Committee refined the statement just prior to its adoption by the WPA. It is clear from those "conversations" that they struggled with this problem. One planned solution that apparently fell through was to include hyperlinks on the Web version of the Outcomes Statement which could lead a reader to different explanatory examples.

    It is also clear that they were fully aware of the complexity of the term and its implications. At various points the group considered alternative terms such as "multiple formats." But they ultimately rejected such terms because they do not get at the variety of processes and awarenesses the statement is meant to succinctly express. Finally, genre theory has to be mentioned.

    Keith Rhodes: I'm wondering if "genre theory" is really what was motivating folks so much as just not using the 5P theme for everything. Much simpler idea.

    Rita Malenczyk: I wondered that myself. But we did use the word "genre," which allows us to get genre theory in by the back door.

    Irvin Peckham: I think genre theory is behind it.

    Susanmarie Harrington: Are we agreed on "understand what genres are and how they function"?

    Keith: Agreed, the theory is informing us; but I don't think the ambitions for fyc students are high enough to invoke a great deal of it. "Functions" kinda scares me as an assessment item for fyc.

    Irv: I was suggesting: "understand what genres are and how they function."

    Susanmarie: What about if we just go with "understand what genres are?"

    Keith: I thought it was "know."

    Susanmarie: Well, it's either "know" or "understand"—

    Irv: Either.

    Susanmarie: Are we agreed on ditching the "and" . . .

    Rita: "Understand what genres are" would work for me."

    Irv: One of the problems is: genres "aren't something"—the function is the real key but . . .

    Susanmarie: I think I like "understand," myself. Ok by you, Keith?

    Keith: "That" they function might not scare me as much, but then that's ugly language.

    Susanmarie: "Very ugly. Irv, I take your point, but I think it might be something else we're backed into now. (Harrington et al. 1999)

    I've edited some off-topic chitchat from the above conversation, but the bulk of it remains. It is clear here that the group has a fully theorized understanding of the term *genre and that several of them feel uneasy—to some degree—leaving the word there on its own (with all its connotations of complex social functions left unexplicated).*

3. It is interesting to note that Peckham, in a version of the Outcomes Statement prepared for his own students' use, does not use the word genre at all; among other revisions, he replaces genre with "writing situations."

4. Joy Reid works with her ESL students to find alternatives to "I don't understand what you want" such as 'This is the first paper/review/report I have written at a U.S. university. May I make an appointment to talk with you during your office hours? (Reid 1989, 225–26).

5. While a number of collections on genre have been published, none could really qualify as an introduction to genre theory for nonspecialist composition instructors. The most likely candidate might be Freedman and Medway's Genre and the New Rhetoric (1994).

CHAPTER 13 (TOWNSEND)

1. Among those present at the June 21 meeting were Vivian Davis, Linda Flower, Maxine Hairston, George Kennedy, Richard Lanham, Richard Larson, Richard Lloyd-Jones, Richard Marius, John Munro, James Murphy, Jay Robinson, Harriet Sheridan, Jerry Ward, Thomas Whitaker, and Joseph Williams. Wayne Booth, Shirley Brice Heath, and Phyllis Franklin were invited but did not attend.

2. According to Jossey-Bass editorial assistant Melissa Kirk (November 13, 2002), Engaging Ideas has sold over twenty-two thousand copies in the eight years since it was published. Our experience at the University of Missouri, where a copy is given to each faculty member who attends a WAC workshop, is that instructors continue to use the book after the workshop and to apply WAC principles to their teaching.

3. The National Educational Goals Panel (NEGP) has since been dissolved by Congressional mandate, and its website (http://www.negp.gov) is defunct. A statement of its goals is still available at a North Central Regional Educational Laboratory site (http://www.ncrel.org/sdrs/areas/issues/envrnmnt/go/go4negp.htm), and web searches reveal links to some NEGP publications, although none are directly available from government sites as this volume goes to press.

CHAPTER 14 (HARRINGTON)

1. Indiana University Purdue University Indianapolis (IUPUI) is Indiana's comprehensive urban university campus, housing both Indiana University and Purdue University schools. The writing program is part of the English department, located in the Indiana University School of Liberal Arts. Writing courses serve undergraduate majors in English as well as students in other majors across campus.

2. Indiana University Purdue University Indianapolis (IUPUI) is Indiana's comprehensive urban university campus, housing both Indiana University and Purdue University schools.

CHAPTER 16 (HOKANSON)

1. I would like to thank my Alverno colleagues Carole Barrowman, Nancy Bornstein, and Georgine Loacker for their comments on a draft of this manuscript and especially for their longtime commitment to the development of our students as communicators.

CHAPTER 19 (ELBOW)

1. One of the main premises of the competence-based movement was that outcomes should be worked out locally, either by individual teachers or by teachers working collaboratively in a program, department, or even a whole college. The movement was based on the idea that teaching could be revitalized if teachers themselves figured out what outcomes they are teaching toward. In contrast, the Outcomes project, though impressively collaborative, aims to provide outcomes to teachers who had no hand in devising them. For the purposes of this essay I set to one side this important difference.

2. This is a structure where all students must have at least half a semester's experience in a writing workshop, but where students who make good progress earn the right to leave as early as halfway through the semester, while others may have to stay longer—maybe even well more than a semester. When a student is judged competent (by means of a portfolio) and exits, a new student enters. In this model, students have more incentive to improve their writing than in the standard semester-long, lockstep course. And the admittedly startling structure gives relief from what strikes me as the hardest thing about teaching writing: starting off each semester with a brand-new class where all are strangers to each other and none has internalized the culture of a writers' workshop. In the yogurt model, half or two-thirds of the class would always be experienced members of the culture—even on the first day of the semester. In effect, the yogurt model simulates the writers' group—where some people leave and others enter. The model also suggests experimenting with smaller "classes" of "group" size. A single teacher would be responsible for multiple groups—and thus they would have to function more autonomously than standard classes. I speak more about this in my 1996 essay, "Writing Assessment in the Twenty-first Century: A Utopian View."

CHAPTER 20 (HASWELL)

1. Not that plasticity is a concept alien to biology, far from it. As just one luminous example, see Gerald M. Edelman's book (1992) on the individual human brain as a organ physiologically modifying in reaction to daily experience.

2. The interpretive or hermeneutic approach to adult development is well established. In developmental and life-history studies, see Bruner 1986a and Freeman 1993. In composition, see Green 1985; Haswell 1991; and Phelps 1988.

3. Jameison and David's entry on "Cognitive Developmental Theory" in Kennedy's *Theorizing Composition* (1998) is a good example of the way the field of composition brackets or trivializes developmental thinking. The entry restricts itself to outdated cognitive developmentalists, and mentions none of the outpouring of social, culture, and situational studies of the last three decades. They cite only six studies in composition from the 1990s; three of the pieces argue against the use of developmental theory and the other three don't refer to it at all. None of the developmentalists cited in the present piece appear in Jameison and David. Development does not appear as an entry in Heilker and Vandenberg's Keywords in Composition Studies (1996), or in Enos's Encyclopedia of Rhetoric and Composition (1996).

AFTERWORD (YANCEY)

1. Personal communication with institutions.

2. Ironically, in this critique we see a continuing tension between the individualism of the teacher (expressivism) and the collective of the program (Marxism).

3. All too often we aren't noticed, as is all too clear. As I finish writing this chapter, the WPA listserv is exploding with discussion about the recent removal of the University of Florida composition program from the English department to the provost's office, under the codirection of a professor of classics. The WPA was, it seems, not consulted, either before the removal or as the program took a new form.

4. Composition has been informed by other communities of practice: one of the first is Portnet, a group of teacher-researchers from across the country who studied portfolios in theory and practice (see Allen 1995). For a more sustained discussion of community of practice in composition, see Yancey's "Bowling Together: Communities of Practice and the Knowledge-Making Function of Reflection" (forthcoming).

REFERENCES

Allen, Michael. 1995. Valuing Differences: Portnet's First Year. *Assessing Writing* 2.1: 67–89.

Alverno College Communication Ability Department. 1981. *Criteria for Effective Writing.* Milwaukee, WI: Alverno College Productions.

———. 1988. *Criteria for Effective Writing.* Milwaukee, WI: Alverno College Productions.

Alverno College Faculty. 1994. *Student Assessment-as-Learning at Alverno College.* Milwaukee, WI: Alverno College Institute

Astin, Alexander W. 1993. *What Matters in College? Four Critical Years Revisited.* San Francisco: Jossey-Bass.

Atkin, J. Myron. 1994. Developing World-Class Education Standards: Some Conceptual and Political Dilemmas. In Cobb 1994, 61–84.

Bakhtin, Mikhail. 1952 (reprint, 1986). The Problem of Speech Genres. Translated by Vern W. McGee. In *Speech Genres and Other Late Essays,* edited by Caryl Emerson and Michael Holquist, 60–102. Austin: University of Texas Press.

———. 1981. *The Dialogic Imagination.* Edited by Michael Holquist. Translated by Michael Holquist and Caryl Emerson. Austin: University of Texas Press.

Ballenger, Bruce and Michelle Payne. 2003. *The Curious Reader: Exploring Personal and Academic Inquiry.* New York: Longman.

Baron, Dennis. 1999. From Pencils to Pixels: The Stages of Literacy Technologies. In Hawisher and Selfe 1999, 15–33.

Bartholomae, David. 1989. Freshman English, Composition, and CCCC. *College Composition and Communication* 40: 38-50.

Bauman, Zygmunt. 1993. *Postmodern Ethics.* Oxford: Blackwell.

Baxter-Magolda, Marcia B. 1992. *Knowing and Reasoning in College: Gender-Related Patterns in Students' Intellectual Development.* San Francisco: Jossey-Bass.

Bazerman, Charles. 1988. *Shaping Written Knowledge: The Genre and Activity of the Experimental Article in Science.* Madison: University of Wisconsin Press.

Bean, John. 1986. *Engaging Ideas : The Professor's Guide to Integrating Writing, Critical Thinking, and Active Learning in the Classroom.* San Fransisco CA: Jossey Bass.

Bearison, David J., and Herbert Zimiles. 1986. Developmental Perspectives on Thought and Emotion: An Introduction. In *Thought and Emotion: Developmental Perspectives,* edited by David J. Bearison and Herbert Zimiles, 1–10. Hillsdale, NJ: Erlbaum.

Beers, Kylene. 2003. *When Kids Can't Read: What Teachers Can Do.* Portsmouth, NH: Heinemann.

Belanoff, Pat, and Peter Elbow. 1991. Using Portfolios to Increase Collaboration and Community in a Writing Program. In *Portfolios: Process and Product,* edited by Pat Belanoff and Marcia Dickson, 17–36. Portsmouth, NH: Boynton/Cook.

Berkenkotter, Carol, and Thomas N. Huckin. 1995. *Genre Knowledge in Disciplinary Communication.* Hillsdale, NJ: Erlbaum.

Bishop, Wendy. 2000. *The Subject is Reading.* Portsmouth, NH: Heinemann.

Bitzer, Lloyd. 1968. *The Rhetorical Situation.* Philosophy and Rhetoric 1: 1–14.

Bizzell, Patricia. 1997. Foreword to *Constructing Knowledges: The Politics of Theory-Building and Pedagogy in Composition,* by Sidney I. Dobrin. Albany: State University of New York Press.

Black, Laurel, Donald A. Daiker, Jeffrey Sommers, and Gail Stygall, eds. 1994. *New Directions in Portfolio Assessment.* Portsmouth NH: Boynton/Cook.

Blau, Sheridan. 2003. *The Literature Workshop: Teaching Texts and Their Readers.* Portsmouth, NH: Heinemann.

Bleich, David. 1978. *Subjective Criticism.* Baltimore, MD: Johns Hopkins University Press.

Bloom, Lynn. 2000. Advancing Composition. In *Coming of Age: The Advanced Writing Curriculum,* edited by Linda K. Shamoon, Rebecca Moore Howard, Sandra Jamieson, and Robert A. Schwegler, 3–18. Portsmouth, NH: Boynton/Cook.

Boyer Commission. 1998. *Reinventing Undergraduate Education: A Blueprint for America's Research Universities.* http://naples.cc.sunysb.edu/Pres/boyer.nsf/.

Boyer, Ernest L. 1990. *Scholarship Reconsidered: Priorities of the Professoriate.* Princeton: Carnegie Foundation for the Advancement of Teaching.

Brereton, John C., ed. 1995. *The Origins of Composition Studies in the American College, 1875–1925: A Documentary History.* Pittsburgh: University of Pittsburgh Press.

Bruce, Bertram, and Maureen P. Hogan. 1998. The Disappearance of Technology: Toward an Ecological Model of Literacy. In *Handbook of Literacy and Technology: Transformations in a Post-typographic World,* edited by David Reinking, Michael C. McKenna, Linda D. Labbo, and Ronald D. Kieffer, 269–81. Mahwah, NJ: Erlbaum.

Bruner, Jerome. 1986a. *Actual Minds, Possible Worlds.* Cambridge, MA: Harvard University Press.

———. 1986b. Value Presuppositions of Developmental Theory. In *Value Presuppositions in Theories of Human Development,* edited by L. Cirillo and S. Wapner, 19–28. Hillsdale, NJ: Erlbaum.

Castells, Manuel. 1996. *The Rise of the Network Society.* Vol. 1 of *The Information Age: Economy, Society, and Culture.* Malden, MA: Blackwell.

———. 1997. *The Power of Identity.* Vol. 2 of *The Information Age: Economy, Society, and Culture.* Malden, MA: Blackwell.

———. 1998. *End of the Millenium.* Vol. 3 of *The Information Age: Economy, Society, and Culture.* Malden, MA: Blackwell.

Cobb, Nina, ed. 1994. *The Future of Education: Perspectives on National Standards in America.* New York: College Entrance Examination Board.

Conference on College Composition and Communication. 1989. *Statement of Principles and Standards for the Postsecondary Teaching of Writing.* http://www.ncte.org/groups/cccc/positions/107680.htm.

Cooper, Marilyn M. 1986. The Ecology of Writing. *College English* 48: 364–75.

———. 1999 . Postmodern Pedagogy in Electronic Conversations. In Hawisher and Selfe 1999, 140–60.

Cope, Bill, and Mary Kalantzis, eds. 2000. *Multiliteracies: Literacy Learning and the Design of Social Futures.* New York: Routledge.

Coulter, Lauren. 2003. Re: Outcomes Statement. E-mail to Patricia Ericsson, 30 March.

Council of Writing Program Administrators. 1998. Evaluating the Intellectual Work of Writing Administration. *WPA: Writing Program Administration* 22.1: 2: 85–104.

Cross, Christopher T. 1994. Implications of Subject-Matter Standards. In Cobb 1994, 43–50.

Crowley, Sharon. 1991. A Personal Essay on Freshman English. *Pre/Text* 12: 155-176.

Deibert, Ronald. 1997. *Parchment, Printing, and Hypermedia: Communication in World Order Transformation.* New York: Columbia University Press.

Doe, John. 2003. Re: Outcomes Stmt. E-Mail to Patricia Ericsson, 31 March.

Edelman, Gerald M. 1992. *Bright Air, Brilliant Fire: On the Matter of the Mind.* New York: Basic Books.

Eisner, Elliot W. 1998. Standards for American Schools: Help or Hindrance? In *The Kind of Schools We Need: Personal Essays by Eisner,* 175–87. Portsmouth, NH: Heinemann.

Elbow, Peter. 1979. Trying to Teach while Thinking about the End. In *On Competence: A Critical Analysis of Competence-Based Reforms in Higher Education,* edited by Gerald Grant et al., 95–137. San Francisco: Jossey-Bass.

————. 1996. Writing Assessment in the Twenty-first Century: A Utopian View. In *Composition in the 21st Century: Crisis and Change,* edited by Lynn Z. Bloom, Donald A. Daiker, and Edward M. White, 83–100. Carbondale: Southern Illinois University Press.

Enos, Theresa, ed. 1996. *Encyclopedia of Rhetoric and Composition.* New York: Garland.

Faigley, Lester, 1992. *Fragments of Rationality: Postmodernity and the Subject of Composition.* Pittsburgh: Univerisy of Pittsburgh Press.

Feenberg, Andrew. 1999. *Questioning Technology.* New York: Routledge.

Feldman, Carol, Jerome Bruner, David Kalmar, and Bobbi Renderer. 1993. Plot, Plight, and Dramatism: Interpretation at Three Ages. *Human Development* 36: 327–42.

Feldman, David H. 1980. *Beyond Universals in Cognitive Development.* Norwood, NJ: Ablex.

Foucault, Michel. 1983. *Beyond Structuralism and Hermeneutics.* 2nd ed. Chicago: University of Chicago Press.

Fox, Tom. 1999. *Defending Access: A Critique of Standards in Higher Education.* Portsmouth, NH: Heinemann.

Freebody, Peter. 1992. A Socio-Cultural Approach: Resourcing Four Roles as a Literacy Learner. In *Prevention of Reading Failure,* ed. Alan Watson and Anne Badenhop. Lindfield, NSW: Scholastic Australia. http://www.myread.org/readings_freebody.htm.

Freedman, Aviva. 1994. "Do As I Say": The Relationship between Teaching and Learning New Genres. In Freedman and Medway 1994, 191–210.

Freedman, Aviva, and Peter Medway, eds. 1994. *Genre and the New Rhetoric.* Bristol, PA: Taylor and Francis.

Freeman, Mark Philip. 1993. *Rewriting the Self: History, Memory, Narrative.* London: Routledge.

Freire, Paulo. 1989. *Pedagogy of the Oppressed.* Translated by Myra Bergman Ramos. New York: Continuum.

Fulkerson, Richard. 1980. Conjectures on (Advanced?) Composition and Its Teaching. *Journal of Advanced Composition* 1: 30–34.

Gee, James Paul. 1996. *Social Linguistics and Literacies: Ideology in Discourses.* 2nd ed. Bristol, PA: Taylor and Francis.

Giddens, Anthony. 1984. *The Constitution of Society: Outline of a Theory of Structuration.* Berkeley and Los Angeles: University of California Press.

Giele, Janet Z. 1980. Adulthood as Transcendence of Age and Sex. In *Themes of Work and Love in Adulthood,* edited by J. Smelser and Erik H. Erikson, 151–73. Cambridge, MA: Harvard University Press.

Glassick, Charles E., Mary Taylor Huber, and Gene I. Maeroff. 1997. *Scholarship Assessed: Evaluation of the Professoriate.* San Francisco: Jossey-Bass.

Glau, Greg. ASU Stretch Program Web site. http://www.asu.edu/clas/english/composition/cbw/stretch.htm.

Gleason, Barbara. 1997. When the Writing Test Fails: Assessing Assessment at an Urban College. In *Writing in Multicultural Settings,* edited by Carol Severino, Juan C. Guerra, and Johnella E. Butler, 307–24. New York: MLA.

Gollin, Eugene S. 1981. *Developmental Plasticity: Behavioral and Biological Aspects of Variations in Development.* New York: Academic Press.

Goodman, Kenneth. 1967. Reading: A Psycholinguistic Guessing Game. *Journal of the Reading Specialist* 4: 126–35.

Goodman, Kenneth and Yetta Goodman. 1989. *The Whole Language Evaluation Book.* Toronto, ON: Irwin.

Goodman, Yetta, Carolyn L. Burke, and Barry Sherman. 1980. *Reading Strategies: Focus on Comprehension.* New York: Richard C. Owen.

Goodman, Yetta and Sandra Wilde. 1996. *Notes from a Kidwatcher: Selected Writings of Yetta M. Goodman.* Portsmouth, NH: Heinemann.

Grant, Gordon. 1996. Program Outcomes Statements. Writing Program Administration List (WPA-L) Archives, 13 March. http: //lists.asu.edu/cgi-bin/wa?A2=ind9603&L=wpa-l&O=D&P=12283.

Graves, D., and J. Hansen. 1983. The Author's Chair. *Language Arts* 60: 176–83.

Green, Michael. 1985. Talk and Doubletalk: The Development of Metacommunication Knowledge about Oral Language. *Research in the Teaching of English* 19: 9–24.

Haas, Christina. 1994. Learning to Read Biology: One Student's Rhetorical Development in College. *Written Communication* 11: 43–84.

Harrington, Susanmarie, et al. 1999. Revising the WPA Outcomes Statement Draft. MOO session transcript, 11 August.

Harste, Jerome C. 1984. The Winds of Change: Examining Assumptions in Instructional Research in Reading Comprehension. Paper read at the National Council of Teachers of English Conference, Detroit, November.

Hartwell, Patrick. 1985. Grammar, Grammars, and the Teaching of Grammar. *College English* 47: 105–27.

Haswell, Richard H. 1991. *Gaining Ground in College Writing: Tales of Development and Interpretation.* Dallas: Southern Methodist University Press.

———. 1994. Student Self-Evaluations and Developmental Change. In *Student Self-Evaluation*, edited by J. MacGregor, 83–100. San Francisco: Jossey-Bass.

———. 2000. Documenting Improvement in College Writing: A Longitudinal Approach. *Written Communication* 17: 307–52.

Haswell, Richard and Janise Tedesco Haswell. 1996. Gender Bias and Critique of Student Writing. *Assessing Writing* 3.1: 31-84.

Havighurst, R. J. 1973. *Developmental Tasks and Education.* 3rd ed. New York: David McKay.

Hawhee, Debra. 1999. Composition History and the Harbrace College Handbook. *College Composition and Communication* 50: 504–23.

Hawisher, Gail, and Cynthia L. Selfe, eds. 1999. *Passions, Pedagogies, and 21st Century Technologies.* Logan: Utah State University Press.

Heilker, Paul, and Peter Vandenberg. 1996. *Keywords in Composition Studies.* Portsmouth, NH: Boynton/Cook.

Helmers, Marguerite, ed. 2003. *Intertexts: Reading Pedagogy in the Composition Classroom.* Mahwah, NJ: Lawrence Erlbaum Associates.

Henry, Ronald. 2000. Standards-Based Curricular Planning. *Peer Review* 2.2: 19–20

Hesse, Doug. 2005. Who Owns Writing? Chair's Address. Annual Convention of the Conference on College Composition and Communication. San Francisco, California.

Hillocks, George. 1986. *Research on Written Composition: New Directions for Teaching.* Urbana, IL: NCTE.

Hochman, Will. 2003. Re: A.W Review of CCCC Session on WPA OS (+ More If Interested). E-mail to Patricia Ericsson, 30 March.

Hogan, Michael P. 1980. Advanced Composition: A Survey. *Journal of Advanced Composition* 1: 21–29.

Jameison, Carol, and Denise David. 1998. Cognitive Developmental Theory. In *Composition: A Critical Sourcebook of Theory and Scholarship in Contemporary Composition Studies*, edited by Mary Lynch Kennedy, Westport, CT: Greenwood Press. 26–37.

Johns, Ann M. 1997. *Text, Role, and Context: Developing Academic Literacies.* New York: Cambridge University Press.

Johnson Foundation. 1993. *An American Imperative: Higher Expectations for Higher Education.* Racine, WI: Johnson Foundation.

Jones, Elizabeth A., et al. 1995. *National Assessment of College Student Learning: Identifying College Graduates' Essential Skills in Writing, Speech and Listening, and Critical Thinking—Final Project Report.* U.S. Dept. of Education Office of Educational Research and Improvement, NCES 95-001.

Keene, Ellin and Susan Zimmerman. 1997. *Mosaic of Thought: Teaching Comprehension in a Reader's Workshop*. Portsmouth, NH: Heinemann.

Kegan, Robert. 1994. *In Over Our Heads: The Mental Demands of Modern Life*. Cambridge: Harvard University Press.

Kennedy, Mary Lynch, ed. 1998. *Composition: A Critical Sourcebook of Theory and Scholarship in Contemporary Composition Studies*. Westport, CT: Greenwood Press.

Kitchener, Karen. S. 1983. Cognition, Metacognition, and Epistemic Cognition: A Three-Level Model of Cognitive Processing. *Human Development* 26: 222–32.

Klein, Stephen P., Laura S. Hamilton, Daniel F. McCaffrey, and Brian M. Stecher. 2000. *What Do Test Scores in Texas Tell Us?* http: //www.rand.org/publications/IP/IP202/.

Kress, Gunter. 1999. "English" at the Crossroads: Rethinking Curricula of Communication in the Context of the Turn to the Visual. In Hawisher and Selfe 1999, 66–88.

Labouvie-Vief, Gisela. 1994. *Psyche and Eros: Mind and Gender in the Life Course*. Cambridge: Cambridge University Press.

Larson, Richard L. 1993. Portfolios in the Assessment of Writing: A Political Perspective. In White, Lutz, and Kamusikiri, 271–83.

Latour, Bruno. 2000. When Things Strike Back: A Possible Contribution of Science Studies to the Social Sciences. *British Journal of Sociology* 51: 1: 107-124.

Light, Richard. 1993. *Second Report of the Harvard Assessment Seminars*. Cambridge, MA: Harvard Graduate School of Education.

Light, Richard J. 2001. *Making the Most of College: Students Speak Their Minds*. Cambridge: Harvard University Press.

Levine, Mel. 2002. *A Mind at a Time*. New York: Simon and Schuster.

Loacker, Georgine, ed. 2000. *Self-Assessment at Alverno College*. Milwaukee, WI: Alverno College Institute.

Lofty, John. 2000. "We Are Doing This Already": Teacher Talk about Standards in Britain and America. *English Journal* 89.4: 97–105.

Logan, Shirley Wilson. 2003. Changing Missions, Shifting Positions, and Breaking Silence. Chair's Address. Annual Convention of the Conference on College Composition and Communication. New York, New York.

Loveless, Tom. 1994. The Politics of National Standards. In Cobb 1994, 51–54.

Lowe, Kelly. 2003. Re: Cs Panel. E-mail to Patricia Ericsson, 7 April.

Lu, Min-Zhan. 1999. The Vitality of the Ungrateful Receiver: Making Giving Mutual between Composition and Postcolonial Studies. *JAC: A Journal of Composition Theory* 19: 335–57.

Matsuda, Paul Kei. 1999. Composition Studies and ESL Writing: A Disciplinary Division of Labor. *College Composition and Communication* 50: 699–721.

McClelland, D. C. 1973. Testing for Competence Rather Than for Intelligence. *American Psychologist* 28: 1–14.

McCormick, Kathleen. 1994. *The Culture of Reading and the Teaching of English*. Manchester: Manchester UP.

McLeod, Susan. 1997. *Notes on the Heart: Affective Issues in the Writing Classroom*. Carbondale: Southern Illinois University Press.

Miller, Carolyn R. 1984. Genre as Social Action. In Freedman and Medway 1994, 23–42.

———. 1994. Rhetorical Community: The Cultural Basis of Genre. In Freedman and Medway 1994, 67–78.

Murnane, Richard. 2000. The Case for Standards. *Boston Review* 24.6. http: //bostonreview.mit.edu/BR24.6/murnane.html.

Murphy, Sandra, and Barbara Grant. 1993. Portfolio Approaches to Assessment: Breakthrough or More of the Same? In White, Lutz, and Kamusikiri, 284–300.

Myers, Miles. 1994. Problems and Issues Facing the National Standards Project in English. In Cobb 1994, 259–76.

National Council of Teachers of English and the International Reading Association. 1996. *Standards for the English Language Arts.* Urbana, IL: NCTE and IRA.

Newberry, R. A. 1967. Objective Indices in the Assessment of Essays. *British Journal of Educational Psychology,* 37: 403–5.

Norgaard, Rolf. 2002. Re: Outcomes Modeled on WPA Statement. In Writing Program Administration List (WPA-L) Archives, July 17. http: //lists.asu.edu/cgi-bin/wa?A2=ind0207&L=wpa-l&D=1&O=D&F=&S=&P=13762.

Ohanian, Susan. 1999. *One Size Fits Few: The Folly of Educational Standards.* Portsmouth, NH: Heinemann.

O'Neill, Peggy, Angela Crow, and Larry W. Burton, eds. 2002. *A Field of Dreams: Independent Writing Programs and the Future of Composition Studies.* Logan: Utah State University Press.

Outcomes Statement Steering Committee. 1998–2003. The Outcomes Statement Archives. http: //comppile.tamucc.edu/WPAoutcomes/index.htm.

———. 2001. WPA Outcomes Statement for First-Year Writing. *College English* 63: 321–25.

Peckham, Irvin. 1999. Re: Opposed to Outcomes Statements. In Writing Program Administration List (WPA-L) Archives, May 17. http: //lists.asu.edu/cgi-bin/wa?A2=ind9905&L=wpa-l&D=1&O=D&F=&S=&P=21709.

———. Unpublished. The Rhetorical Situation of the Outcomes Statement.

Peterson, Linda H. 1991. Gender and the Autobiographical Essay. *College Composition and Communication* 42: 170–83.

Petrosky, Anthony. 1982. From Story to Essay: Reading and Writing. *College Composition and Communication* 33: 24–25.

Phelps, Louise Wetherbee. 1988. *Composition as a Human Science: Contributions to the Self-Understanding of a Discipline.* New York: Oxford University Press.

Pope, Rob. 1995. *Textual Intervention: Critical and Creative Strategies for Literary Studies.* New York: Routledge.

Purves, Alan C., Joseph A. Quattrini, and Christine I. Sullivan. 1995. *Instructor's Manual for Creating the Writing Portfolio.* Lincolnwood, IL: NTC.

Purves, Alan, Theresa Rogers, Anna O. Soter. 1990. *How Porcupines Make Love II: Teaching a Response-Centered Literature Curriculum.* New York: Longman.

Putnam, Robert. 2001. *Bowling Alone: The Collapse and Revival of American Community.* New York: Simon & Schuster.

Qualley, Donna. 1993. Using Reading in the Writing Classroom. In *Nuts and Bolts,* Ed. Thomas Newkirk. Portsmouth: Boynton/Cook. 101-127.

Ramage, John. 1992. *Proposal to Improve Writing Instruction at ASU.* Photocopy. Tempe: Arizona State University.

Reid, Joy M. 1989. English as Second Language Composition in Higher Education: The Expectations of the Academic Audience. In *Richness in Writing: Empowering ESL Students,* edited by Donna M. Johnson and Duane H. Roen, 220–34. New York: Longman.

Reiff, Mary Jo. 2003. Accessing Communities through the Genre of Ethnography: Exploring a Pedagogical Genre. *College English* 65: 553–58.

Rhodes, Keith. 2000. Help with the OS Section. E-mail to Ruth Overman Fischer, 1 August.

Rosenblatt, Louise. 1978. *The Reader, the Text, the Poem: The Transactional Theory of the Literary Work.* Carbondale: Southern Illinois University Press.

Sabatier, Paul, and Hank C. Jenkins-Smith. 1993. *Policy Change and Learning: An Advocacy Coalition Approach.* Boulder, CO: Westview Press.

Salvatori, Mariolina. 1996. Conversations with Texts: Reading in the Teaching of Composition. *College English* 58.4 (April 1996): 440-454.

Salvatori, Mariolina. 2003. Conversations. In *Intertexts: Reading Pedagogy in the Composition Classroom,* ed. Marguerite Helmers. Mahwah, NJ: Lawrence Erlbaum Associates. 443-444.

Scalzo, Mary Jo, Anne Koenig, and Stephen Wilhoit. 2003. Writing across the Curriculum: Hatching an Owl to Foster Student Writing. *Today's School* 3.4: 15–18.

Schön, Donald. A. 1987. *Educating the Reflective Practitioner.* San Francisco: Jossey-Bass.

Schuster, Charles I. 1994. Climbing the Slippery Slope of Assessment: The Programmatic Use of Writing Portfolios. In Black et al. 1994, 314–24.

Schwalm, David. 1999. Re: Outcomes Statement—Motive, Procedure, and Text. In Writing Program Administration List (WPA-L) Archives, May 28. http: //lists.asu.edu/cgi-bin/ wa?A2=ind9905&L=wpa-l&D=1&O=D&F=&S=&P=41206.

Schwegler, Robert A. 2000. Curriculum Development in Composition. In Shamoon et al. 2000, 25–31.

Selfe, Cynthia. 1999. *Technology and Literacy in the Twenty-first Century: The Importance of Paying Attention.* Carbondale: Southern Illinois University Press.

Seymour, Daniel. 1995. *Once upon a Campus: Lessons for Improving Quality and Productivity in Higher Education.* Phoenix: Oryx Press.

Shamoon, Linda K., Rebecca Moore Howard, Sandra Jamieson, and Robert A. Schwegler, eds. 2000. *Coming of Age: The Advanced Writing Curriculum.* Portsmouth, NH: Boynton/ Cook.

Shaughnessy, Mina. 1977. *Errors and Expectations.* New York: Oxford University Press.

Smith, Frank. 1978. *Understanding Reading.* New York: Holt, Rinehart, and Winston.

Smith, Michael, and Jeffrey Wilhem. 2002. *Reading Don't Fix No Chevys.* Portsmouth, NH: Heinemann.

Smitherman, Geneva.1999. CCCC's Role in the Struggle for Language Rights. *College Composition and Communication* 50: 349–76.

Soles, Derek. 2002. A comment on the "WPA Outcomes Statement for First-Year Composition." *College English* 64.3: 377-378.

Sommers, Nancy. 1982. Responding to Student Writing. *College Composition and Communication* 33.2: 148-156.

Stacey, David. 2003. Re: List of Schools That Have Used OS. E-mail to Patricia Ericsson, 15 March.

Sternglass, Marilyn S. 1986. Commitment to Writing and Complexity of Thinking. *Journal of Basic Writing* 5.1: 77–86.

———. 1997. *Time to Know Them: A Longitudinal Study of Writing and Learning at the College Level.* Mahwah, NJ: Erlbaum.

———. 1999. The Importance of Writing to Second-Language Learners. Paper read at the Conference of the New York State Teachers of English to Speakers of Others Languages, Manopac, New York, 15–17 October.

Straub, Richard and Ronald F. Lunsford. 1995. *Twelve Readers Reading: Responding to College Writing.* Cresskill, NJ: Hampton Press.

Straub, Richard. 1996. Teacher Response as Conversation: More than Causal Talk, An Exploration. *Rhetoric Review* 14.2: 374-399.

Stryker, Sheldon. 1987. Identity Theory: Developments and Extensions. In *Self and Identity: Psychological Perspectives,* edited by K. Yardley and T. Honess, 89–103. Chichester: John Wiley.

Swales, John M. 1990. *Genre Analysis: English in Academic and Research Settings.* New York: Cambridge University Press.

Townsend, Martha A. 1991. Instituting Changes in Curriculum and Teaching Style in Liberal Arts Programs: A Study of Nineteen Ford Foundation Projects. Ph.D. diss., Arizona State University. Abstract in Dissertation Abstracts International, 52: 06A, University Microfilms no. 91-34898.

Trachsel, Mary. 1992. *Institutionalizing Literacy: The Historical Role of College Entrance Examinations in English.* Carbondale: SIUP.

Trimbur, John. 1989. Consensus and Difference in Collaborative Learning. *College English* 51: 602–16.

Walvoord, Barbara E., Linda Lawrence Hunt, H. Fil Dowling Jr., and Joan D. McMahon. 1997. In *The Long Run: A Study of Faculty in Three Writing-across-the-Curriculum Programs.* Urbana, IL: NCTE.

Weaver, Constance. 1996. *Teaching Grammar in Context.* Portsmouth, NH: Heinemann.

Wenger, Etienne, Richard McDermott and William Snyder. 2002. *Cultivating Communities of Practice: A Guide to Managing Knowledge.* Boston: Harvard Business School Press.

White, Edward M. 1994. Portfolios as an Assessment Concept. In Black et al. 1994, 25–39.

———. 1995. The Rhetorical Problem of Program Evaluation and the WPA. In *Resituating Writing,* edited by Joseph Janangelo and Kristine Hansen, 132–50. Portsmouth, NH: Boynton/Cook.

———. 1996. Power and Agenda Setting in Writing Assessment. In White, Lutz, and Kamusikiri 1993, 9–24.

White, Edward M., William D. Lutz, and Sandra Kamusikiri, eds. 1993. *Assessment of Writing: Politics, Policies, Practices.* New York: MLA.

Wiley, Mark. 1999a. Response [to the Outcomes Statement]. *WPA: Writing Program Administration* 23.1–2: 67–68.

———. 1999b. Theorizing the Outcomes Statement (Version 3). E-mail to Ruth Overman Fischer, 16 June.

Wilhelm, Jeffrey. 1997. *You Gotta Be the Book: Teaching Engaged and Reflective Reading With Adolescents.* New York: Teachers College Press.

Williams, Joseph. 1999. *Style: Ten Lessons in Clarity and Grace.* 6th ed. New York: Longman.

Wineberg, Samuel S. 1991. On the Reading of Historical Texts: Notes on the Breach between the School and Academy. *American Educational Research Journal* 28: 495–519.

Wise, J. Macgregor. 1997. *Exploring Technology and Social Space.* Thousand Oaks, CA: Sage.

Wolf, Dennie Palmer. 1994. Curriculum and Assessment Standards: Common Measures or Conversations? In Cobb 1994, 85-106.

Wolff, Donald. 1999. Outcomes Statement—Motive & Procedure. In Writing Program Administration List (WPA-L) Archives, 24 May. http: //lists.asu.edu/cgi-bin/wa?A2=ind9905&L=wpa-l&D=1&O=D&F=&S=&P=36775.

Yancey, Kathleen Blake. 1999. Response. *WPA: Writing Program Administration* 23.1–2: 67.

———.2003a. Promising Developments and Innovations in Science, Writing, and Psychology. Paper read at the American Association of Higher Education Assessment Conference, Seattle.

———. 2003b. Re: Your Recollections. E-mail to Patricia Ericsson, 30 March.

———. Forthcoming. Bowling Together: Communities of Practice and the Knowledge-Making Function of Reflection. In *Rethinking Reflection in Composition Studies,* edited by Michael Neal, Tony Baker, Brian Huot, and Ellen Schendel.

Zemsky, Robert. 1989. *Structure and Coherence: Measuring the Undergraduate Curriculum.* Washington, DC: Association of American Colleges.

CONTRIBUTORS

SUSANMARIE HARRINGTON is professor of English and director of writing at Indiana University-Purdue University Indianapolis. Her research interests focus on the ways literacy is shaped by assessment and technology. With Linda Adler-Kassner, she is co-author of *Basic Writing as a Political Act: Public Conversations about Writing and Literacies* (Hampton, 2002) and co-editor of *Questioning Authority: Stories Told in School* (U. of Michigan, 2001).

After an earlier career as a lawyer, KEITH RHODES completed a master's and doctorate in rhetoric and composition. He served as coordinator of composition at Northwest Missouri State University from 1994-1999. He then moved to Missouri Western State College, where he served as director of developmental writing and writing placement. He has now returned to the practice of law.

RUTH OVERMAN FISCHER received her PhD in English with an emphasis in rhetoric and linguistics from Indiana University of Pennsylvania in 1997. She has taught in the English Department at George Mason University since 1987 and was the director of composition from 1998-2003. She has three short essays in *Strategies for Teaching First-Year Composition* (Roen et al, 2002) and coauthored an essay with Chris Thaiss in *Coming of Age: The Advanced Writing Curriculum* (ed by Shamoon et al, 2000).

RITA MALENCZYK is associate professor of English and director of the University Writing Program at Eastern Connecticut State University. Her scholarly work, which has appeared in various publications including *WPA: Writing Program Administration*, is focused primarily on the politics and rhetoric of administering writing programs.

LINDA ADLER-KASSNER teaches first-year writing and composition pedagogy at Eastern Michigan University. With Heidi Estrem, she also directs Eastern's first-year writing program. With Susanmarie Harrington, she is co-author of *Basic Writing as a Political Act: Public Conversations about Writing and Literacies* and co-editor of *Questioning Authority: Stories Told in School.*

LINDA S. BERGMANN, associate professor of English at Purdue University and director of the Purdue Writing Lab, has started writing-across-the-curriculum programs and writing centers at the University of Missouri-Rolla, the Illinois Institute of Technology, and Hiram College. She has published articles in such journals as *Language and Learning Across the Disciplines, Feminist Teacher, A/B: Auto/Biography Studies,* and *American Studies.*

WILLIAM CONDON has been engaged with writing assessment as a WPA at a wide variety of institutions—the University of Oklahoma, Arkansas Tech University, the University of Michigan, and Washington State University, where he is director of Campus Writing Programs and professor of English. He has published extensively and is principal investigator of a three-year FIPSE grant devoted to faculty development and statewide accountability assessment around teaching critical thinking.

PETER ELBOW is professor of English emeritus at University of Massachusetts, Amherst. He directed the writing program there and at SUNY Stony Brook, and taught at M.I.T., Franconia College, and Evergreen State College. His recent book, *Everyone Can Write: Essays Toward a Hopeful Theory of Writing and Teaching Writing*, was given the James Britton Award by the Conference on English Education. NCTE recently gave him the James Squire Award "for his transforming influence and lasting intellectual contribution."

PATRICIA FREITAG ERICSSON is assistant professor in the English department at Washington State University, where she works with the Digital Technology and Culture Program. Her work has appeared in a variety of venues including *Computers and Composition*, *The ACE Journal*, *Text Technology*, and several edited collections.

HEIDI ESTREM teaches first-year writing, courses for future English teachers, and graduate courses in writing pedagogy and theory at Eastern Michigan University. She is also associate director of first-year writing. Currently, she is working on a variety of projects stemming from her interests in how and why students read in writing classes. Her recent publications include co-authored essays in *WPA: Writing Program Administration* and *Rhetoric Review*.

GREGORY GLAU is director of writing programs at Arizona State University, where he has taught since 1994. Before being appointed WPA, he directed ASU's basic writing Stretch Program. With Linda Adler-Kassner of Eastern Michigan University, he is co-editor of the *Bedford Bibliography of Basic Writing* and has co-authored and published numerous books and articles.

RICHARD HASWELL is Haas Professor of English at Texas A & M University, Corpus Christi. At Washington State University, he served as director of writing and director of the University Office of Writing Assessment, and played significant roles in the revision of the undergraduate curriculum and the development of the junior portfolio examination. He is the author and coauthor of numerous books and articles on writing assessment and interpretation, including *Gaining Ground in College Writing*.

ROBERT O'BRIEN HOKANSON is associate professor of English and coordinator of the Communication Ability department at Alverno College. He also serves as co-chair of the college's Council for Student Assessment. He has published and presented on a range of topics including digital portfolios, communication across the curriculum, American poetry, and teaching and assessing for student learning outcomes.

BARBARA LITTLE LIU is assistant professor of English at Eastern Connecticut State University, where she also coordinates the first-year writing program. Her teaching and research focus on composition theory and pedagogy and rhetorical theory and criticism, especially political and religious rhetorics.

BARRY M. MAID is professor and head of technical communication at Arizona State University East, where he developed a new program in multimedia writing and technical communication. At the University of Arkansas at Little Rock, he directed the first year composition program, chaired the department of English, and helped create the department of rhetoric and writing. Though most of his time is now spent in program administration, he keeps in touch with his interests in computers and writing, writing program administration, and academic/industry partnerships.

J.L. McClure is professor of English at Kirkwood Community College in Cedar Rapids, Iowa. He teaches composition, various literature classes, and creative writing. He also serves as coordinator of English assessment.

Irvin Peckham is an associate professor at Louisiana State University, where he directs the first-year writing program. He has published articles in *Composition Studies, Computers and Writing, Pedagogy,* and in several collections of essays. He has recently co-edited (with Sherry Linkon) a special edition of *College English* on working-class writing and literature. His research interest is the function of writing instruction in social class reproduction.

Duane Roen, professor of English, currently serves as Head of Humanities, Arts, and English at Arizona State University East. From 1999 to 2004, he directed the Center for Learning and Teaching Excellence at Arizona State University, where he also served as WPA. In addition to six books, including *Strategies for Teaching First-Year Composition,* he has authored or co-authored more than 170 chapters, articles, and conference papers.

Cynthia L. Selfe is professor of Humanities at Michigan Technological University and the co-editor of *Computers and Composition.* In 1996, Selfe was recognized as an EDUCOM medal award winner for innovative computer use in higher education. In 2000, Selfe, along with long-time collaborator Gail Hawisher, was presented with the Outstanding Technology Innovator award by the CCCC Committee on Computers. Selfe has served as Chair of CCCC and Chair of the College Section of NCTE.

Marilyn Sternglass was professor emeritus of English at City College of City University of New York and author, most notably, of *Time to Know Them,* which won both the 1998 Mina P. Shaughnessy Medal from the Modern Language Association and the 1999 CCCC Outstanding Book Award. She was, in the words of her CCCC colleagues, "a tireless advocate of educational access and the study and teaching of literacy" (*CCC* June 2004). She died in January 2004.

Martha Townsend is associate professor of English and director of the University of Missouri's twenty-year-old Campus Writing Program. Her publications include chapters and entries on WAC/WID in numerous volumes, most recently *The Writing Program Administrator's Resource.* Her work in writing and general education has taken her to universities across the U.S. as well as Romania, Korea, Thailand, South Africa, China, and Costa Rica.

Edward M. White has written or edited eleven books and about 100 articles or book chapters on writing, writing instruction, and writing assessment. His best-known books are *Teaching and Assessing Writing,* whose second edition in 1994 won an award from the MLA for "outstanding research in teaching," and *Assessment of Writing: Politics, Policies, Practices.*

MARK WILEY is professor of English and director of the Faculty Center for Professional Development at California State University-Long Beach, where he also coordinated the composition program for eight years. Presently, he is part of a faculty team to assess writing in CSU-LB's General Education Program. Most of his research and publications, which include *Composition in Four Keys,* have been in rhetoric and composition.

STEPHEN WILHOIT is associate professor of English at the University of Dayton. He serves as the department's director of writing programs and is a teaching fellow in the university's Ryan C. Harris Learning Teaching Center. His research focuses on composition pedagogy, TA education, and faculty development, and he has authored two books, *A Brief Guide to Writing from Readings* and *The Allyn & Bacon Teaching Assistant's Handbook.*

DONALD WOLFF is professor of English at Eastern Oregon University, where he directs the Oregon Writing Project. He has worked in assessment for most of the twenty-five years he has been teaching at the university level. Recent publications include "Asynchronous Computer Conferencing" in *Strategies for Teaching First-Year Composition,* edited by Duane Roen et. al., and *Some Days,* a poetry chapbook.

Past Chair of CCCC and the NCTE College Section, and past president of WPA, KATHLEEN BLAKE YANCEY is the R. Roy Pearce Professor of Professional Communication at Clemson University, where she directs the Pearce Center for Professional Communication and the Pearce Center Studio. She has co-edited, edited or authored eight books; has delivered numerous plenary and keynote addresses; and has authored over 40 articles and book chapters.

INDEX